# The End of Theology

To my good friend
Andrew

with best wishes

Paul.

1. xii 16

# The End of Theology

Shaping Theology for the Sake of Mission

Jason S. Sexton and Paul Weston, editors

Fortress Press
*Minneapolis*

THE END OF THEOLOGY

Shaping Theology for the Sake of Mission

Cover design: Tory Herman

*Library of Congress Cataloging-in-Publication Data*

Print ISBN: 978-1-5064-0591-9

eBook ISBN: 978-1-5064-0592-6

The paper used in this publication meets the minimum requirements of American
National Standard for Information Sciences — Permanence of Paper for Printed
Library Materials, ANSI Z329.48-1984.

Manufactured in the U.S.A.

This book was produced using Pressbooks.com, and PDF rendering was done by
PrinceXML.

*To Richard Bauckham and Ruth Padilla DeBorst*


*Whose tireless, inspiring work of scholarship and service have done much for the good of the church and for the sake of its mission in the world.*

# Contents

# Contributors

Jonny Baker is the mission education director for Church Mission Society (London) and oversees their pioneer training. He is a longtime blogger, one of the early worship leaders influencing the emerging church conversation. He has published *Curating Worship* (2010) and recently coedited with Cathy Ross, *The Pioneer Gift: Explorations in Mission* (2014).

Mark W. Elliott (PhD, University of Cambridge) is professor of historical and biblical theology at St. Mary's College in the University of St. Andrews. His research and teaching focus on historical theology and the theology of biblical exegesis. He has published *The Reality of Biblical Theology* (2008) and *The Heart of Biblical Theology* (2012), and he directs the Institute for Bible, Theology, and Hermeneutics.

Michael W. Goheen (PhD, University of Utrecht) is director of theological education and scholar in residence at the Missional Training Center in Phoenix, Arizona. He recently authored *A Light to the Nations: The Missional Church and the Biblical Story* (2011) and *Introducing Christian Mission Today: Scripture, History, and Issues* (2014).

Bradley G. Green (PhD, Baylor University) is associate professor of christian thought and tradition at Union University in Tennessee. Having edited *Shapers of Christian Orthodoxy: Engaging with Early and Medieval Theologians* (2010), he is also the author of *Covenant and*

*Commandment: Works, Obedience and Faithfulness in the Christian Life* (2014).

Krish Kandiah (PhD, Kings College, University of London) is founder and director of Home for Good and a vice president at Tearfund. Formerly he was president of London School of Theology and has previously served with the Evangelical Alliance as their executive director for churches in mission. His recent books are *Paradoxology* (2014) and *Home for Good: Making a Difference for Vulnerable Children* (2013), which highlights his heart for the vulnerable as an adoptive father.

Kirsteen Kim (PhD, University of Birmingham) is professor of theology and World Christianity at Leeds Trinity University. She serves as editor of *Mission Studies*, the journal of the International Association for Mission Studies, and also edits the Edinburgh Regnum Centenary series. With Paul Grogan, she recently edited *The New Evangelization: Faith, People, Context and Practice* (2015), and with Sebastian Kim, authored *A History of Korean Christianity* (2014).

David C. Kirkpatrick (PhD, University of Edinburgh) is the T. Gannon postdoctoral associate in religion at Florida State University. He was previously a teaching fellow at the University of Edinburgh, where he taught a variety of courses on religion in the Global South and was part of the academic staff of the Centre for the Study of World Christianity.

Andrew Marin (PhD cand., University of St. Andrews) teaches at St. Mary's College, the divinity school in the University of St. Andrews. He is an advisor to the United Nations on Christian involvement in social and political reconciliation, and is the author of three books, including the award winning *Love Is an Orientation* (2009) and *Us Versus Us* (2016).

Daniel Strange (PhD, University of Bristol) is academic vice principal and lecturer in culture, religion, and public theology at Oak Hill College, London. His specialty is in the area of Christianity's relationship to other religions, and his recent book is *Their Rock Is Not Like Our Rock: A Theology of Religions* (2015).

Justin Stratis (PhD, University of Aberdeen) is tutor in christian doctrine and director of postgraduate research at Trinity College, Bristol. His research focuses on the doctrine of God, and he is coeditor of *Theological Theology: Essays in Honour of John Webster* (2015).

Jason S. Sexton (PhD, University of St Andrews) is lecturer in the honors program at California State University, Fullerton, and has held visiting fellowships at USC, UC Riverside, and at Ridley Hall, Cambridge, and is a visiting scholar at UC Berkeley's Center for the Study of Religion. He is secretary of the Tyndale Fellowship Christian Doctrine study group, convener of the Theological Engagement with California's Culture Project, and coeditor of *Theology and California: Theological Refractions on California's Culture* (2014).

Brian Stanley (PhD, University of Cambridge) is professor of world christianity and director of the Centre for the Study of World Christianity in the University of Edinburgh. He has authored *The Global Diffusion of Evangelicalism* (2013), is working on a world history of twentieth-century Christianity for Princeton University Press, and is editor for *Studies in World Christianity* (Edinburgh University Press).

Pete Ward (PhD, King's College, University of London) is professorial fellow in ecclesiology and ethnography at Durham University and professor of practical theology at MF the Norwegian School of Theology Oslo, Norway. He is the author of several books including *Liquid Church* (2002) and *Participation and Mediation* (2008), and is one of the coordinators of the Ecclesiology and Ethnography network.

Paul Weston (PhD, King's College, University of London) is director of the Newbigin Centre for Gospel and Western Culture, Ridley Hall, Cambridge. He lectures in mission studies in the Cambridge Theological Federation, and is an affiliated lecturer in the Cambridge University Divinity Faculty. His PhD was on Lesslie Newbigin's missionary engagement with Western culture, and he has written widely on his work. He is editor of *Lesslie Newbigin, Missionary Theologian: A Reader* (2006), and coeditor of *Theology in Missionary Perspective: Lesslie Newbigin's Legacy* (2012).

Emma Wild-Wood (PhD, University of Edinburgh) is lecturer in world Christianities in the University of Cambridge. She has also served as director of the Cambridge Centre for Christianity Worldwide. Her research focuses on religious encounter in sub-Saharan Africa, and the impact of contemporary global migration on the Christian church and the ecclesiological responses that may emerge.

Christopher J. H. Wright (PhD, University of Cambridge) is the international ministries director of Langham Partnership International, which provides literature, scholarships, and preaching training for pastors in Majority World churches and seminaries. He has served as principal of All Nations Christian College and is the author of *The Mission of God* (2006) and John Stott's updated, *Christian Mission in the Modern World* (2015).

# Acknowledgments

This book began with a friendship that started in 2011. Jason was finishing up his PhD at the University of St. Andrews in theology and eager to take up postdoctoral study with a missiologist, rounding out a British PhD experience that might prepare him well for meaningful engagement with California's culture, which he had already begun to pursue. Paul was at the early stages of developing the idea of a Lesslie Newbigin Centre to sit in the heart of Cambridge, committed to themes revolving around the gospel and Western culture. Through a mutual friend, fellow student of Trinity Hall with Paul and member of St. Andrews Baptist Church with Jason, Neill Fraser made the connection. Paul was eager to have Jason along as a postdoctoral fellow, helping with the early development of the Newbigin Centre. Through the hospitality of Andrew Norman, faculty and staff colleagues at Ridley Hall, space was created; and through the generous financial support of Mike and Amy Shane, the partnership and postdoctoral fellowship was enabled. Indeed, without the kindness of Mike and Amy, this book, arising from the Tyndale Fellowship Christian Doctrine group's renewed and concentrated focus around mission and theology, might not have happened at all.

It was during the subsequent academic year (2012–2013) that Jason was asked to be the next secretary of the Tyndale Fellowship Christian Doctrine study group, replacing David Rainey. As a result of developing conversations between us about the relationship between theology and mission, Jason suggested that Tyndale Fellowship's Christian Doctrine group set out to explore the idea of bringing missiologists into conversations with key theological themes. This led to the 2014 Tyndale doctrine study group's focus on the subject of methodology for mission theology, bringing together theologians, missiologists, and others for the conversation. Referred to as a "revolutionary" move, this brought missiologists into conversation with theologians at the Tyndale group, creating an invigorating and generative partnership.

Of course, this book would have never come about without the enthusiastic support of Mike Gibson, an editor who takes the subject of theology, mission, and ecclesiology as seriously as any editor in the business. For the organizing efforts of the earlier meeting, we have especially to thank Enid Instone-Brewer, Rob McDonald, Preston Parsons, and Karen Sunabacka, as well as other participants in that summer's study group: Andrew McGowan, Mike Moynagh, David Rollings, Graham McFarlane, Mark Pickett, Tom Creedy, Ian Randall, and of course, the chair of the CD group, Tom Noble. Since then, California State University, Fullerton, has supported Jason's work and research, providing space and academic encouragement throughout the finishing of this project, as has a fellowship at UC Riverside's Center for Ideas and Society, Fall of 2015. At Cal State Fullerton, Peter Nwosu, Susan Jacobsen, Sandra Perez, and Alison Wrynn have provided an amicable context for thinking through many of the things contained in this book and for editing its proceedings, and Jennifer Scheper Hughes has been a constant collaborator in thinking through what theology might mean in the wider public university context. For these wonderful colleagues, we are profoundly grateful, as indeed we are to our colleagues in mission and theology, Emma Wild-Wood and Chris Wright, who provided the excellent and insightful foreword and afterword for this book.

A portion of chapter 10 appear as Jason S. Sexton, "Confessional Theology in Public Places," *International Journal of Public Theology* 10, no. 2 (2016): 232–46.

# Foreword

## Emma Wild-Wood

Twin changes in global demography propel many of the assumptions that run through this volume: the growth in Christianity in the global South, and its decline in the global North. Moreover, this demographic shift takes place at a time when the speed of travel and communication allows a virtual crossing of geographical boundaries with the click of a mouse and thus creates the perception that parts of the world are desirable destinations for refuge, vacations, employment, or evangelism. Christians and people of other faiths move around the world taking their beliefs and practices with them, creating more religiously plural environments. While analysis of these changes is not the focus of this book, the intellectual debates and practical Christian responses that have emerged through the changes we call secularization, pluralization, and globalization prompt the scholars contributing here to call for change in the theological status quo. It is no accident that Lesslie Newbigin is often referenced in these pages. Having spent much of his life working with Christian communities in a religiously plural India, he returned to Europe and made the incisive observations on Western society and Christian mission for which he remains so well-respected. The current landscape of Christian churches provides new angles and aspects on the familiar ground of the nature and economy of God, and the proper response of God's creation and God's people, the analysis of which is the work of theologians and missiologists.

The aim of the book is to address essential methodological questions for developing the kind of theology that will fuel Christian mission. It assumes that this is best done by clearing the ground, by starting from first principles, rather than rushing ahead. This is no "how-to" handbook. Jason Sexton and Paul Weston have brought together thoughtful scholars who have engaged thoroughly with the ways in which the disciplines of theology and missiology may inform each other. Categories and terms are scrutinized, clear meanings are provided, genealogies of thought are explored, and new approaches are detailed. The underlying concern of the book is best articulated in Mike Goheen's quotation of Richard Bauckham, that academic theology and biblical studies often propound a "self-generated agenda [that] increasingly excludes the church from its context and implied audience." The antidote to this malaise is a recourse to missiology, defined as the reflection on the gospel in a particular context, not a form of "timeless" theology. Through missiological reflection, the contributors perceive new ways of comprehending the Creator actively loving the creation. They reexamine how we bear witness to Christ, and explore how we live with diversity, both within the church and outside it. Yet this volume provides no unthinking acceptance of missiology. While the contributors assume that contemporary missiologists have uncoupled contemporary missional thought from negative historical assumptions associated with the word "mission" and that they benefit from cross-cultural insights, Kirsteen Kim and Brian Stanley both critically examine the intellectual antecedents of cultural studies in the Western world.

It is pleasing to see that the call for collaboration between systematic theologians and missiologists is not unique. It perhaps represents a recent trend. A recent special edition of *Theology Today* took a similar approach to a related issue. It called for interdisciplinary collaboration as Western theologians engage with the "World-Christian turn." Paul Kollman, one of the contributors, argued for missiology "to serve as a master discipline" facilitating enquiry among church historians and systematic theologians. Missiology, he said, "is ecumenical, engages theological subfields . . . embraces the social sciences, and attends to Christian manifestations everywhere." Concerned that theologians either judge theologies emerging from the global South as "chaotic, syncretistic and superficial," or enthusiastically "laud the proliferation of theological creativity and inspiring discipleship as social and cultural differences generate new Christianities," he urged that "historical and theological understanding of the diversity and vitality of the world Christian movement will be well served by deeper attention to contemporary missiology."[1] Another enthusiastic proponent of the world-Christianity turn in theology declared, "I see enormous theological potential in exploring the polycentric nature of world Christianity," giving as an example the fact that "it revolutionizes the notion of 'tradition' as a source for doing constructive theological work . . . tradition becomes a more fluid, heterogeneous, and politically inflected category for constructive theological work."[2] Missiologists have examined the adaption and reinterpretation of Christian tradition around the globe. They are used to situations where—to push Jonny Baker's metaphor—the conceptual maps to hand appear misleading and they require the orientation skills of those they meet to help them comprehend the landscape anew. The present volume includes articles that take their impetus from the Western world and its need for Christian mission, and the insights drawn from a discipline that has engaged with peoples and their theologies worldwide. The West may be perceived as having particular attributes and requirements. It is also—particularly in an era of globalization and mass migration—interconnected with the whole world.

1. Paul Kollman, "Understanding the World-Christian Turn in the History of Christianity and Theology," *Theology Today* 71 (2014): 174–75.
2. Joy Ann McDougall, "Contemporary Landscapes and New Horizons: The Changing Maps of World Christianity," *Theology Today* 71 (2014): 162.

This book benefits from the face-to-face meeting of its contributors, which enabled them to engage with each other's contributions. The chapters often maintain the conversational style of a small conference while delving deeply into issues that prepare the way for greater collaboration. Their perspectives are fresh and engaging. They cover a wide range of ground that reaches beyond theology into biblical studies, history, and world Christianity. Together, they encourage the reflective practice of mission theology that shapes the Christian life lived as the body of Christ in the world.

# Introduction

## Jason S. Sexton and Paul Weston

### An Overdue Conversation

Theologians and missiologists do not often talk to each other. This means that as time passes, they may become increasingly unaware of each other's questions and concerns in their respective quests to do theology in ways that serve the church effectively. Some efforts have been set forth in recent years to address this, but with little real success.

In a desire to contribute to the development of this interdisciplinary conversation, a conference was organized by the Tyndale Fellowship Christian Doctrine study group, a consortium of scholars and practitioners, leading systematic theologians, and seasoned missiologists from different parts of the world. The conference took place at Wolfson College, University of Cambridge, July 3–5, 2014.

### The Aim of the Conversation

The aim of the conversation was to bring together key players from the two groups to seek a greater mutual understanding on the question of how to *do* theology in the service of the church's mission. This book allows you to listen in on some of the discussions we had during the 2014 gathering. It was not an entirely easy conversation. Each participant brought particular perspectives to questions about the nature of theology: how it is most meaningfully constructed, and how its outcomes are applied and carried out. Accordingly, in truly interdisciplinary fashion, this volume covers a host of considerations about the relationship between theology and mission, incorporating perspectives from contextual and systematic theology, missiology and mission studies, World Christianity and historical studies, biblical studies, missional hermeneutics, ethnography, pastoral practice, and social justice. However, at every point, the focus of the authors was the central question of what it means to *do theology* for the sake of mission.

Ordinarily, systematic theology is done in ways that have tended to pay little practical attention to matters "on the ground." At the same time, the missional conversation (both at local and global levels) can often lack the depth and seriousness that a close-range conversation between systematic theologians and missiologists has the potential to generate. Yet one of the abiding issues in evangelical Christianity today relates to questions about evangelical identity—including matters of ministry practice and mission—and how these relate to the wider Christian traditions out of which they arise. These are vital concerns, and they require a number of voices to make sense of the issues involved (certainly more than those who have already been at the table, as it were). In our increasingly globalized world, with burgeoning local theologies in various forms of development, putting the conversation off any longer is a luxury that Christians of all persuasions can ill-afford. After all, missiologists and theologians are engaged in the same task, working together for the same outcome—helping the church do its theology better for the sake of the gospel.

As will be apparent from the chapters that follow, the contributors disagree on a number of things—sometimes quite strongly. We will leave it to our readers to discern precisely where these tensions are, and who has made the better case about how best to do theology for the sake of mission in our fast-changing world. This serves as a reminder that the task of doing theology faithfully as part of the calling to make disciples is never an easy one, requiring not just the best participants that can be found, but a variety of perspectives as well.

The subtitle's phrase from this book's title, "Shaping Theology," is, at first sight, a strange way to talk about this. Isn't theology somehow fixed? Does it not involve a number of nonnegotiable and immutable truths, "once and for all delivered to the saints" (Jude 3)? For our part, theology is indeed a matter of the first order, for it affirms a number of things that are possible to know and have been made known by God. These are common core commitments shared by this volume's contributors, and they form a vital part of our collective understanding of reality. Humans are a special part of a universe created by God, who is triune; God has acted decisively in Christ as Savior; the church is the community in which God's special presence as Spirit abides today; Jesus will return to heal everything broken.

But what is the nature of these claims set forth as theological commitments? What *is* theology? Is it doctrine, something to be taught and passed on? Is it dogma, reflecting unwavering beliefs that cannot be revised in light of other considerations? And how is it *shaped* for mission? This is where theology also emerges as a second-order enterprise, an ongoing activity of the church. There remain fundamental features of our theology that are nonnegotiable, and yet the church is called to be active in *shaping* these commitments for the purposes of God for the world. This book therefore sets out to explore what this *shaping* might involve, so that the people of God might be better equipped for the mission to which they are called.

## The Shape of the Conversation

The contributions in the book are arranged in three sections. Section 1—entitled "Theology and Mission in Dialogue"—arises out of the conversation between mission theologians and systematic theologians about the nature of theological enterprise, and in particular, about the three sources from which theology has to draw: Scripture, tradition, and culture.

Mike Goheen begins with a restatement of a missional hermeneutic of Scripture, viewing the Bible not just as a missional text in its own right, but one that gives rise to—and energizes—the ongoing work of mission, with attendant implications for the way Scripture should therefore be read today. In spite of broad agreement with the thrust of Goheen's argument, systematician Justin Stratis offers a corrective, noting that if mission is one of the divine names, as it were, it is only such because it is grounded in God's free life-giving being. In other words, there is more to God than is told in the Bible, and this is something Stratis finds missing in the desire of missiologists to attempt to draw directly from the divine life—however inadvertently —in making everything about mission.

Brad Green offers an exposition of a Protestant understanding of the role of tradition for doing theology, with a strong affirmation of *sola scriptura* as the propositional core of this tradition. Having much sympathy with Green's approach, missiologist Paul Weston offers a corrective by insisting that theology is always more than a mere restatement of earlier statements from the tradition. Theological traditions, Weston argues, are both contextual and dynamic in their present articulations. Their formulation bears a consciousness of the pressing issues of the day, and carries an ability to respond to these with both realism and expectant hope.

With the conversation well underway, Kirsteen Kim strengthens Weston's argument for the cultural-locatedness of all theology (as well as theological traditions) with a thoroughgoing and rigorous treatment of how culture has been understood from evangelical, ecumenical, and Catholic perspectives. To this largely historical treatment, Dan Strange considers the implications of Kim's work for ministerial training and contexualized mission. As a systematician, Strange offers an alternative proposal, highlighting the gospel as the subversive fulfillment of culture, enabling a renewed calling for Christians to function as transformative agents in light of the future re-creation of all things.

The second section of the book (titled "Assessing the Shape of

Theology and Mission in Dialogue") builds on the first, but develops a different kind of conversation. Taking stock of the various proposals already set forth, it explores the ways in which the enterprises of theology and mission operate in the church and in the world. To begin, Mark Elliott gives a critical biblical-theological assessment of current trends in missional hermeneutics, urging the church toward better forms of discipleship. Next, leading historian of world Christianity Brian Stanley offers his reading of the discussion thus far, topped off with a challenging plea for evangelical theological reflection on a number of key issues emerging from the current state of global Christianity.

Pete Ward follows this with a similar plea to pay attention to the life of the church and its lived experience. In true ethnographic fashion, his is a challenge to theologians, historians, and missiologists alike to draw interpretive theology from the reality of actual ecclesial practices. The final chapter in this section is Jason Sexton's exposition of a dynamic evangelical public theology, which sketches the various ways in which theology operates in public spaces in so-called secular Western cultures, and lays out a reflexive agenda by which the church might better live out its theology as a witnessing community.

The final section is titled "The Practice of Shaping Theology for Mission" and moves the conversation out of the primarily critical, abstract, and methodological realm in order to present glimpses of differing ways in which theology and mission have worked together from an international and regional perspective. First, David Kirkpatrick offers a critical study of Ecuadorian theologian René Padilla's theology of *misión integral* (integral mission). The chapter accounts for Padilla's fascinating role within both Western (and non-Western) Evangelicalism, and explores how Western evangelicals have continued to lack significant engagement with partner evangelicals in the majority world. Next, Andrew Marin explores the issue of reconciliation in the context of alienated relationships among members of the LGBT and evangelical communities. Drawing from his work in Chicago and beyond, he offers a proposal that seeks to take sufficient account of psychological realities among victims, and makes healing and forgiveness possible through embodiment.

Continuing with the practical mission proposals, Jonny Baker employs his practitioner's lens to develop a pioneer theology for people living beyond where Christ is usually proclaimed. He explores the kind of education needed to facilitate this gift to the church, emphasizing the need to cultivate greater attention to mission and how it works. Krish Kandiah's contribution develops a vision of mission that cares for vulnerable children—especially pertinent in an era of refugee crisis. This chapter reflects on Kandiah's work with the UK-based organization Home for Good, which focuses on a theology of adoption and care, but calls for the church to develop a more robust theology for this kind of mission work.

Finally, Christopher J. H. Wright offers a valuable afterword, which serves to locate the context of this book in current discussions about mission. In doing so, he draws attention to what, in our estimation, is his own considerable contribution to the enterprise—without which the present book would surely be much poorer.

### Where the Conversation May Be Headed

We believe that the kind of critical conversation taking place in this book offers something of major importance to the future of Christian witness, especially in the context of the pressing questions raised by colonialization, globalization, forms of diaspora, the refugee crisis, and the mass migrations occurring on an unprecedented scale. In our fast-changing and challenging world, we may often wonder where and how God is working. We will also very naturally ask what we are doing as those called in mission, as well as those claiming to do academic theology in the service of the church. What is it all for? What is its end? And how might we best shape theology to serve God's purposes for the world? In spite of strong and various impulses calling us to fear others, we are called, instead, to labor with the desire to see others flourish alongside members of our own ecclesial communities, to pursue a vision of radical hospitality and vulnerability. And so, the questions addressed in this book matter massively for the ongoing dynamic life of the church and its calling.

In an ever-changing world—sometimes called "post-Christian"—in which significant challenges remain about the nature of theological education and its future, these kinds of conversations must be developed and deepened. While they may often be challenging, requiring us to learn new things and to be transformed (even sanctified!), it is our conviction that what must remain central is the significance of the church's mission as the aim of theological education. The practicality of theology is certainly something that the churches need more and more. Yet, at the same time, churches and those involved in the frontlines of missionary work in its variety of forms need the depth of tradition and theological reflection to strengthen and direct their work. We trust that this book will provide a model for the kind of rigorous engagement needed if the church is to do theology for mission, both in the academy as it continues to change, and in the churches that the academy serves.

# PART I

# Theology and Mission
# in Dialogue

1

———

# A Missional Approach to Scripture for the Theological Task

## Michael W. Goheen

### An Opening Excursus on Missional

The title employs the term "missional" as an adjective to describe the way we are to approach Scripture when doing theology. The terminology of "missional" has become pervasive in North America. It is used to describe church, theology, hermeneutic, theological education, and more. We could respond the way one editorial in a British newspaper did when referring to the word "postmodernism": "The word has no meaning. Use it as often as possible." Of course, a word can be used so much that it becomes banal. However, its ubiquity may also indicate that there is something important that has long been obscured and is now being recovered. I believe this to be the case with the term "missional."

Darrell Guder is correct when he speaks of the term "missional" as a kind of scaffolding that, at least for some of us employing the term, is holding up our ecclesiology, or theology, our interpretation of Scripture, and our theological education. There would be no need for that scaffolding if those things were already being shaped as they should be by the *missio Dei* and by a robust understanding of the church's missional nature. Speaking of theology in particular, Guder says, "If mission were truly the mother of our theology, if our theological disciplines were intentionally conceived and developed as components of the formation of the church for its biblical vocation, we would never need to use the term 'missional.'"[1] The trouble is, of course, that it is not, and so this word points us to something important that is missing. Likewise of biblical hermeneutics, Guder says that the "practice of 'hermeneutics' should be missional by its very nature. But it clearly is not, and so we must speak of 'missional hermeneutics,' propping up the enterprise with this conceptual scaffolding."[2]

The problem is that our churchmanship and our theology developed at a time when mission was not a central concern. As Lesslie Newbigin observes, "The period in which our thinking about the Church received its main features was the period in which Christianity had practically ceased to be a missionary religion. . . . It was in this period, when the dimensions of the ends of the earth had ceased to exist as a practical reality in the minds of Christians, that the main patterns of churchmanship were formed."[3] Similarly, David Bosch says of the theological curriculum: "A major problem is that the present division of theological subjects was canonized in a period when the church in Europe was completely introverted."[4]

And so I will use the word "missional" throughout this chapter as

---

1. Darrell Guder, "*Missio Dei*: Integrating Theological Formation for Apostolic Vocation," *Missiology: An International Review* 37 (2009): 66.
2. Ibid.
3. Lesslie Newbigin, *Honest Religion for Secular Man* (Philadelphia: Westminster, 1966), 102.
4. David J. Bosch, "Theological Education in Missional Perspective," *Missiology: An International Review* 10 (1982): 26.

scaffolding that draws attention to the biblical understanding of the nature of the church as it exists for the sake of the world (missional ecclesiology), to the kind of faithful theology whose content is shaped by the mission and whose goal is to equip the church for its vocation (missional theology), and to a kind of faithful biblical interpretation that takes seriously the participation of God's people in his redemptive mission as a central theme in Scripture (missional hermeneutic). Of course, scaffolding is a temporary structure that supports a building until it can stand on its own. Hopefully, someday, our understanding of church, of theology, of scriptural interpretation, and of theological education will be so suffused with our missional vocation that we no longer need the term. Perhaps, one day, we may even be able to say, as Christopher Wright often does, that to speak of "missional church" (or we might add, theology or hermeneutic) is like saying "female woman"—that's the only kind there is!

## Missional Ecclesiology, Missional Theology, and Missional Hermeneutic

The theme of this book is the task of theology. And so, before speaking of how to appropriate Scripture for that task, let me offer a brief description of what I believe missional theology to be—that is, how this scaffolding can support the task of theology. This will give us a clue about what a missional approach to Scripture for the theological task should be. Bosch says of theology: "We are in need of a missiological agenda for theology rather than just a theological agenda for mission; for theology rightly understood, has no reason to exist other than critically to accompany the *missio Dei*."[5] Similarly, Harvie Conn says that the "question is not simply, or only, or largely, missions and what it is. The question is also theology and what it does."[6] If this is so, then Bosch is correct when he says that "unless we develop a missionary theology, not just a theology of mission, we will not achieve more than

---

5. David J. Bosch, *Transforming Mission* (Maryknoll, NY: Orbis, 1991), 494.
6. Harvie Conn, "The Missionary Task of Theology: A Love/Hate Relationship?" *Westminster Theological Journal* 45 (1983): 7.

merely patch up the church."[7] These are all rather bold statements, but I believe them to be correct. So, in line with them, I describe missional theology with the following five features.

Missional theology, in the first place, explores the implications of the church's missional identity as participants in the *missio Dei*. The starting point for missional theology is the central theme of mission in the biblical story. The Bible tells one unfolding story of God's mission to restore the whole creation and entire life of humankind. At the center of God's work is his election of a people: He works *in* them and *through* them for the sake of the world. This covenant people exists to participate in God's mission, to take up their role in the biblical drama for the sake of the world. Theology accompanies them on their way, taking account of this vocation and equipping them for it.

Theological reflection explores this missional identity, besides, in all areas of the theological curriculum. Traditionally, the theological curriculum has manifested a fourfold division: biblical studies, systematic theology, church history, and practical theology. In all of these areas, the question is pressed: How does the centrality of mission in the biblical story affect the content of these disciplines? How do these disciplines equip the church for its ongoing mission?[8]

Missional theology, moreover, explores the significance of the missional vocation in all areas of the congregational life of the church. This includes the church's gathered or institutional life in which our new life in Christ is nurtured for the sake of the world (preaching, prayer, worship, sacraments, pastoral visitation, counseling, fellowship, formation, and so on), our new life in the midst of the world (evangelism, mercy and justice, involvement in our neighborhoods, cross-cultural missions, training laity for their callings, living as a contrast community, equipping to understand culture and other religions, and so on), and the structures that enable and equip the

---

7. David J. Bosch, *Believing in the Future: Toward a Missiology of Western Culture* (Valley Forge, PA: Trinity Press International, 1995), 32
8. I have probed this question in a chapter titled "A Missional Reading of Scripture, Theological Education, and Curriculum," in *Reading the Bible Missionally*, ed. Michael W. Goheen (Grand Rapids: Eerdmans, 2016), 299-329. See also, Bosch, "Theological Education in Missionary Perspective," and Newbigin, *Honest Religion for Secular Man*, 102-3.

nurturing and outward ministries to thrive (leadership, congregational, ecumenical, and financial).[9]

The fourth component of missional theology is that its goal and purpose is to form God's people to be faithful to their missional calling. Richard Bauckham laments that too often, "the academic guild of biblical scholars" has a "largely self-generated agenda [that] increasingly excludes the church from its context and implied audience." Biblical scholarship, he insists, must "address the church in its mission to the world" and even make the church in the West, which is now waking up to its mission, not simply its audience, but its primary dialogue partner.[10] Bauckham's observation is true not only of biblical studies, but of other theological disciplines as well.

Finally, missional theology rejects the notion of a *theologia perennis*—a timeless theology valid for all times and places—and is alert to the fact that all theology takes place in a particular historical and cultural context. There is no supra- or meta-cultural theology; there is only theology that reflects on the gospel in a particular context and is directed to the particular needs of a church. While the gospel has universal validity, our particular theologies do not. While particular contextual theologies may well enrich churches in other cultural contexts—in fact, they always will if they are rooted in Scripture since the gospel is universally true—they will be formed by particular historical and cultural traditions in response to the needs of the church in that setting.

There is a danger that since the very nature of theology is contextual reflection, it might become parochial and accommodated to the idolatry of particular cultures. And so missional theology will need the mutually correcting and enriching voices of Christians from other settings: from other cultures, from other historical eras, and from other confessional traditions. But theology will also require the voice

---

9. This is how I structured a course I taught at Calvin Theological Seminary, 2012–2015, titled "Introduction to Missional Ministry." It is also the way we structure the whole "congregational theology" component of our curriculum at Missional Training Center—Phoenix. We ask: If the church is missional by its very nature, how does that affect these areas of congregational life?

10. Richard Bauckham, "Mission as Hermeneutic for Scriptural Interpretation," in *Reading the Bible Missionally*, ed. Michael W. Goheen (Grand Rapids: Eerdmans, 2016), 29.

of missiology as a particular discipline to offer a critical voice that can act as a gadfly or leaven to call it to its missional vocation.[11] To quote the striking words of Harvie Conn: "Missiology stands by to interrupt at every significant moment in the theological conversation with the words 'among the nations.'"[12]

What is fundamental to these five components of missional theology is the recognition of the missional identity of the church as defined by the role it is called to play in the unfolding story of God's mission. Indeed, this is the rocket launcher that sends a missional theology into orbit. As one traces the role of God's people in the biblical story and interprets the various books of the canon in this context, two things emerge. First, the Bible is a *record* of God's mission in and through his people. Mission is so central that to ignore it is to miss a very important part of the story the Bible tells. Mission is a hermeneutical key that unlocks the biblical story. Second, the Bible is a *product* and *tool* of God's mission, in and through his people. That is, the various canonical books find their origin in God's intention to shape and equip a people for his purposes. These are the two dimensions of a missional hermeneutic.

I have now erected a missional scaffolding in a preliminary way for three interrelated things: an ecclesiology that sees its missional identity as central to its being; a theology that works out the implications of this identity to form the church for its vocation; and a hermeneutic that reads Scripture as a record and tool of God's mission, in and through his people. In fact, if we were now to take the time to trace historically a small slice of the concept of mission in the twentieth century, we would see precisely this. That is, the development of the *missio Dei* and a consequent missional ecclesiology in the middle part of the twentieth century has led inexorably on to questions about the significance of this missional identity for theology, for theological education, for the life of the church, and for reading Scripture. A missional ecclesiology has, in turn, led to a missional theology and a missional hermeneutic. A missional approach to

---

11. Bosch, "Theological Education in Missionary Perspective," 27.
12. Harvie Conn, *Eternal Word and Changing Worlds: Theology, Anthropology, and Mission in Trialogue* (Grand Rapids: Zondervan, 1984), 224.

Scripture for the task of theology comes by way of a missional hermeneutic.

## Messianic and Missional Reading of Scripture

It is not just the accidents of twentieth-century mission history that lead us to read Scripture in a missional way. Jesus himself points us to a narrative reading of Scripture with mission at the center. At the close of Luke's Gospel, the resurrected Jesus met with the disciples and "opened their minds so that they could understand the Scriptures" (Luke 24:45). To speak with contemporary terminology, Jesus gives them a hermeneutical key to unlock the biblical story. That key is disclosed in his subsequent words: "This is what is written: The Messiah will suffer and rise from the dead on the third day, and repentance for the forgiveness of sins will be preached in his name to all nations, beginning at Jerusalem" (vv. 46–47). In these words, Jesus offers a twofold hermeneutical key.[13] The first is messianic: the Messiah will suffer and rise from the dead on the third day. The second is missional: and repentance for the forgiveness of sins will be preached in his name to all nations. The grammar of Jesus's words is clear: both Christ *and* the subsequent mission of the church are referred to in "This is what is written" that is now being fulfilled. Together, they form a key to interpret the Scriptures.

The Old Testament story is one of restoration and renewal. God set out on the long road of redemption to restore the whole creation, a people from all nations, and the whole of human life from sin and its effects. Jesus stood with the other Jews of his day in reading the Old Testament as a story waiting for an ending. According to Jesus's words, that story finds its climactic telos in himself, Jesus the Messiah who accomplishes this salvation. "What is written" is fulfilled by the work of the Messiah, especially in his death and resurrection. However, the Old Testament story is also one of the restoration and renewal *of all nations through God's chosen people.* The whole Old Testament story

13. Christopher J. H. Wright, *The Mission of God: Unlocking the Bible's Grand Narrative* (Downers Grove, IL: IVP Academic, 2006), 30, 41.

has in view, from the outset, the salvation of all nations, indeed, of the entire creation. And this will be accomplished through a chosen people. God's particularist means in choosing Abraham and Israel ultimately have a universal goal in the salvation of all nations. Thus Jesus discloses the climactic moment of the Old Testament story, not only in how salvation has been accomplished (in the Messiah), but also in how that salvation is to now include all nations through his chosen people (in mission). "What is written" is fulfilled by the work of Jesus and by mission of the church to the ends of the earth.

These words of Jesus invite a twofold response as we read Scripture, and both are important for appropriating and approaching Scripture for the theological task. The first is to look back and read the Old Testament story with a messianic and missional lens. The second is to look forward and read the New Testament with the same lens. In other words, if we are to read the Bible aright, we must recognize, not only the centrality of Christ, but also the essential missional thread that weaves its way through the whole Scripture. A missional hermeneutic is not simply a matter of tracing the theme of mission throughout the biblical story the way we might trace, say, the theme of work or marriage. Rather, it posits mission as an indispensable lens for reading the whole. Richard Bauckham puts it nicely when he says that a "missionary hermeneutic . . . is a way of reading the Bible for which mission is the hermeneutical key. . . . A missionary hermeneutic of this kind would not be simply a study of the theme of mission in the biblical writings, but a way of reading *the whole of Scripture* with mission as its central interest and goal."[14]

## Scripture as a Record of God's Mission in and through His People

Scripture is a historical record of God's mission to restore the whole creation from sin through the mission of his chosen covenant people. Bauckham further identifies two approaches in biblical scholarship that are especially favorable for developing a missional hermeneutic

14. Bauckham, "Mission as Hermeneutic," 28.

—narrative and canonical. We may also observe that the biblical theology movement dominated the ecumenical tradition in the 1940s and 1950s, and was a major factor in the rise of the *missio Dei* as the framework of a missionary ecclesiology at the Willingen conference of the International Missionary Council (1952). Like both the narrative and canonical approaches to Scripture, biblical theology attends to Scripture as one unfolding story of God's redemptive work in history. The redemptive-historical tradition of Dutch Calvinism, which shaped the missional hermeneutic and theology of folks such as J. H. Bavinck and Harvie Conn, also reads Scripture as a canonical and narrative whole. A missional hermeneutic is dependent upon reading Scripture in this way—as one unfolding story of redemption.

We can briefly highlight three important components. The first is the importance of the Old Testament in a missional hermeneutic. Johannes Blauw rightly observes:

> When we speak about the Church as "the people of God in the world" and enquire into the real nature of this Church, we cannot avoid speaking about the *roots* of the Church which are to be found in the Old Testament idea of Israel as the people of the covenant. So the question of the *missionary* nature of the Church, that is, the real relationship between the people of God and the world, cannot be solved until we have investigated the relation between Israel and the nations of the earth.[15]

Attending to the centrality of mission in the Old Testament will mean that by the time we reach the mission of the new covenant people, it is fully informed by several millennia of Israel's history that have shaped the identity of God's people as a light to the nations evident across the full spectrum of their lives.

The second feature is the scope of the salvation that is central to and the goal of the biblical story. A "soteriological self-centredness"[16] has marginalized the cosmic scope of the biblical story and has led to an emaciated understanding of mission, which, in turn, shapes a missional hermeneutic. Newbigin complains that we have abstracted

---

15. Johannes Blauw, "The Mission of the People of God," in *The Missionary Church in East and West*, ed. Charles C. West and David M. Paton (London: SCM, 1959), 91.
16. G. C. Berkouwer, *The Return of Christ* (Grand Rapids: Eerdmans, 1972), 211.

the individual from God's bigger story that gives the person's story meaning. Many read the biblical story, he says, starting with the question of individual salvation, and in so doing, privatize God's mighty work of grace and talk "as if the whole cosmic drama of salvation culminated in the words, 'For me; for me.'" This is a perversion of the Gospel, he says.[17] But not only have we isolated the individual from the cosmic scope of the biblical story, we have also diminished the central role of the community of which the individual is a part. This way of reading Scripture has deeply influenced our theology.

The logic of the biblical story that will nourish a robust missional hermeneutic and rich theological reflection is cosmic-communal-personal. God's redemptive goal is a *cosmic*, creation-wide renewal; he chooses a *community* to embody and make known that future salvation; and we are *personally* summoned to respond to God's Word, join this community, and take responsibility for our role in the bigger story. This places the people of God at the center of the story with the vocation of embodying a creation-wide, cosmic salvation.

And so these first two observations lead to the third, a point that I have already alluded to—the centrality of a people chosen for the sake of the world.[18] Somehow Israel was to be God's solution to the sin that infected his very good creation as a result of Adam's rebellion. Both election and covenant have a missional aim—the restoration of all creation and a people from all nations. God employs a particular means to accomplish his universal purpose; he walks a particularist road to reach a universal destination. I noted above Blauw's insistence of the importance of not bypassing Israel as a people of the covenant. Indeed, the covenant emphasizes the election of a people to serve God's purpose to recover his world. Both election and covenant are fundamentally missional. Election was never about Israel being chosen for its own sake—that was a distortion—but always for the sake of the world. Likewise, the purpose of the covenant was that Israel might be

17. Lesslie Newbigin, *The Gospel in a Pluralist Society* (Grand Rapids: Eerdmans, 1989), 179.
18. Cf. Michael W. Goheen, *A Light to the Nations: The Missional Church in the Biblical Story* (Grand Rapids: Baker Academic, 2011).

a light to the nations. To forget the missional aim of the covenant, says Tom Wright, is to "betray the purpose for which that covenant was made. It is as though the postman were to imagine that all the letters in his bag were intended for him."[19]

The unfolding of Israel's history is rooted in the Abrahamic and Sinaitic covenants. Together, they set a narrative trajectory for the rest of the Old Testament. God calls Abram and sets out a twofold blueprint for redemptive history: first, he promises to restore the blessing of creational life to him and his descendants, so that, second, they might be a channel of that blessing to all nations (Gen 12:2-3; 18:18-19). Blessed to be a blessing—that is the identity of God's chosen people from the beginning. At Sinai, on the heels of rescuing Israel from the dominion of Egyptian idolatry, he calls them to be a holy nation on display to all peoples and a priestly kingdom that mediates God's blessing to the nations (Exod 19:3-6). Israel is given the Torah so that they might "function as a people who would show the rest of humanity what being human was all about" (Exod 20-23).[20] The remainder of the Old Testament is a commentary on how well Israel fulfilled this calling for the sake of all nations.

Israel failed, treating both election and the covenant as an exclusive privilege. Called to model God's original creational design for human life in the midst of the nations, Israel was unfaithful to that commission, served idols instead of the living God, and thus, rather than being the solution, became part of the problem. The lifeguard God sent out to save the drowning world now also was drowning. But God promises through his prophets that his plan to bless all nations and restore the whole creation *through his chosen people* will not be foiled; he will gather and renew his people to successfully complete their missional role.

In keeping with God's promise, Jesus takes upon himself Israel's vocation to be the light of the world. In his ministry, he gathers the

---

19. N. T. Wright, *What Saint Paul Really Said: Was Paul of Tarsus the Real Founder of Christianity?* (Grand Rapids: Eerdmans, 1997), 108.

20. Tom Wright, *Bringing the Church to the World: Renewing the Church to Confront the Paganism Entrenched in Western Culture* (Minneapolis: Bethany House, 1992), 59.

scattered sheep of Israel, inviting them to join him afresh in their vocation, and showing and teaching them what that would look like. In his life, death, and resurrection he fulfills the covenant, dealing with the sin of the world, including the sin and failure of Israel so that they might now fulfill their original calling. The newly gathered and renewed Israel, the new covenant people of God, is the beginnings of the new humanity restored in Christ, called now to fulfill their original vocation, which they had failed to attain. Jesus sends them to the nations to continue his own mission, the original mission of Israel. "As the Father has sent me, I am sending you" (John 20:21) defines the very identity of this disciple community. They are to discharge their mission to the world as he had to Israel.

With the outpouring of his Spirit, God calls into being the eschatological people of God, the restored Israel for the sake of the world. This renewed Israel transformed through Jesus, and by the Spirit, is sent into the world. It is now a nongeographically based and multiethnic people called to continue Jesus's mission, to witness to his reign in life, word, and deed to the ends of the earth. And it is this mission that gives the church its very identity. The church is called to make known the end of universal history as a sign, foretaste, and instrument of the kingdom. It is a sign and foretaste of the goal of salvation history: it is to be a preview of what God will do for the entire cosmos. But the church is also an instrument, the means by which God's renewing work comes into the world.

This all too brief summary of the biblical story highlights the centrality of mission—God's mission, in and through his people. And it is essential to stress again that mission is not simply a subsidiary theme in the biblical narrative, but a hermeneutical lens on the whole of Scripture. And so, our approach to Scripture for the theological task must take seriously this missional direction and framework of the biblical story. "A missional hermeneutic," says Christopher Wright, "will work hard to read any text in the [scriptural] canon within this overarching framework, discerning its place within that framework, assessing how the shape of the grand narrative is reflected in the text in question, and conversely, how the particular text contributes to and moves forward the grand narrative itself."[21]

## Scripture as a Tool of God's Mission in and through His People

Scripture is not only a *record* of God's mission, in and through his people, to bring salvation to the world; it is also a *tool* to effectively bring it about. Or perhaps better, Scripture is a toolbox with many genres, all of which function to bring salvation through faith in Jesus the Christ. They don't just tell us the story but also take an active part in actually accomplishing it. Thus the nature and authority of Scripture may be understood in terms of its place and role in this story, or as Tom Wright puts it, biblical authority is a "sub-branch . . . of the mission of the church." He continues: "God's self-revelation is always to be understood within the category of God's mission to the world, God's saving sovereignty let loose through Jesus and the Spirit and aimed at the healing and renewal of the creation."[22] To rightly understand the nature and authority of Scripture, then, is to understand its formative role, how it powerfully works to shape a faithful people, and through them, to bring healing to the world. To miss this role and purpose of Scripture is to misunderstand how we are to approach and appropriate it.

And so, an essential question to ask of the text of Scripture, according to Guder, is, "How did this written testimony form and equip God's people for their missional vocation then, and how does it do so today?" He goes on to rightly draw out the implication for all biblical studies: "All the resources of historical, critical, and literary research on the biblical testimony can and must contribute to the church's formation by illumining all the dimensions of this fundamental question."[23]

---

21. Christopher J. H. Wright, "Mission and Old Testament Interpretation," in *Hearing the Old Testament: Listening for God's Address*, ed. Craig G. Bartholomew and David J. H. Beldman (Grand Rapids: Eerdmans, 2012), 184.
22. N. T. Wright, *Scripture and the Authority of God* (SanFrancisco: HarperOne, 2011), 27–29.
23. Darrell Guder, "From Mission and Theology to Missional Theology," *Princeton Seminary Bulletin* 24 (2003): 48.

Formation for their missional calling—that is why the various books of the scriptural canon were written. Again, what we mean by formation for mission is not an equipping to carry out various evangelistic and outreach activities. Rather, the vocation of God's people is to be a distinctive people embodying God's original creational intentions for humanity as a sign and preview to the world of where God is taking the whole creation. God works redemptively, first of all *in* his people, and thereafter *through* his people. So, the scriptural books were written to form God's people to be a distinctive people, ultimately for the sake of the nations.

The biblical books are *products* of God's mission in and through his people. They arise out of various needs, threats, and crises that face God's people in the course of living out their calling. Moreover, the various books of the canon are *tools* of God's mission; they form and shape God's people to be faithful to their vocation. For example, the Pentateuch is addressed to a people in danger of being engulfed by the pagan religions of the ancient Near East: thus Genesis 1 is a polemic against ancient Near Eastern creation myths that enables Israel to understand the true God, what it really means to be human, and what the world is really like; and the redemption of Israel from Egypt is portrayed as God's victory over the Egyptian gods. The Torah is designed to shape Israel into a people who embody God's creational purposes for human society in a particular cultural and historical context. Historical and prophetical books are addressed to a people in a crisis of faith so as to shape their identity and call them to faithfulness in a new setting: 1–2 Kings and Jeremiah address a people in exile who wonder what they are doing there after God's promises about a people, land, king, and temple seem to be null and void; Ezra-Nehemiah, Chronicles, and Haggai are addressed to a postexilic people struggling to understand why the grand fulfillment promised earlier in Scripture has not materialized. The prophets are covenant enforcers who call Israel back to their original vocation by warning them of judgment and nurturing hope by forming their imagination with God's marvelous future. The psalms form a covenant mind-set and identity in various ways by giving Israel songs and words for their worship, including pointing them to the nations as the horizon of their vocation.[24] The wisdom literature forms a people to live in accordance with the wisdom of God's creation order across the whole spectrum of human life. The Gospels craft their narratives to proclaim and witness to the Christ event in a way that equips the church for faithful witness. The Epistles address the church in various contexts, bringing the good news of Jesus Christ to bear on their particular context so that they might be a faithful preview of the kingdom. And so on. The Scriptures form Israel and the church to be a faithful covenant people *for the sake of the world.*

I. Howard Marshall draws out the hermeneutical implication for the New Testament in a comment that could also be extended to the Old Testament: "A recognition of this missionary character of the [New Testament] documents will help us to see them in true perspective and to interpret them in the light of their intention."[25] The first step in hermeneutical obedience to discern what the particular text is trying to do. And so, in our approach to Scripture for the theological task we must constantly ask: What is this text trying to do? How is this text or book or genre functioning to equip God's people for their missional calling, then and now?

## Implications of a Missional Reading of Scripture for Theology

Scripture is the main source for theology. If mission is a central theme in the biblical story, then this will form a missional theology. Two distinctions are important if we are to properly understand the word "missional" as an adjective to describe theology. The first, introduced by Lesslie Newbigin in the middle part of the previous century, is between missionary dimension and missionary intention.[26] He is reflecting on the nature of mission itself rather than theology. There

---

24. The "nations" are mentioned some 175 times in the Psalms.
25. I. Howard Marshall, *New Testament Theology: Many Witnesses, One Gospel* (Downers Grove, IL: InterVarsity Press, 2004), 35.
26. Lesslie Newbigin, *One Body, One Gospel, One World* (London: International Missionary Council, 1958), 21, 43–44.

are intentional activities such as evangelism, church planting, and works of justice and mercy that have as their express intent the purpose of making known the gospel in word or deed. However, most of our lives are not aimed deliberately at that goal. Yet all of our lives have a missional dimension. That is, every part of the life of the Christian community—individually and corporately—witnesses to the renewing power of the gospel.

This distinction may also helpfully be applied to theology. Missiology deals explicitly and intentionally with various issues of the missional task of the church. However, not all theology will have mission as its explicit subject matter. Yet theology should have a missional dimension; mission is "not simply yet another subject but a dimension of theology as a whole."[27] Mission raises new questions and formulates different approaches to the same subject matter. It brings missional questions to bear on the work of the various theological disciplines. It reframes but does not replace theology as it has developed historically. It brings new perspectives, new questions, and new light to familiar issues and themes. It is, to quote Conn again, a matter of *interrupting the theological conversation among the various disciplines with the reminder "among the nations."*[28]

The second distinction important to understanding the adjective "missional" is between the goal and content of theology. Theology must be missional in the sense that its *goal* is to equip the church for its missional calling. Theology plays a role in the formation of leaders and a congregation to more faithfully embody the gospel for the sake of the world. Both phrases are held together: formation "to embody the gospel" and "for the sake of the world." But theology must also be formed in its *content* by the central theme of mission. How does the category of mission shape the various aspects of theological reflection? For too long, theology has primarily treated "to embody the gospel" and neglected "for the sake of the world."

Karl Barth critiques a theology that has forgotten mission as "pious

---

27. Bosch, "Theological Education in Missionary Perspective," 26.
28. Conn, *Eternal Word*, 224.

and sacred egocentricity."[29] He asks a deceptively simple question: What does it mean be a Christian? The "classic answer" is to be a recipient and possessor of the *beneficia Christi* (benefits of Christ). He lists these benefits: regeneration, conversion, peace with God, reconciliation, justification, sanctification, forgiveness of sins, empowerment to live a life of liberation, beloved of God, freedom, adoption as God's children, hope of the resurrection of the body, foretaste and heirs of eternal life, and a new obedience. All these come by grace as gifts of God in Jesus Christ by the Holy Spirit in response to repentance and faith. It is this, he says, that inspires the theology of the church. It is the way the New Testament has been approached and appropriated in theology.

"There can be no disputing," says Barth, "that something true and important is meant and envisaged in all this."[30] Yet it would be all too easy to make the reception, possession, and enjoyment of these benefits what is essential to being a Christian. Barth wonders: Can it really be the end of Christian vocation that I should be blessed, that I should be saved, that I should receive, possess, and enjoy all these gifts and then attain to eternal life without any regard for others? Does this not smack of a pious or sacred egocentricity? Would it not be strange and even contradictory that the selfless and self-giving work of God should issue in a self-seeking concern with our own salvation? Would not this egocentricity stand in stark contrast to the being and action of the Lord? Would this not turn the church into an institute of salvation that forgot its very missional purpose in the world? Does this not make us *pure* recipients and possessor of salvation?[31]

## Conclusion

If, on that final day, the church is found to be a pure recipient and possessor of salvation, it will be justly judged for neglecting its calling given by its Lord. Theology will play a role in forming the church:

---

29. Karl Barth, *Church Dogmatics*, vol. IV, *The Doctrine of Reconciliation*, pt. 3.2, ed. Geoffrey W. Bromiley and T. F. Torrance (1961; repr., Peabody, MA: Hendrickson, 2010), IV/3.2: 554–69.
30. Ibid., 563.
31. Ibid., 568.

it may either either foster this pious egocentricity or help equip the church for its missional calling. But to faithfully fulfill the latter, it must recover a missional approach to Scripture—a covenant people chosen and blessed for the sake of the world.

2

———

# Widening the Frame on Redemptive History: A Response to Michael Goheen

### Justin Stratis

I am grateful for the opportunity to offer some brief words of response to Michael Goheen's provocative chapter, "A Missional Approach to Scripture for the Theological Task." Before beginning, however, I would like to highlight that, in terms of the work's practical effect, I am in total agreement. Like Goheen, I believe a church that mutes its missiological impetus, or indeed, treats mission as a mere appendix to its activities, is a disobedient church. I also agree that Holy Scripture, particularly the New Testament, was written in what we might call a "missional context," and thus any reasonable historical interpretation of the Bible cannot ignore this fundamental factor.[1] Finally, I believe

1. On this point, see Christopher J. H. Wright, "Mission as a Matrix for Hermeneutics and Biblical

that, as an essentially ministerial discipline (that is, a discipline that is not an end in itself but rather trades in what David Kelsey calls "second order" discourse),[2] theology ought to do the work of equipping the saints to fulfill their divine commission in the world. Consequently, in offering critique, my aim is only to broaden or expand the backdrop against which these points of agreement might find even more theological coherence.[3]

I will structure this chapter in three small sections that roughly correspond to what I understand to be the three main *doctrinal* points in Goheen's essay. First, I will interact with the claim that "mission" is the hermeneutical "key" to the narrative of Scripture. Second, I will explore the nature of the church, and more specifically, whether "mission" ought to be that aspect of the church's existence from which we infer its primary identity. And third, I will suggest an alternative paradigm, which may bring Goheen and me closer together, namely, seeing mission under the imperative of creaturely obedience before the Creator of the world.

## 1. Mission and the Grand Narrative

One of the more intriguing aspects of Goheen's chapter is his claim that the crimson thread running through the "grand narrative" of the Bible is precisely mission—specifically, God's mission to restore creation to harmonious fellowship with its Creator in light of sin. From a theological perspective, there is much to commend this thesis. For example, I resonate strongly with the idea that what brings coherence to the canon is not simply a singular religious history (that is, the assumption of certain "canonical" approaches), but rather, a consistency of divine activity. As Goheen rightly emphasizes, the primary concern of Holy Scripture is to narrate something that *God*

Theology," in *Out of Egypt: Biblical Theology and Biblical Interpretation*, ed. Craig Bartholomew et al. (Grand Rapids: Zondervan, 2004), 120–22.

2. See, for instance, David H. Kelsey, *Eccentric Existence: A Theological Anthropology* (Louisville: Westminster John Knox, 2009), 1:20–27.

3. For a more critical reading of Goheen's chapter, see chap. 7 of the present vol., Mark W. Elliott, "Theology, Bible, and Mission."

is doing. And so, among the impressive variety of peoples, events, and perhaps even religious ideologies depicted in the biblical text, what remains consistent is the presence of a principal actor—God himself—who, in the words of St. Paul, "worketh all things after the counsel of his own will" (Eph 1:11 KJV). The Bible, then, *is* a "grand narrative"; in the broadest sense, it is the story of God's dealings with all that is not God. Consequently, when, as Christian disciples, we aim to "emplot" ourselves in such a tale, we can only do so in relation to the actual nature of such dealings. The question, then, is whether the full measure of the particular relationship between God and creation depicted in the Bible is rightly captured by the term "mission," and that is what I would like to explore presently.

According to Goheen, the story Scripture tells is chiefly one of "redemption." Indeed, he says, "A missional hermeneutic is dependent upon reading Scripture—as one unfolding story of redemption." This is surely true, but I wonder if beginning the story with a creation in need of such redemption leads us to neglect certain key threads in the narrative. In particular, what is it about creation that makes it so worthy of divine favor, even in the face of its blatant rebellion? Obviously, it is the case that all of Scripture was composed in a post-lapsarian context, and moreover was written for the benefit of a world desperately in need of salvation; nevertheless, there are moments when the frame is pulled back to reveal a much broader perspective. The Son was indeed sent to atone for our sins, but he was also slain "from the foundation of the world" (Rev 13:8). Jeremiah was called to execute a particular task in the history of Judah, and yet he was known by God even before his conception (Jer 1:5). Paul praises God for redeeming the pagans in Ephesus, but then reveals that their new identity "in Christ" is actually the fruit of a divine decision that preceded creation itself. There are hints, it seems, that the redemptive history presented in Scripture finds its narrative coherence in a context far greater than that which it specifically depicts.

This ought not to surprise us, of course, because the principal actor of redemption, namely, the God of Jesus Christ, is himself described as radically exceeding the creation in which he undertakes his mighty works. "Where were *you*," this One asks of Job, "when I laid the foundation of the earth?" (Job 38:4). The answer is, of course, *nowhere*. While it may *not* be said of the divine Son, it surely *could* be said of us, on the grounds of Holy Scripture: *there was a time when we were not.*[4] Whatever happens in history, then, is preceded, radically and incomparably, by the being of God. And to the extent that Scripture attributes certain actions and activities to *this* God, we are obligated to designate his identity, beyond, above, and even without us, with all due fittingness and care. This too is a responsibility laid upon those to whom God has chosen to give himself in Christ, and theology helps us to offer just such a faithful response.

Now, this ought not to be heard as a plea to reinstate all manner of speculative theology to the detriment of mission. It is, instead, an attempt to put redemptive history in its proper context. There is only a *missio Dei* because there is a first a *Deus*, and second, a *voluntas Dei in creatione*, that is, a divine will for creation. The Bible invites us to consider this order when it tells us that God is not a constituent, but the creator of the world and, consequently, that there is *no one* like him (1 Chron 17:20). For this reason, I would prefer to reverse Goheen's claim that "election and covenant are fundamentally missional" to read, instead, that "mission is essentially covenantal and therefore based upon divine election." Put another way: mission occurs within the context of covenant, and as such, it serves the ends of that fundamental feature of the divine will for creation.

Therefore, we should consider creation not only as the theater for, or even the object of, redemption but also, and primarily, as a divinely commissioned reality fitted from the beginning with certain ends. To answer the question, "why did God create the world?" with the response, "to redeem it" is insufficient precisely because it tells us nothing of the real nature of creation, and by extension, the Creator whose will it reflects. Jonathan Edwards is helpful here when he suggests a distinction between what he calls an "original" end and a

---

4. I use temporal language here to indicate the contingent nature of human existence.

"consequential" end. In his essay, "Concerning the End for Which God Created the World," Edwards argues that while certain aspects of God's relationship to creation are essential to understanding the testimony of Scripture—for instance, "his faithfulness, or his inclination to fulfill his promises to his creatures"[5]—they are ultimately *consequent* upon God's decision to create a certain type of world with a certain type of end, that is, the world's *original* end. Moreover, he suggests, enquiring into such an end is not superfluous to the concerns of Scripture, because the very coherence of the biblical narrative depends upon the ultimate context in which it sits. If, for instance, God created the world simply for his own amusement (as is the case in certain mythologies), it would be difficult to explain why he would go to such extremes to redeem it. On the contrary, if God created the world to manifest his glory, as Edwards ultimately concludes, redemption can be shown to make much more sense.[6] Similarly, in his *De Incarnatione*, St. Athanasius argues that before one can offer an explanation for the coming of the Word to redeem the world, one must first speak of the nature of creation "so it may be duly perceived that the renewal of creation has been the work of the selfsame Word that made it at the beginning."[7] In other words, a doctrine of redemption must show itself to flow from the doctrine of creation, and, furthermore, a doctrine of creation will be intelligible only in light of the doctrine of God.

Hence, while I agree with Goheen that the Bible tells the story of a loving God who undertakes a grand mission to rescue the world from sin, there are yet a few chapters, as it were, that precede and follow this tale—chapters upon which I suggest that redemptive history itself depends on. And if this is the case, then it would seem that the engine that drives the biblical plot forward is not *primarily* mission, but rather the nature of creation itself, or, more specifically, the covenant that God made with creatures at the very beginning. And if this very specific

---

5. Jonathan Edwards, "Concerning the End for Which God Created the World," in *Works of Jonathan Edwards*, vol. 8, *Ethical Writings*, ed. Paul Ramsey (New Haven: Yale University Press, 1987), 412.
6. I am not necessarily affirming Edwards's view in this chapter.
7. Athanasius, "On the Incarnation of the Word," in *Christology of the Later Fathers*, ed. Edward R. Hardy (Louisville: Westminster John Knox, 1954), 56.

Creator-creature relationship lies at the heart of the narrative, then mission can only be seen as a theme that contributes to something much higher, that is, the end of creation, or, the purpose for which God elected to extend his perfect triune life beyond himself. That, I believe, is the context in which the biblical narrative ultimately takes place and which, consequently, generates the proper hermeneutic for its interpretation. What is creation, and who is the Creator? These are the questions theology asks and that are illumined, yet not finally answered, by the *missio Dei*.

## Excursus: Mission and the Being of God

I pause here in my dialogue with Michael Goheen to engage briefly the thought of another missiologist whose work may attenuate the force of the argument I have just made, and that is John Flett. In his fascinating and lucid study *The Witness of God*, Flett suggests that one of the reasons why the church has often regarded world-facing mission as secondary to its supposedly core identity as a worshiping community is that it assumes a similar "cleavage" between God's identity in himself and God's good will for the world. Thus, he writes:

> The problem of the church's relationship to the world is consequent on treating God's own mission into the world as a second step alongside who he is in himself. With God's movement into his economy ancillary to his being, so the church's own corresponding missionary relationship with the world is ancillary to her being.[8]

Flett's contention is that, for nearly half a century, ecumenical missiologists struggled (quite rightly) to ground their mission theory in the doctrine of God, particularly the Trinity, as a consequence of their commitment to *missio Dei* as a controlling paradigm. The fact that none succeeded in doing so, despite the frequent verbal deployment of the phrase in the literature, was due precisely to a lack of attention paid to the doctrine of God itself. A solution to this confusing state of

---

8. John G. Flett, *The Witness of God: The Trinity, Missio Dei, Karl Barth, and the Nature of Christian Community* (Grand Rapids: Eerdmans, 2010), 3.

affairs, Flett suggests, can be found in the theology of Karl Barth, who realized that the revelation of God in Christ entails the doing away of any cleavage between God's being and act.

The debate among specialists regarding Barth's supposed "actualistic ontology" is thorny and need not be engaged fully here.[9] Suffice it to say, for Flett and others, Barth's genius was to recognize that God's benevolent will for humanity is based on a prior and concrete divine *self*-determination to *be* God-for-humanity *in* Jesus Christ. Put another way: there is no God outside of God's eternal decision to include humanity in his very being, hence no appeal can be made to any nonchristologically determined being of God in the Christian confession (for example, God's eternal triune being *simpliciter*). Consequently, we ought to say, with Flett, that "God is a missionary God"—a God who, to the depths of his being, faces others in love and with hospitality.[10]

On the face of it, this scheme seems to call into question my claim that God's being radically exceeds his history with humanity (and thus qualifies the story of redemption, rather than vice versa). Moreover, if seeing the Bible as a witness to God in himself forces one into the realm of a dehistoricized, natural theology (as Flett argues such a position entails), then I would agree that I am in violation of a key consequence of the revelation of God in Christ. However, such a consequence is not inevitable if one disciplines oneself to define God's being in the personalist terms that the biblical narrative particularly highlights.

In my view, the aseity of God, or the theological defensibility of the thought "God in himself," is very specifically a concomitant of God's eminently personal being.[11] God's being is God's act, as Barth insists,

9. For a collection of some of the more influential essays in the debate, see Michael T. Dempsey, ed., *Trinity and Election in Contemporary Theology* (Grand Rapids: Eerdmans, 2011).

10. Flett, *Witness of God*, 196–239. For another defense of this divine name, and for different reasons, see Stephen R. Holmes, "Trinitarian Missiology: Towards a Theology of God as Missionary," *International Journal of Systematic Theology* 8 (2006): 72–90.

11. It is not incidental that Barth himself once titled the so-called Perfections of Love and Freedom from the *Church Dogmatics* Die personalichen Vollkommenheiten Gottes and *Die aseitätischen Vollkommenheiten Gottes*, respectively. Barth used this terminology in his dogmatics lectures given in Münster during 1926–1927, which are unfortunately unpublished, but housed in the Barth-Archiv in Basel, Switzerland (relevant sections are §§30–33; titles are on lecture cards 214 and 290).

not because God's will has an especially definitive purchase on his being (leading to such strange ideas as God "constituting" himself), but because there is no gap between *who* and *what* God is.[12] Unlike created persons, God is not a person-in-formation—a person who is arriving at his personhood—but a person *in* becoming. In other words, because God is already "himself," so to speak, he is also the only person who can *be himself* in a history, particularly a history that involves other persons. This enables God to give himself to humanity without, as it were, "giving himself away."[13] God's ability to give himself fully to his creation is predicated on the fact that he is infinitely and eternally beyond and above his creation. Indeed, the purity and unreservedness with which God can and has given himself to us in Christ reveals to us that God does not merely love, but is the very act in which he loves us; God is love (1 John 4:8).

In the following sense, therefore, I can agree with Flett that God *is* a missionary God: God is what he does in his outgoing movement toward humanity because God cannot acquire any more identity by such external acts than that which he already has in himself. Hence, because God is himself without humanity, so can he include humanity in his personal being—as, in fact, he has done in Jesus Christ.

If this is true, however, it is misleading to say that God's personal being is logically *determined* by his decisions vis-à-vis humanity. It is not as if God "found himself" in his eternal decision to be for humanity; it is rather more like God elected to be himself *with us*. Similarly, it is misleading to suggest that the being of the church must, and thus, *can* correspond to the kind of unique personal existence that God enjoys

---

12. Cf. Wilfred Härle: "Barth is able to define God not only as a 'person'; he can also ascribe to God a 'nature.' This does not contradict the description of the divine being as act, but rather, is possible because of it. Here, it is crucial that the concepts of 'person' and 'nature' are not defined by a general, created understanding of person and nature, but . . . on the grounds of an analysis of the actual divine being as person and nature." *Sein und Gnade: Die Ontologie in Karl Barths Kirchliche Dogmatik* (Berlin: Walter de Gruyter, 1975), 49.

13. Karl Barth, *Church Dogmatics*, vol. IV, *The Doctrine of Reconciliation*, pt. 1, ed. Geoffrey W. Bromiley and T. F. Torrance (London: T&T Clark, 2003), 185. Cf. Barth's comments from an earlier volume: "God gives Himself entirely to man in His revelation, but not in such a way as to make Himself man's prisoner. He remains free in His working, in giving Himself." *Church Dogmatics*, vol. I, *The Doctrine of the Word of God*, pt. 1, ed. Geoffrey W. Bromiley and T. F. Torrance (London: T&T Clark, 1975), 371.

as God—an existence wherein *what* we are (the people of God) corresponds exactly to that which we do (mission). Creatures are simply of a different order than God the Creator; whereas God's identity is fully realized, enabling him to be himself fully in all of his acts, we must live *into* our God-given creaturely vocation.

Consequently, Flett is right to insist that the church ought not to view mission as "ancillary" to its identity, yet this is only because the vocation of God's people to serve the world has been determined by God as constitutive of the identity toward which the church is moving eschatologically. There is no church in the eschaton that has not obeyed the divine command to bear witness to Christ, and so there is no present church that can ignore this command. Or: just as creation cannot be without observing the divine "Let there be . . . ," so the church cannot exist without reference to her commission, even if at the end of all things she will see rest from her labors.[14] Such leads me to my next section, engaging Goheen on the church and mission.

## 2. Mission and the Church

Several times in his chapter, Goheen refers to the church's "missional identity" as the foundation of a "missional ecclesiology." In general, I can see the logic of this perspective: the church is indeed commissioned to make disciples through the proclamation of Christ by word and deed, and to the extent that creatures owe their existence fundamentally to a divine command ("Let there be . . ."), I can see how being the recipient of a divine commission entails that one's identity has now become linked to this command (in the sense described above). My question, however, has to do with the force of the term "identity." For instance, when Goheen says that the sending of the

---

14. Notably, Flett is aware of the "eschatological objection" to the church's missional identity that I raise here. His response involves the claim that because "witness is the nature of the Son's relationship with the Father (John 14:10), the Father's relationship to the Son (John 5:32), the Spirit's relationship to the Son (John 15:26), the Son's relationship to the disciples (Acts 26:16–18), and the disciples' relationship to the Son (Rev. 7:9–10)," so "witness is not something beyond which the community will move in the *eschaton*" (*Witness of God*, 224–25). In one sense, I agree with Flett that the church will continue to testify to God's glory in the *eschaton*; nevertheless, it seems to me that some equivocation is necessary to regard such a state of affairs as the extension of "mission" as an ecclesial *act* to the consummated history of divine and human fellowship.

disciples by Christ in John 20:21 "defines the very identity of this disciple community," does he mean to emphasize that the church now participates in mission by "being" in the world (for example, as a "counter-polis"), or does he mean that the church simply *is* its mission, such that all aspects of its calling, existence, and essence are properly bounded within this particular vocation. I can reconcile myself, to a certain extent, to the former option, but the latter raises some questions.

If the church *is* its mission, then I wonder, first of all, how this relates to Christology. "As my Father hath sent me, even so send I you," Jesus tells his disciples. This *is*, surely, an invitation and authorization for the church to join with the *missio Dei*, particularly in the power of the Holy Spirit. But, of course, Jesus's own identity, upon which the disciples' identity is predicated, is not *finally* missional—the reality of the ascension informs us that the incarnational identity of the Son endures forever, even *after* he has redeemed the world. Consequently, it is not the "working" of John 5:17 that determines the Son's incarnational life in an ultimate sense, but rather the *rest* of the incarnate Son in the favor of the Father, a reality that also speaks to our fundamental identity, even as we participate in Christ's mission now, prior to the establishment of the new heavens and the new earth. Like Christ's identity, the identity of the church is not *ultimately* determined by her mission, but fundamentally by her relationship to the Father, established by grace through adoption. As Jesus instructs Mary, "Go to my brothers and say to them, 'I am ascending to my Father and your Father, to my God and your God'" (John 20:17). Similarly, for St. Paul, to be "in Christ" means, in part, to enjoy the *visio Dei* in the company of the Son, such that "when Christ . . . is revealed, then you also will be revealed with him in glory" (Col 3:4). Again, it is only because we are predestined to be joint heirs with Christ in the covenant of creation that we may serve his kingdom in the present under the banner of the *missio Dei*. The church's identity is "in Christ," and what Christ offers—indeed what Christ *is*—finally and in correspondence to God's unchanging will, is *peace*. Thus, it is only *after* God enables his people "to successfully complete their missional role" (as Goheen puts it) that the church will embody her identity in the fullest possible sense, when, as the hymn writer puts it, "with the vision glorious, [our] longing eyes are blest, and the great church victorious, shall be the church at rest." As with the doctrine of creation, it is the end of the church that determines even its contemporary identity, and not vice versa. The church may indeed emerge *in time* from the redemptive mission of God, but its eschatological destiny, born of the eternal divine decree, *is*, in an unqualified sense, determinative of its immutable essence.[15]

### 3. A Place for Mission in the Grand Narrative

As stated earlier, I am wholly sympathetic with Goheen's desire to encourage the church to live out its missional vocation. So what theological rationale might enable us to join in this shared vision? Here, I think that Karl Barth offers some wise counsel. In an essay titled "Theology and Mission in the Present," published in 1932, Barth inquires into the nature of both theology and mission, wondering, in particular, how these two seemingly disparate church activities might be brought together into a more coherent relationship.[16] He suggests that what unites them is the fact that both activities share the aim of bringing all things under the lordship of Christ. Both the world *and the church*, Barth says, err in that they do not correspond to their created ends; both, in differing respects, "exchange the truth about God for a lie and worship and serve the creature rather than the Creator" (Rom 1:25). While it may perhaps be easier to envision this problem with respect to the world, Barth is clear that the church is often equally guilty of such idolatry; we are, in his unhappy phrase, a "pagan church" (*Heidenkirche*).[17] Hence, while we might distinguish between mission and theology as the "outward" and "inward" ministries of the church,

---

15. This is reflected, I think, in the careful wording of *Ad Gentes*, which states that "the *pilgrim* church is missionary by her very nature" (I.2)—a concept that is explicated in *Lumen Gentium* in relation to the church's "eschatological" nature as the worshiping community in the heavenly City (§§ 48–51).
16. Karl Barth, "Die Theologie und die Mission in der Gegenwart," *Zwischen den Zeiten* 10 (1932): 189–215.
17. Ibid., 191.

respectively, both share an identical aim: laying the Word of God before rebellious creatures in order to incite repentance and reconciliation with their Creator in the power of the Holy Spirit. In this respect, Barth can say both that "everything that the church does is mission,"[18] and "mission conditions everything that the church does,"[19] since even the church's own internal discourse aims for the conversion of human hearts to God.

What I like about Barth's model is that it blurs the lines between church and world, such that the primary engine driving redemptive history is precisely the Creator-creature relationship. God *is* the lord of his creation, and the temporal relationship between the two parties serves only to reinforce this *fact* in the drama of history. Missional theology, then, is the church's attempt to bring its speech and action under the sovereignty of God and thereby to announce the lordship of Christ to the world. This call to obedience finds its rationale in the very identity of God, emerges from the heart of the covenant, and extends beyond this "time between the times" into all eternity, when God's glory in Christ will be evident to all. Implied in this model, then, are a doctrine of God, a doctrine of creation, and an account of redemption as a consequence of God's fundamental commitment to the creature. Moreover, I would suggest, it frees us to read Scripture "missionally," as Goheen desires, because we see in this model every aspect of the biblical metanarrative as a working out of God's identity as the Creator. To put it another way, the long narrative arc of the Bible, a feature both Goheen and I are zealous to highlight, begins to make sense when we attend not only to the internal logic of the story, but also, and especially, to the God whose identity gives rise to its possibility, duration, and final consummation.

### 4. Conclusion

In the end, I am encouraged by the work of those such as Michael Goheen, Christopher J. H. Wright, Craig Bartholomew, David Bosch,

18. Ibid., 190.
19. Ibid., 204.

and others as they highlight the Bible's missional context/aim through attendance to the metanarrative of redemption. In no way do I want to challenge this general observation. In order to make such a narrative work, however, I suggest that we need a bit more focus on the being of God and the nature of creation as the rubrics under which the story sits. And here, we may indeed find a constructive way for the work of theologians and missiologists to complement each other in fruitful ways.

3

---

# More Scripture, Please! A Protestant Approach to Appropriating Tradition for Theology Today

## Bradley G. Green

The intent of this chapter is to explore the importance of tradition in the Christian theological task. While a more programmatic statement is warranted by the topic, the exploration in this chapter will, by necessity, be something of a sketch of the major issues as I understand them.

The topic itself brings to mind an aphoristic quip in Richard Muller's four-volume *Post-Reformation Reformed Dogmatics.*[1] In his section on theological method, Muller suggests that rarely (ever?) did a

---

1. Richard A. Muller, *Post-Reformation Reformed Dogmatics: The Rise and Development of Reformed Orthodoxy, ca. 1520 to ca. 1725*, 4 vols., 2nd ed. (Grand Rapids: Baker Academic, 2003).

theologian *first* formulate a method and *then* apply the method. Rather, theologians tried their best to say something true of God and his ways with men and *then* (perhaps) wrote of their "method." In short, the Protestant scholastics *first* "did theology" and *then* said, "Now, this is my method." When I first read Muller on this a number of years ago, I concurred. And over the years, my concurrence with him has only been strengthened by my own attempts to read, teach, and write Christian theology.

I have just finished seventeen years of teaching theology, so I write as someone who is perhaps at the beginning of mid-career—I am no longer a complete beginner, but I still have a lot to learn. But if I may be forgiven, an initial anecdotal reflection on the state of evangelical theology is warranted here. As I see it, one of the tendencies among some evangelical theologians is an increasing appreciation for the theological past—in particular, the church fathers. I think this general trajectory is good, essential, and right on target. Indeed, there is no path to being a good theologian unless one has some knowledge of the last two thousand years of theologizing. We all have strengths and weaknesses, but it is absolutely essential that evangelicals theologize in the light *of* and in conversation *with* the whole Christian tradition. I still remember devouring Tom Oden's *After Modernity . . . What? Agenda for Theology*[2] as a young seminary student studying at Southern Seminary (and Oden was *truly* a breath of fresh air). And I am indeed thankful for Oden's massively significant multivolume *Ancient Classic Commentary on Scripture.* My own dissertation focused heavily on Augustine, and my interests continue to revolve around how evangelicals might appropriate and benefit from Augustine today.

At the same time, I must admit that I am sometimes a tad anxious when a bright-eyed student begins to dip into the church fathers and begins to develop something of a white hat/black hat mentality. That is, I sometimes see students or others develop something of a "If it was written in the first five centuries, it must be good. And if it springs from my own Protestant tradition it must be bad, modern, and somehow

---

2. Thomas C. Oden, *After Modernity . . . What? Agenda for Theology* (Grand Rapids: Zondervan, 1992).

tied to the Enlightenment—which is always a very bad thing." And of course, this appreciation for the theological past, at times, leads folks to head to Rome or to head to Eastern Orthodoxy. And when such a convert writes about such a conversion, I rarely find their reflections on Reformation theology particularly illuminating or helpful.

An anecdote might illustrate. At Baylor University in Waco, Texas (I am an alum), the honors college is a particularly strong and vibrant community. Some of the finest Christian academics anywhere teach in the honors college at Baylor. A few years ago, a story circulated that some students made T-shirts that said, "Baylor's Honors College Made Me a Catholic." I am not sure if this anecdote communicates from the United States to the United Kingdom, but for those of us in the United States, this is easy to understand. Some bright-eyed and smart eighteen-year-olds (many of these Baptist) come to Baylor as freshmen, and join the honors college. They begin to read—perhaps for the first time—the classic works of the (largely) Western tradition. They are going to First Baptist Church, or Second Baptist Church, or XYZ Baptist Church on Sunday (and Wednesday night, if they are *truly* Baptist kids). They are falling in love with learning, fascinated with a particular novel, or political tract, or philosophical exploration. Then they go to church, and they perhaps do not find a vibrant wrestling with the past, and with the history of Christian and non-Christian thought. They discover serious thought journals such as *First Things*, and discover that many contributors are Roman Catholic. A romance develops, then some flirting, and next thing you know, the Baptist boy or girl is quietly attending the local Catholic Church. What has happened? Perhaps many things, and I do not want to be reductionistic. But at least *part* of what has happened is that these students have discovered the importance of the past, and the importance of coming to terms with a whole tradition of thinking. More pointedly, they have discovered that a lot of what they have been taught over the years was hammered out over a long period of time by some of the finest minds in the history of the Christian tradition. Faced with the option of remaining within a slice of Protestantism that (as they see it) does not take tradition seriously, versus joining the "true Church"—what real choice do they have?

Thus I suspect that while it is right and proper *and necessary* to engage the patristic and medieval eras, I sometimes have the sneaking suspicion that some evangelicals who have engaged in project of *retrieval* from the patristic era—and have felt compelled to head to Rome or to the East—have perhaps not engaged in a project of retrieval from their own Protestant heritage. A part of what I want to do in this paper is encourage Protestants in what it means to be Protestant.

But let us turn to the task at hand: the importance of tradition in the theological task. And to clarify, I am speaking as a Protestant, so I might slightly rework the title: "The Protestant Theological Task, and the Importance of Tradition in Such a Task." I will try and do the following. First, I will explore the place of Scripture in the theological task. Second, I will explore the role of tradition in the theological task. Third, I will try and offer something of a constructive proposal on the place of tradition in the Christian theological task.

### Scripture and the Task of Theology

To begin, I ask a question J. I. Packer asked some twenty-three years ago: "Is Systematic Theology a Mirage"?[3] That is, is systematic theology simply something of a fantasy? This is the right question. In a chapter dealing with the role of *tradition* in the theological task, one must back up and ask a more fundamental question: What is theology? Or, what is the theological task? And our understanding of the nature of theology will lead to, or include within it, an answer to the question of the place of tradition in the theological task.

Let me not be coy. I think something like a traditional Protestant understanding of theology is viable and worthy of our commitment. Certainly, any understanding might be improved, deepened, sharpened, and indeed, corrected. But it is naive to think that it is the

---

3. J. I. Packer, "Is Systematic Theology a Mirage? An Introductory Discussion," in *Doing Theology in Today's World: Essays in Honor of Kenneth S. Kantzer*, ed. John D. Woodbridge and Thomas Edward McComiskey (Grand Rapids: Zondervan, 1993), 17–37.

responsibility of the current generation of thinkers to constantly seek to overturn all things in terms of this or that discipline. To be an academic is not ipso facto to be a revolutionary. That is, theologians are not somehow required to wear the equivalent of a Che Guevara T-shirt as they engage in the theological task.[4] Nonetheless, I want to suggest that something like the traditional position is still worthy of our allegiance. But let us try and work our way there.

Scripture, as traditionally understood, is the Word of God written, and therefore trustworthy and true. I will not here seek to justify or argue for this. Attendant to this is the affirmation that God has spoken, and that Scripture is therefore an expression of his will and mind. And back behind this is the notion that, as mysterious as God is, he nonetheless communicates—in his Word—in a way that is ultimately coherent. Unlike you or me, who might utter contradictions on a daily if not hourly basis, God is able to speak, and he speaks in a noncontradictory way. Since it is God who has spoken in Scripture, and since God himself is true, trustworthy, coherent, and does not lie or contradict himself, then Scripture likewise is true, trustworthy, coherent, and does not contradict itself.

If theology, then, is the explication of Scripture—as Protestants (and Catholics and Eastern Orthodox also in their own way) have traditionally believed—and if Scripture is true, trustworthy, coherent, and does not contradict itself, then theology is a possibility. That is, theology is possible because God has (1) so spoken in Scripture such that Scripture is a trustworthy communication of the mind and will of God, and God has (2) created humankind with the capacity to understand this communication of God.

Also, of course, related to this are other—and not insignificant! —convictions. Namely: not only that God speaks, and speaks in and through human authors, but also that God has created humankind with the capacity to understand such communication, *and* to then "talk

---

4. But to even say such a thing requires us to bump into our topic: the role of *tradition*. Protestants indeed have a *tradition*. But before a tradition can be truly or fully embraced, it must be understood.

back" to God in a coherent way, in light of what God has spoken to humankind.

But once we take up the question of tradition, we inevitably bump into the traditional cleavage between traditional Protestants and traditional Roman Catholics (not to mention Eastern Orthodoxy). It is tempting to explore the work of John Henry Newman and his work on the development of doctrine, as well as a Protestant response, but I will only touch briefly on such questions here. My question is not primarily whether tradition *matters*, or whether tradition *influences* one's theologizing. It would seem obvious that in the process of theologizing, it is inevitable that one will theologize *in the light of*, and *in conversation with*, the now two thousand years of Christian theologizing that precede us. (The only exception to this, I suppose, is the person who theologizes who is *genuinely and truly* ignorant of all that has preceded him.) The question really, I suspect, is the exact place of tradition in the theological task. In principle, I would think virtually every traditional Protestant would affirm that Scripture is the touchstone of all theologizing, and that theology is ultimately concerned with what we say about God and his ways in response to what he has spoken in Scripture. As we engage in this task, we realize that many Christian thinkers precede us, and we must attend to former attempts at theologizing as we engage in the task of theology.

Over against Rome, the Protestant does not theologize with the notion that there is *always* fundamental continuity between (1) Holy Writ and (2) official church dogma. Of course, *in fact*, many of us take the Nicene Creed, Apostles' Creed, Athanasian Creed, and all of the ecumenical councils with a high degree of seriousness. Nonetheless, such documents are, *in principle*, capable of revision. Thus, in practice, an evangelical will generally look to the central creeds as true and worthy of allegiance, but recognizes that they are not on the same level as Scripture *and* are, in principle, capable of revision. And thus evangelicals can debate—and have debated—whether the "descent into hell" clause from the Apostles' Creed need be believed or recited. But also, most evangelicals would likely say that there is something of an onus upon the one who would deny or question this or that component of one of the classic Christian creeds.

Another brush-clearing exercise: It is perhaps necessary to make clear what *is* and is *not* being said concerning tradition. *First*, all theologians (whether they recognize it or not) do, in fact, theologize in the light of tradition. We are born of certain parents, in a certain time period, in a certain place, are taught a certain language, are raised a certain way, among others. And we thus think and deliberate accordingly. I was raised Lutheran, and then became a Baptist as a twelve-year-old. I have been shaped by my teachers, by the persons I have read, and others. I theologize in light of various traditions, and am shaped by them.

*Second*, even if Protestants do not affirm an infallible tradition or infallible magisterium, that does not mean there are not numerous informal traditions that develop and play a significant role in Protestant theologizing. And likewise, it is necessary to point that there is, indeed, a *tradition* of Protestant theologizing. And perhaps it is unnecessary to point out that this is completely in keeping with a traditional understanding of *sola Scriptura*. Scripture is the only infallible authority under God. It is the *norma normans non normata*. It is the norming norm that is not normed by any other norm (and in fairness to Rome, many Roman Catholics could indeed—especially after Vatican II—affirm *norma normans non normata*). But there are, nonetheless, other norms—although the Protestant does not believe that these norms are infallible. I, for example, had the privilege of studying with Millard J. Erickson as a theological student—both at the master's and doctoral levels. When I first began teaching a one-semester introduction to theology course, my teaching notes looked and sounded a lot like Erickson's big green systematic theology. I still make recourse to certain analogies, certain particularly compelling anecdotes, and certain insightful illustrations—from Erickson—when I teach theology.

But what has happened along the way? Since I first started teaching theology some seventeen years ago, I have continued to read, write, and learn. So notes that were originally pretty much Erickson have, over time, taken on an increasingly (Bradley) Greenish hue. This is proper and inevitable. In a sense, I have worked in the "Erickson tradition" while reworking, rethinking, and rewriting my notes for close to two decades now. Have I worked "within" a tradition? Of course I have. But the Protestant principle is not therefore vanquished or invalidated. Rather, I have worked within a tradition, but I have constantly sought to turn to Scripture as I have theologized. I have traveled with certain guides—ranging from Henri Blocher to Gerald Bray, from Cornelius Van Til to Augustine, from Calvin to Aquinas. I have often turned to the Old Princetonians, as well as the contemporary evangelical stalwarts such as J. I. Packer. I have been helped by a profound insight from Hugh of St. Victor: "Read everything, later you will find that nothing was superfluous."[5] But the Protestant principle shines through: we look at the past, and learn from others, all along the way working with a commitment that Scripture is the Word of God written, and thus true, and our only infallible authority.

### The Place and Centrality of Scripture

In the background of any discussion of the role and place of tradition is the question of canon, and concomitantly, the nature of redemptive history. Protestants—especially within the Reformed trajectory—have historically believed that as one moves from the Old Testament era to the New Testament era, there is a paradigmatic shift with the incarnation, life, death, burial, and resurrection of Jesus. In short, the incarnation, life, death, burial, and resurrection of Jesus is the fulcrum of all of history. And these realities are certainly the fulcrum of the Bible. Although the Baptist and the paedo-baptist will argue about certain very important fine points, they are united in affirming a once-for-all significance and shift as we move from *before* the incarnation to *after* the incarnation, life, ministry, death, burial, and resurrection

---

5. Hugh of St. Victor, *De beatae Mariae Virginis* 6.3.115.

of Jesus. This is perhaps captured particularly well in Hebrews 1:1–4: "Long ago, at many times and in many ways, God spoke to our fathers by the prophets, but in these last days he has spoken to us by his Son, whom he appointed the heir of all things. . . ." Likewise, when Paul teaches that God sent forth his Son "when the fullness of time had come" (Gal 4:4), there is something unique and important (indeed, "once-for-all") about the first century.

In short, informing a Protestant understanding of the role of tradition is an understanding of the Bible in Christian theology. And in a Protestant understanding of the Bible, there is a certain way of thinking about what God has done in history, and in particular, a certain understanding of the development or progression of history— such that at least many, if not most, Protestants affirm that God's revelation reached a climax or high point in the first century. Indeed, in the ministry of Jesus, we have the high point of revelation, and this led to the emergence of certain documents—the New Testament documents—as a certain kind of literature. And these documents would eventually be collected into a canon.[6]

To illustrate, Malcolm Muggeridge once wrote a book titled A Third Testament.[7] The book was about certain particularly important Christians who, in their faithfulness to God, could be seen to be a "third testament" of sorts. As a title of a popular book, such a title might be fine. But if pressed, it is problematic, at least for the Protestant. For, to cut to the chase, the Protestant is not interested in a "third testament," and indeed sees such a notion to be riddled with problems.

---

6. And lest I be thought to dodge an important issue. On the question of canon, the traditional Protestant believes that those documents which would eventually be seen as a canon—an official collection of religious literature bearing the imprint of divine authority—exists. And this collection—as a Protestant sees it—is composed of documents having intrinsic authority, not simply extrinsic authority. That is, the documents, because they were authoritative, would eventually be collected and become—formally—a canon. They were not declared by the church to be authoritative and thus thereby gained their authority. Intrinsic authority led to the church seeing and recognizing this authority. One can see the older works of Bruce and Metzger, although the more recent work of Michael Kruger brings this out more explicitly. Likewise, an older essay by Richard Gaffin is still very helpful: "New Testament as Canon," in Inerrancy and Hermeneutic: A Tradition, a Challenge, a Debate, ed. Harvie Conn (Grand Rapids: Baker, 1988).

7. Malcolm Muggeridge, A Third Testament: A Modern Pilgrim Explores the Spiritual Wanderings of Augustine, Blake, Pascal, Tolstoy, Bonhoeffer, Kierkegaard, and Dostoevsky (New York: Little, Brown, 1976).

This is not to somehow muzzle God, or to dogmatically claim that God is *unable* to speak today. Nonetheless, it *is* to say that in a Christian (here, Protestant) understanding of God and his ways with humankind, there is an implicit (at least) biblical notion or philosophy of history, whereby one confesses that there is something special indeed about the first century. Revelation reached a climax, or high point of sorts. We do not await a future era that will relate to the themes and truths of the New Testament in the same way that the New Testament relates to the Old Testament. That is, Protestants will generally happily say with Luther: "What lies in the Old Testament concealed, is in the New Testament revealed." But is the Protestant now waiting or looking for new developments in the contemporary era that will develop and fulfill and flesh out the New Testament in the way that the New Testament develops or fulfills or fleshes out the Old Testament? Most would say: No. But this no is not because of a curmudgeonly conservatism that resists any change in the status quo. Rather, the Protestant believes that there was something unique and special, indeed something "once-for-all," about the first century and the incarnation, life, ministry, death, burial, and resurrection of Jesus.

In short: attention to the Bible has led at least many Protestants to affirm a type of biblical philosophy of history, or of the history of redemption. In this understanding of history, we cannot flatten out every era, and see all eras the same. Rather, God throughout history was preparing God's people for the coming of the Son (indeed, "in the fullness of time"). With the incarnation, life, ministry, death, burial, and resurrection of Jesus, we reach a high point in the history of redemption. The canon of Scripture emerges out of those first-century events, and is then the verbal and written vouchsafing of the testimony concerning those events. This canon is therefore worthy of exploration and study. And because of the nature of its emergence—flowing from a unique period in history—the Protestant sees these documents as unique and "once-for-all."

Another brush-clearing exercise: A word about "tradition" on the New Testament itself. The New Testament is replete with various references to "tradition," "that which is passed on," and other references. While sometimes the New Testament condemns various human traditions, "tradition" (and similar words) are often spoken of wholly positively. We read in the New Testament that the "traditions" are to be held on to (2 Thess 2:15). Likewise, in Jude (v. 3), the recipients are to contend for the faith once delivered (= "handed on") to the saints. Paul's own gospel message is something he is "delivering" to his listeners/readers (1 Cor 15:3; 11:23). And Paul commends his readers/ listeners for holding fast to the traditions (1 Cor 11:2). For our purposes, it is simply worth noting that these traditions are sometimes oral (Paul and the apostolic preaching: 1 Thess 2:13), and sometimes written (for example, a letter: 2 Thess 2:2, 15). That is, in the New Testament tradition can be a good thing, and this tradition can be seen in the apostolic preaching and in apostolic written communication. As Leonhard Goppelt could write: "The tradition of the Christ event is taken up in the Canon. Every 'spiritual' or apocryphal addition to that tradition is to be rejected."[8]

But, as Herman N. Ridderbos has written, this "tradition" is coming from God through the apostles to the people. That is, at the heart of the tradition is divine self-disclosure through human agents. Hence, Ridderbos can write, in a summative way:

> God's authority as Canon is not limited to His great deeds in Jesus Christ but extends to their communication in the words and writings of those He specially chose and equipped to be the bearers and instruments of divine revelation, and the written tradition they established, in analogy with the writings of the Old Testament, thereby became the foundation and standard of the coming church.[9]

Let us turn to the Old Testament. One of the key themes in the Old Testament is the call to remember. Even in the closing lines of Malachi, we read: "Remember the laws of my servant Moses, the statutes and rules that I commanded him at Horeb for all Israel" (Mal 4:4). That

---

8. Leonhard Goppelt, "Die Tradition nach Paulus," *Kerugma und Dogma*, 1958; quoted in G. C. Berkouwer, *Second Vatican Council*, trans. Lewis B. Smedes (Grand Rapids: Eerdmans, 1965), 107n53.
9. Herman N. Ridderbos, *Redemptive History and the New Testament Scriptures*, trans. H. De Jongste, rev. Richard B. Gaffin, Jr. (Philipsburg, NJ: P&R, 1963), 24.

is, Israel had forgotten the law of God, and needed to remember the law that had been given to them. Indeed, the Old Testament prophets emerged in the first place because the people of God had forgotten God and his law, and needed to be constantly called back to God's prior revelation. The Israelites were indeed the people of God, but because of their sin, the prophets were sent to warn, instruct, remind, and at times to offer a word of impending judgment.[10] One can affirm a real *development* of Christian doctrine over time, but yet still recognize the possibility (the inevitability in a fallen world?) of times of decline, corruption, and error. But, given the example of the Old Testament, Christians should also recognize that the history of God's people over time—if the past is any predictor of the present and future—might very well be marked by decline and failure, as much as by progress and success.

## The Importance of Tradition

When we speak of the first century as being a high point of revelation, are we thereby forced to say that there is no development of doctrine, or no progress of the Christian church in history, or the like? Not at all. Rather, I suspect that to affirm the uniqueness of the first century is to compel one to affirm a type of biblical theology or philosophy of history that affirms God's sovereign rule over all things. And there is no reason to limit this rule to (or end this rule with) the first century. The first century does seem unique—for reasons I have stated earlier. But to say that the first century was unique is *already* to be committed that God is ruling history, and has purposes, plans, and goals. And God's sovereign rule—and his purposes, plans, and goals—can (indeed, must!) continue on throughout history.

That being said, I suspect it best to be something like the following: while the first century was unique—and serves as something like a climax or high point of revelation, God continues to lead and guide

10. In summarizing the work of one of his own critics (James Bowling Mozley), John Henry Newman points out that for Mozley there was no meaningful category of the possibility of "corruption through excess or exaggeration" (Peter Toon, *The Development of Doctrine in the Church* [Grand Rapids: Eerdmans, 1979], 20).

his church throughout the ages (John 16:13). The Bride is still the Bride, and the Bride has not been jilted. Rather, the Son intercedes for his people, for his priesthood is perpetual (Heb 7:24–25; 9:24–25). Throughout postapostolic history, God shepherds his people, raises up gifted speakers and teachers, and continues to conform his people more and more to the image of the Son. God shepherds with his Word, and leads his people—by the Spirit—to continue to plumb the depths and riches of his Word. As God's people continue to mine Holy Writ, God's people cast around (now) to over two thousand years of Christian reflection and deliberation. God's people in the present age look back and discover Irenaeus, Origen, Tertullian, Athanasius, the Cappadocians, Augustine, (et al.!) and discover that the last two thousand years have seen rich explorations and articulations of the meaning of the Christian canon, as well as scripturally soaked reflection on challenges and issues facing the church throughout her history.

All of this is compatible with the fundamental Protestant principle of *sola Scriptura*. Indeed, I suspect that it is a certain understanding of the canon (where the New Testament canon is seen as reflecting the high point of revelation), that undergirds and can account for an understanding of God's continued shepherding of his people over time, as he leads them into a fuller and clearer understanding of Scripture. The position I am staking out here is not too different from that outlined by James Orr in 1901:

> I believe also, with more direct relation to our present subject, that so far from the history of dogma being the fatuous, illusory thing that many people suppose, there is a true law and logic underlying its progress, a true divine purpose and leading in its developments, a deeper and more complete understanding of Christianity in its many-sided relations being wrought out by its labours; and that, while its advance has not been without much conflict, much error, much implication with human sin and infirmity, and is yet far from complete, that advance has in the main been onward, and has yielded results which further progress will not subvert, any more than the future developments of science will subvert, say, such discoveries as the circulation of the blood, or the law of gravitation.[11]

11. James Orr, *The Progress of Dogma* (London: Hodder and Stoughton, 1901), 8–9; quoted in Toon, *Development of Doctrine*, 64–65.

Similarly, Peter Toon, in his book *The Development of Doctrine in the Church*, outlines three convictions, that guide his own constructive proposal for understanding the development of doctrine.[12] They are:

1. First, the authority of the Bible: "for Christians the only authoritative basis for faith and doctrine is the revelation of God of which the books of the Bible are the written, unique record."
2. Second, the importance of forming doctrine: "one part of the work of the Church on earth involves the making of doctrine."
3. Third, on the relationship of doctrinal development in the Scriptures to doctrinal development after the Scriptures: "Whatever development of doctrine exists within the Bible, such as, from the Old to the New Testament and from the Gospels to the Epistles, it has no *direct* bearing on the development of doctrine in the historical Church after the days of the apostles." In other words, there is something particularly unique about the first century in the history of redemption.

Protestants can, and should, affirm that key to the Christian life is the knowledge of God. We know from John 17:3 that eternal life, in fact, *is* to know God. And we know that while we now know in part, that one day we will see God face-to-face, and will know God fully and be fully known (1 Cor 13:12). So we can affirm that one of the things God is doing in history is calling, shaping, and forming a people to glorify and know him. This people, the church, is being more and more conformed to the image of the Son. If this is indeed the case, it makes sense to affirm that the people of God will indeed continue to know God more and more fully over time, and in heaven will continue to get to know God more fully—that is, when we see God face-to-face (1 Cor 13:12), we will know fully, but this full knowing will somehow continue on throughout eternity. But all of *this* is to say: perhaps it is inevitable and necessary to say that, *of course*, there will be a development of doctrine over time. While God has given us a deposit in the biblical documents,

---

12. Toon, *Development of Doctrine*, 105–6.

this deposit is mined, more deeply understood, more fully explicated over time. Protestants need not follow John Henry Newman and affirm an infallible magisterium. However, it is completely consistent with Protestant principles to affirm that God's people will continue to grow in their understanding of the triune God of Scripture over time. And it is during this already-but-not-yet period in which tradition will inform God's people as they continue to explicate and submit to Holy Writ. Protestants—whether laypersons or not, whether possessing formal theological training or not—should look to tradition. We should seek to understand what Christians over the past two thousand years have said, what they have argued, and what they have concluded. And indeed, we believe God cares for his church and is at work in his church. But again, we need not conclude—with Newman—that a magisterium is ipso facto necessary to ensure a correct doctrinal and theological development. That is, the church can—and does—get it wrong at times.

Nonetheless, a knowledge and grounding in the theological tradition is of virtually inestimable value. We know—from Holy Writ—that we are both *finite* and *fallen* creatures. Therefore, we know that we are prone to get things wrong. We read the Scriptures, think we have discovered an insight, then realize we are bumping into the Arian heresy, or the Apollinarian heresy, or the Nestorian heresy, or the Eutychian heresy. So we return to the Scriptures, wondering if we have misunderstood them. We *think* we have an insight, but at least a knowledge of the tradition can encourage us to study and think and pray further, realizing that if our supposed insight is true, then it would mean the overturning of the first five centuries of Christian theologizing. *Sola Scriptura* is true, in my view. But by theologizing in light of two thousand years of tradition, I can at least be aware if my supposed insight is in accord with, or not, some of the finest minds in the history of the Christian faith.

## Tradition on Tradition

G. C. Berkouwer, in prescient style, wrote: "Time was when the word

49

tradition alone was enough to evoke negative responses. For, within the polemical situation, it was the word tradition that overshadowed the gospel. At present, theologians are able to think about tradition without the negative emotional accompaniments and as a result are rethinking the matter of Scripture and tradition themselves."[13] Berkouwer has also written: "The question that counts is how the Lord of the Church, the Lord of this tradition, leads His people through the past into the present."[14]

We cannot go into detail here, but it is worth pointing out that something such as the Protestant principle, understanding, or method by all means has precedent in the pre-Reformation church. For example, Heiko Oberman, in describing a certain strand of medieval theology, can write: "The same does not seem to apply to the medieval doctor of theology, however. Theology is understood as the science of Holy Scripture. And notwithstanding the constant and growing temptation to comment on the comments, Holy Scripture is understood to be the authoritative source—the final test of the interpretation of later interpreters."[15] Oberman continues: "Tradition I, then, represents the sufficiency of Holy Scripture as understood by the Fathers and doctors of the Church. In the case of disagreement between these interpreters, Holy Scripture has the final authority."[16] This view, that theology is ultimately the "science of Holy Scripture," is what Oberman calls "Tradition I." He distinguishes between "Tradition I" and "Tradition II" as follows:

**Tradition I:** single-source, or exegetical tradition of Scripture, held together with its interpretation.

**Tradition II:** two-source theory, which allows for an extrabiblical oral tradition.

---

13. Berkouwer, *The Second Vatican Council and the New Catholicism*, 99.
14. Ibid., 100.
15. Heiko Augustinus Oberman, *The Harvest of Medieval Theology: Gabriel Biel and Late Medieval Nominalism* (Cambridge, MA: Harvard University Press, 1963), 369.
16. Ibid., 372. Similarly: "While it proved to be characteristic for Tradition I that Tradition was seriously heard but that the canonical books of Holy Scripture were definitely given the final authority in matters of faith . . . " (ibid., 389).

Tradition I and Tradition II vied for dominance in the Middle Aages, as Oberman understands the issue. We might simply add, the Protestant Reformation was ultimately the victory of a form of Tradition I among the Protestant churches.

Oberman also notes that advocates of Tradition I by no means sought to ignore the history of interpretation. So, according to Oberman: "The representatives of the first concept of Tradition [= Tradition I] by no means isolate Holy Scripture by divorcing it from Tradition understood as the history of interpretation of Scripture."[17] Indeed, although Oberman argues that Gabriel Biel was himself closer to a Tradition II position, even Biel can, at times, sound remarkably Protestant. Note Oberman's summary of Biel:

> Only Holy Scripture teaches all that is to be believed and hoped and all other things necessary for salvation. Scripture is the Word of God, the very mouth of God, the standard by which we can measure the distance by which we are removed from God or our nearness to Him. This word is instruction, consolation, and exhortation which reaches us through listening, reading, meditation, and contemplation.[18]

Biel himself writes: "It is sufficient for salvation to believe in general that everything revealed by God is true in the sense intended by the Holy Spirit. All these truths of revelation are contained in Holy Scripture."[19]

The relation of Scripture to tradition is an old issue, and something such as *sola Scriptura* predates the Reformation era, as shown by Oberman. We should also note that, for Oberman, "Once theologians were faced with the option between Tradition I and Tradition II, neutrality was to prove impossible."[20]

## Protestant Theology and Tradition: A Template

Let me now try and offer something of a construal of the place of

---

17. Ibid., 391.
18. Ibid., 394.
19. Gabriel Biel, *I Sent.* Prol. 1 I a nota 3 D; quoted in Ibid., 394.
20. Ibid., 393.

tradition in the Protestant theological task. More could be said about each of the following, but hopefully this will suffice as a sketch of a Protestant understanding of the place of tradition in the theological task.

First, Protestant theologians must continue to mine and plumb the Scriptures, believing and affirming that the Scriptures are the touchstone of theology, and are the *norma normans non normata*. At a prima facia level, the traditional Roman Catholic would say the same thing. However, in reality, there is a different emphasis, and indeed, a different principle is at work, as we have seen. But we should not begrudge, for partisanship's sake, that there is at least at one level a common commitment to Scripture as God's Word written (at least among traditional Protestants and traditional Catholics). As treated above, the nature and place of the canon is inescapable at this point. For the Catholic (and, of course, there are variations!), *revelation* has a priority, and *revelation* leads to *tradition,* and ultimately, *Scripture.* This is at least how a traditional, if moderate, Catholic such as Avery Dulles summarizes the issue. And within this Catholic understanding, it is the *church* that produces *Scripture.* For the Protestant, God creates the church through his Word. God certainly has revealed himself, and this revelation of himself has become inscripturated. But most importantly, there was a uniqueness in what God was doing in the first century, and certain documents—the New Testament documents—emerged out of these first-century events. For the Protestant, there is an inscripturation of the "traditions" being handed down, and the canon—recognized as divinely authoritative—is the collection of these traditions in inscrip-turated form.

Related to this, Protestant theologians should affirm that while Scripture is the only infallible norm under God, God has been active in and among his people from the formation of the canon to the present. That is, there is nothing within the Protestant framework that brings to an end in the first century (or after the canon is recognized as canon) God's sovereign rule, or guidance, or care. Therefore, the Protestant theologian should read and study the history of Christian thought with an openness to how God might have led his people to explicate the Scriptures over time. Again, key to the whole affair is a certain understanding of the Christian canon. There is a "once-for-all" aspect to the first century, which seems to be seen in the way the New Testament itself speaks about the first century, in terms of "in the fullness of time." To affirm God's ongoing providential care and guidance of his people throughout the centuries is not to sneak in a Roman Catholic understanding through the back door. Rather, it is simply to be upfront with the obvious. Christ is Lord of his church, and did not resign his lordship in the first century, or when the canon was recognized as canon. It is thus the case that Protestant theologians should seek to understand how God's people have interpreted and explicated the meaning of the Scriptures over time. Protestants do this knowing that the history of Christian thought is a mixture of the good, the bad, and the ugly, and are always seeking to be reformed. They are affirming, denying, correcting, finetuning, for Protestant theologians do indeed believe that they have a moral and ethical responsibility to always seek to reform themselves, their theology, and their church according to the infallible Word of God.

Third, the Protestant theologian should—ultimately—be jack of all trades, and master of as many trades as one is able: knowledge of biblical languages and biblical theology, knowledge of the history of Christian thought and church history, knowledge of the history of philosophy, knowledge of contemporary cultural, sociological, and ideological currents. The task of theology is serious business, and requires a wide range of knowledge if one is to do it well.

Protestant theologians, fourth, should recognize that we all indeed theologize out of certain contexts, and in the places where we find ourselves. One can *pretend* that one is simply moving from Bible to theological construal, and in so doing has sequestered oneself from every other possible influence. But this is to pretend, and frankly, to be dishonest. One need not slip into theological relativism in recognizing the influence of one's own background and upbringing, and historical situatedness—even if in our own day certain despisers of the faith have appealed to historical situatedness as a not-so-subtle reason to dodge the clear teaching of Holy Writ. Nonetheless, we are shaped by where we find ourselves, and it is best to recognize this. Again, this is not a postmodern move. B. B. Warfield, for example, could argue that in preparing the biblical writers to pen Scripture, God had provided the writers with varied experiences, and had shaped the lives of the biblical writers in preparing them for their roles as authors of Scripture. But God had done so *providentially* and *with purpose*, such that the experiences of the biblical writers prepared them for their role as the human authors of Scripture. Thus the tree planted by streams of water (Ps 1:3) is not somehow less capable of being a means of revelation because the psalmist had *really* experienced such trees in his lifetime.[21] All of this is to say: if God is sovereign, he can shape and guide all of life such that all of our experiences and learning—including our knowledge of tradition—can be aids as we seek to theologize in the light of Holy Scripture. As Hugh of St. Victor could say: "Read everything, later you will find that nothing was superfluous."

Fifth, Protestant theologians should affirm that the first century was the high point of revelation, and that there is thus a "once-for-all" aspect to the biblical canon. This does not mean that what we find in the Old Testament and New Testament is a developed and fully realized set of doctrines. But neither are the Old Testament and New Testament simply "nontheological" data upon which we force doctrinal understandings (à la Harnack). Rather, there is a finality to the canon, and the canon is indeed closed. It is the high point of revelation. The Protestant theologian has the responsibility to explicate what is found in the canon, and to tease out implications and apply to current situations, among other things. Thus certain doctrines can be ultimately developed over time, but it will be necessary to make sure that all doctrines to be confessed and believed must be seen to follow from the Scripture themselves. There is no extrascriptural

---

21. Besides Warfield, I was helped early on my studies by Moisés Silva, *God, Language, and Scipture: Reading the Bible in the Light of General Linguistics*, vol. 4, *Foundations of Contemporary Interpretation* (Grand Rapids: Zondervan, 1991). He, in turn, references the work of Geerhardus Vos. Hugh of St. Victor (twelfth century) is fascinating along these lines. Cf. his *De tribus diebus* 4.

line flowing through something like apostolic succession to which Protestant theologians owe allegiance. We can both praise and shake our head at Augustine, in the very same sitting. We can be gobsmacked and embarrassed by any number of theologians, in the very same minutes of study. We trust that God is sovereignly guiding his church, and is using his infallible Word as he does so. We can look to two thousand years of Christian theologizing with a high degree of respect and awe, nonetheless knowing that the Protestant theologian has the moral and ethical responsibility to return—repeatedly—*ad fontes,* believing that it is right and necessary and morally required, if necessary, to speak a word of correction and rebuke when necessary. Such words of correction and rebuke will often be interspersed with words of praise and affirmation. But we are a people always desiring to be reformed according to the Word of God. And to be reformed is to be, at times, correcting the past and, at times, affirming the past.

### Tradition and the Missionary Imperative

I have attempted in this chapter to outline a position where (1) the traditional Protestant perspective of *sola Scriptura* is upheld, and (2) where the importance of tradition in the theological task is affirmed—and affirmed robustly. Given the forum in which this paper was originally given—a Tyndale Fellowship gathering of the Christian Doctrine study group, where participants engaged in discussion of the nature of theology and the missiological imperative of the church—a word about the church's missionary endeavor is important.

One of evangelicalism's challenges in the twentieth century was an ongoing endeavor to articulate, defend, and propagate a certain understanding of the doctrine of revelation and Scripture. As a theological student, it was commonplace to hear a traditional evangelical position criticized and (frankly) caricatured as "modern," "rationalist," "foundationalist," or something else. "Propositional" revelation was something of a bogeyman. To affirm propositional revelation was tantamount—according to some critics—to denying the majesty of God, to putting God in a box, and to denying the personal nature of revelation. I raise this because some reading this chapter might seem to be reading an implicit defense of propositional revelation, and the notion that God reveals himself such that we truly know certain things about God. Mea culpa. I am guilty as charged. And at times, this affirmation of propositional revelation is seen to diminish the dynamic and powerful and life-changing nature of Scripture—and hence, ultimately hinder the missionary imperative.

To affirm that God has spoken—and that God has spoken in such a progressively revealed way such that the New Testament documents are the high point of revelation, and that in speaking God has spoken truthfully about himself and his ways with humankind—is not thereby to say that what we have in the Scripture is *simply* a set of propositions that must be passed down from generation to generation. It is to say, with Paul for example, that the gospel "is the power of God for salvation to everyone who believes, to the Jew first and also to the Greek" (Rom 1:16). It is also, with Paul, to able to summarize the gospel in a shorthand manner at times, such that the gospel can be summarized as the death, burial, resurrection, and appearances of Jesus (1 Cor 15:3–11).[22]

My point would be as follows. As Christians seeking to advance God's purposes in the world—that is, to advance the missionary imperative —we must ask a fundamental question: What has God provided that guides us in missionary endeavor? Why is Paul so animated in the first chapter of Galatians, when he says that anyone who preaches a different gospel should be "accursed" (Gal 1:6–11)? In writing to the Corinthians, why does Paul say that he chose to know nothing among them "except Jesus Christ and him crucified" (1 Cor 2:2)? It appears that for Paul there was a certain apostolic message, a message that could be summarized, repeated, and passed on. To lose the gospel was indeed something worthy of curse. This is not because Paul or the other biblical writers were simply concerned with being "right" about

---

22. Of course, in this classic passage, both the *death* and *resurrection* of Christ are "in accordance with the Scriptures"—showing us that these central first-century events are part of a larger plan and story, and that such Pauline shorthand summaries can only be *ultimately* understood in the light of this larger plan and story.

a certain doctrinal formula or "proposition." It was because in God's mysterious and sovereign plan, he has chosen to bring sinners to faith, to make all things new, in and through the proclamation of a certain message—*a certain message that can indeed be summarized in doctrinal/ propositional terms.* With Herman Ridderbos and others, we confess that what we have in our New Testament[23] is the high point of revelation. While this revelation is ultimately "final" in one sense, we still learn from tradition and from two thousand years of church history—as I have affirmed above. It is in and through the proclamation of the apostolic gospel that God has chosen to accomplish his purposes in the world—his purpose of blessing all nations through Abraham (Gen 12), and of bringing persons from every tribe and tongue into the presence of God (Rev 5:9). The gospel is the power of God because in and through his gospel, God accomplishes his purposes in the world.

## Conclusion

David Wells recently published a book titled *The Courage to Be Protestant.*[24] When I saw the title of the book, I thought, "Great, here is a book I have been waiting for. A book that is forthright, and makes the case for being a Protestant." Alas, as strong as the book is, it is not really a theological treatise, but rather extends Wells's sociological—and sociology of knowledge—analysis of the state of evangelical theology. I suspect there is still a book to be written by the same title, one that outlines the strength and logic of what it means to be Protestant. I suspect that one of the most important things Protestants can do is to engage in a deep and intensive study of the Christian tradition. Besides an ongoing wrestling with the Bible, this would mean an ongoing engagement with the church fathers, medieval thinkers, the Reformation, Protestant scholastics, the Puritans, as well as the eighteenth, nineteenth, twentieth, and now, twenty-first centuries. Such an engagement need not encourage one to run to Rome

23. And the New Testament as the culmination and fulfillment of the Old Testament.
24. David F. Wells, *The Courage to Be Protestant: Truth-lovers, Marketers, and Emergents in the Postmodern World* (Grand Rapids: Eerdmans, 2008).

or to the East. Indeed, one aspect of the courage to be Protestant is to wrestle with our own wrestling with tradition. To be a Protestant means continuing to affirm *sola Scriptura,* and to first and foremost say with Barth—exegesis, exegesis, exegesis. But to be a Protestant means engaging with the whole gamut of Christian thought. We benefit in numerous ways from such an engagement, all the while with an eye to the touchstone of all theologizing—Holy Scripture.

4

—

# A Missiological Appropriation of Tradition: A Response to Brad Green

## Paul Weston

I am very grateful for Brad Green's careful chapter, and in particular for its clear-sighted reconstrual of the Protestant theological tradition. In its emphasis upon the centrality of Scripture and some kinds of hermeneutical implication that flow from this, there is much that I want to affirm gladly and wholeheartedly. I agree with him that "inscripturated tradition" is the touchstone within which properly evangelical theological enquiry and construction has to take place; also that in the process of generational doctrinal statement and re-statement, this provides the definitive and normative touchstone by which theological judgments must be weighed and assessed. By way of response, therefore, I do not want to contradict much that Brad has said. I do, however, want to redescribe what I think is going on in the process of engaging with scriptural tradition from a theological and discipleship standpoint, and explore why this is important in relation to the missionary task that lies at the heart of the narrative.

I perhaps ought to state (and confess) from the outset that I have tended to suffer from a deep-seated allergy to certain forms of systematic theology—or more accurately, to the systematization of theology—and continue to do so. The lopsided impression I gained from some of my undergraduate studies was that "doctrine" was rather like an abstract depository of theological thought into which theologians down the ages had each contributed their own particular insight(s). Even the scriptural writers appeared to be on a par at times with their later historical counterparts, with little attention being paid either to historical development, or to historical context. This tendency seemed to be predicated upon a peculiarly Western propensity for systematization and taxonomy, with theological equivalents for concepts such as "genre," "class," or "species" developed by physical scientists. From this sort of approach, a number of inferences and practices could be drawn. To begin with, hermeneutical assumptions deployed meant that one always ended up siding with a particular tradition of doctrinal understanding, depending upon one's social background, theological slant, or seminary training. Some of these streams of thought were large and gregarious. A basic division, of course, was that one was either a Protestant or Catholic theologian, but one could also be a Presbyterian or Anglican theologian. Equally, one might be a Lutheran or Calvinist theologian, even Arminian (rarely both), and so forth.

In this taxonomy, the term *theology* became the most prominent class marker, with other branches of theological knowledge being offshoots of this central stem. You might have a theology *of* almost anything, ranging from doctrinal themes such as "salvation," "grace," or "judgment," to wider fields of classification, such as the theologies of the Old or New Testament. In the latter half of the twentieth century, even "mission" began to develop its own theologies.[1]

There is always a legitimate place for such approaches, and there is much that can be learned from them. But personally, I was always more interested—often intrigued—by the *how* of theological tradition alongside the *what*. How was it that *this* way of understanding God and his purposes in the world came to be? How was it, for example, that Karl Barth came to the theological crisis in relation to his own inherited liberal Protestant tradition of theology that was to produce the barnstorming commentary on Romans of 1918, and provide the "seed" that later flowered into the monumental but unfinished *Church Dogmatics*? At least in part, it was his disillusionment at seeing his former theological mentors in support of Kaiser Wilhelm II's declaration of war in 1914 on the basis of a theological understanding (and deeply Hegelian grasp) of Germany's role in both world history and national destiny. Gradually, Barth began to make more sense to me, both in terms of method and content.[2]

The relationship proper between "historical" and "systematic" approaches to theology is outside the scope of this short chapter, but I have always held on to the conviction that the theological enterprise is nurtured not just by the interrelatedness of its inner and logically constituent parts but also by the power of the historical contexts in which it is developed. Whatever else may be said, the history of the theological enterprise is one in which these two loci are constantly being brought into a symbiotic—if unstated, and even unconscious—relationship with one another. If we ignore these interrelationships, we will always be in danger of developing theological traditions that are "flat" and "linear," rather than dynamic and involving.

A crucial question, therefore, at the heart of this dialogue is what we mean by the word *tradition*. There is a certain inescapability about the term, but plenty of ambiguity about what we mean by it. Is tradition "closed" or "open," and if "open," in what sense "open"? I will arrange my comments around three questions that have arisen in response to Brad's paper. (1) What, in biblical thought, does it mean to engage

---

1. For an early discussion, see Wilhelm Andersen, *Towards a Theology of Mission: A Study of the Encounter between the Missionary Enterprise and the Church and Its Theology* (London: SCM, 1955).
2. See, for example, Eberhard Busch, *Karl Barth: His Life from Letters and Autobiographical Texts*, trans. John Bowden (London: SCM, 1976), 92.

with tradition? (2) How do theological traditions originate and develop biblically? And (3) in what direction do our theological traditions lead us?

## 1. What, in Biblical Thought, Does It Mean to Engage with Tradition?

I want to suggest that in a post-Enlightenment world, the concept of theological *tradition* often suggests a "bounded" set of beliefs or dogmas that can be added to, revised, updated, or rejected. These sets of beliefs may even be thought capable of being transported intact across generations and even cultures. However, this is not the heart of the biblical concept of tradition.

For example, the "handing on" and "receiving" of the tradition (Gk. *paradosis* and cognates) that Paul refers to in texts such as 1 Cor 11:23 and 15:3 is itself integrally related to the good news that God has enacted in the person of his Son, Jesus Christ. It is about what God *has* done already, *is* doing now, and *will* do, through him. It is *this* tradition about Jesus, according to Paul, that constitutes—and must always remain—the central core of the apostolic faith. Brad mentions the reference in 2 Thess 2:15, where Paul tells young believers to "stand firm and hold fast to the traditions [*paradoseis*] that you were taught by us, either by word of mouth or by our letter." The term can carry both positive and negative connotations, as Brad's brief survey of the use of the term by both Paul and Jesus demonstrates. But we may assume here and elsewhere that when Paul uses the word in relation to that which is "received" or is "passed on," he means it in a positive sense.

But what is the nature of this tradition? Here, we need, I think, to recognize that the idea of tradition in biblical terms is neither flat nor one-dimensional. It is not primarily a collection of pieces of information or facts about something or someone, though, of course, there are always highly significant factual and informational elements to it. Neither is biblical tradition simply the record of things that had once been spoken and have since been pulled together and codified. Rather, biblical tradition is a living reality calling for personal engagement and commitment. It is the ongoing record of a divine and living voice that is recorded not just from the perspective of historical memory alone. Neither is it intended as a set of statements to be collected into a program of ideas and principles. Rather it is a living and ongoing tradition of speaking, whose voice continues to be ever-present. Though spoken authoritatively in the past, this speaking invites us into an *open* future, beckoning us toward fresh appropriations and interpretations of what God is doing in his world. Walter Brueggemann puts this well in his book *The Bible Makes Sense*, where he equates Israel's tradition with that of the Bible.

> The central concerns of the Bible are not flat certitudes . . . but assurances that are characterized by risk and open mystery. The quality of certitude offered by the Bible is never that of a correct answer but rather of a trusted memory, a dynamic image, a restless journey, a faithful voice. Such assurances leave us restless . . . always needing to decide afresh. . . . If the Bible is only a settled answer, it will not reach us seriously. But it is also an open question that presses and urges and invites. For that reason the faithful community is never fully comfortable with the Bible and never has finally exhausted its gifts or honored its claims.[3]

Is the tradition that Paul refers to anything less than this? Surely not. There is the same dynamic tension between past and future, between those truths that are being dwelt in as already and authoritatively received, and those things yet to be encountered that will, in turn, continue to shape and sharpen that which has already been received.

At the very heart of this is the fact that the tradition, as Paul understands it, is bound up inextricably with the person and work of Jesus Christ. As the great Cambridge New Testament scholar J. B. Lightfoot put it over a hundred years ago: "Though the Gospel is capable of doctrinal exposition, though it is eminently fertile in moral results, yet its substance is neither a dogmatic system nor an ethical code, but a Person and a Life."[4]

So when Paul warns the Ephesian Christians not to follow the wayward manner of life exhibited by their neighbors ("in the futility

---

3. Walter Brueggemann, *The Bible Makes Sense*, 2nd ed. (Louisville: Westminster John Knox, 2001), 95.
4. J. B. Lightfoot, *Saint Paul's Epistle to the Philippians* (London: Macmillan, 1885), ix.

of their minds," Eph 4:17), he does so not by identifying their lack of systematic doctrinal knowledge but by saying to them: "That is not the way you learned Christ!" (Eph 4:20). Paul uses the language of personal discipleship (the language of the *mathétés*, the "learner-disciple") as the key to doctrinal maturity. The kind of language that follows serves to reinforce the understanding that growing in the tradition means a deeper discipleship *in* Christ. Of course, this includes an informational and factual dimension (it has an "about" referent), but its location is essentially personal and Christocentric; it is *in Christ*, and it is to be personally appropriated. So, Paul can say: "Surely you have heard about him and were taught in him, as truth is in Jesus" (Eph 4:20–21). It seems fair, therefore, to conclude that the interconnected dimensions of Christian discipleship within the tradition are always located within an ongoing relationship with God through Jesus—a relationship that Paul sums up as being "in Christ."

There exists, therefore, a powerful and interactive biblical dynamic between the understanding of tradition as past repository and tradition as ongoing engagement. The danger, perhaps, for some forms of Protestant systematic theology is twofold. First, that in a proper insistence upon the uniqueness of God's actions in the past, tradition can become backward-looking rather than open to the future, and therefore misses the ongoing dynamic of the tradition as discipleship rooted in Christ. A second danger is that in a right insistence on coherence and consistency, tradition can become "flat" and "linear," with discipleship understood, in effect, as a logical application in the present of what has been handed on to us from the past, rather than the urgent personal response to God's overriding presence for both present and future. To quote Walter Brueggemann once again, "Reading the Bible requires that we abandon the subject-object way of perceiving things. It requires that we give up the notion of the Bible as a 'book' to be acted upon, analyzed, studied, and interpreted. Perhaps it will help if we give up thinking of it as a 'book' and regard it as a 'tradition' that continues to be alive and surging among us."[5]

---

5. Brueggemann, *The Bible Makes Sense*, 96–97.

A question arising out of Brad Green's chapter is, therefore, how we properly construe the relationship between past, present, and future in relation to traditions of systematic theology. Brad quotes G. C. Berkouwer as saying, "the question that counts is how the Lord of the Church, the Lord of this tradition, leads His people through the past into the present."[6] But we may also legitimately raise the question of the future. What is the future orientation of the systematic enterprise? And how is it related to that which is past?

## 2. How Do Theological Traditions Originate and Develop Biblically?

Borrowing a phrase from Alister McGrath, we now move on to ask, what is the "genesis of doctrine"?[7] For in order to understand the nature of the tradition that is "handed on" and "received," we have to ask questions about origins. Here my contention is that in the Scriptures, theological traditions begin as responses to divine revelation imparted in specific historical contexts. In fact, the development of biblical tradition is *always*, in this sense, contextual, precisely because the Christian story is one in which God chooses to reveal himself within and through the narrative flow of human history. And, of course, this self-revelation precedes any human attempt to understand or to codify what is being revealed.

To take one illustration of this from the early biblical narrative, it is highly significant that at the beginning of the story of Moses and the liberation of the children of Israel from Egypt, Yahweh introduces himself, first of all, as a subject and as a verb ("I am," Exod 3:14). He is not to be understood primarily as an object to be known, but as the active initiator in the process of revealing. When Moses draws near to him at the burning bush, Yahweh announces himself in terms of relationship ("I am the God of your father, the God of Abraham, the God

---

6. G. C. Berkouwer, *The Second Vatican Council and the New Catholicism*, trans. Lewis B. Smedes (Grand Rapids: Eerdmans, 1965), 100.
7. See Alister E. McGrath, *The Genesis of Doctrine: A Study in the Foundation of Doctrinal Criticism* (Grand Rapids: Eerdmans, 1990).

of Isaac, and the God of Jacob" Exod 3:6). And when Moses asks God to identify himself by name so that the Israelites might recognize him as a god worth following, he gives Moses the rather enigmatic reply, "I am who I am. . . . Thus you shall say to the Israelites, 'I AM has sent me to you'" (Exod 3:14).

By revealing himself, first and foremost, as a verb, God both challenges modern epistemological categories by placing himself at the center of action, and at the same time, shows himself as the prime subject of activity. As Thomas Aquinas puts it: "God is pure act."[8] Thus, Yahweh is not a god who could be possessed by other subjects; he could not be manipulated, bought off, nor necessarily even be understood. He simply was (or rather, *is*), and the path to a deeper knowledge of him was (and still is) that of trust.

The genesis of Israel's tradition starts by revelation, and therefore, it would develop by Israel's continuing trust in the further revelations by which God made himself known. It is a tradition of "journeying trust"—a coming to terms (not always easily) with his acts within Israel's unfolding history. God would go on revealing himself in different contexts—supremely through the liberation of the children of Israel from Egypt—in such a way that the tradition of faith was amplified, corroborated, and deepened. It develops, therefore, as a responsive journey of trust and obedience (and frequent rebellion) in response to the successive acts of divine intervention and rescue. The simple, but enigmatic self-description, "I am who I am," was lesson one in Israel's doctrine course. And deeper understanding required an ongoing commitment to "journeying-trust." Lesson one would soon develop as Israel responded in faith to the actions of Yahweh, and this, in turn, would inform and nourish the community's tradition of theology. The God who was known to Moses at the start of Exodus 3 as the "God of your father, the God of Abraham, the God of Isaac, and the God of Jacob" (Exod 3:6) would become "the LORD who heals you" (Exod 15:26); he would be the God "who brought you out of the land of Egypt,

---

8. Thomas Aquinas, *Summa Theologica* (Pt. I, Q 3, art. 1). See the discussion in Stephen Bevans and Roger Schroeder, *Prophetic Dialogue: Reflections on Christian Mission Today* (Maryknoll, NY: Orbis, 2011), 9.

out of the house of slavery" (Exod 20:2); and—most dramatically—he says to Israel that he would be the "God, who brought them out of the land of Egypt that I might dwell among them; I am the LORD their God" (Exod 29:46).

At each stage in this evolving tradition, context and divine action are the sparking points for both God's revelation of himself and the Israelites' deepening understanding of the divine reality. It is the dramatic experience of liberation through the Red Sea that preeminently reveals God as redeemer and liberator, and it is this redemptive pattern that would ultimately lead to both cross and resurrection; it was the establishment of the tabernacle with all its regulations and detail that introduced into the tradition the core belief that God would "dwell *with* them, and be *their* God," and would find ultimate expression in the vision of Rev 21:1-4. And so forth. But always, the deepening of this understanding is in relation *to* him, and *with* him, for all things are done *through* him.

Biblically speaking, therefore, one can argue that God always makes himself known through acts of divine self-disclosure, and that through the accompanying cycle of responsive obedience, praxis, and doctrinal appropriation, a tradition is brought into being and renewed. Furthermore, this contextual element in the formation of tradition continues throughout the New Testament era. It is, of course, supremely true of the events of the passion and their interpretation. No one who was there would have guessed that the man lifted high and hanging on the tree was winning a cosmic battle. So, to continue to live in the tradition meant engaging with that hermeneutical cycle once again; of reception, trust, obedience, and doctrinal reappropriation. It is the relational move from "we had hoped that he was the one to redeem Israel" on the lips of the travelers to Emmaus (Luke 24:21) to the experience of "hearts burning within . . . while he was opening the scriptures" (v. 32).

This understanding of God's self-revelation continues beyond Easter Sunday, requiring further acts of adaptation, reconstruction, and reappropriation. Here, living in the inherited tradition led the early disciples to expect certain outcomes (note, for example, the disciples' words to Jesus in Acts 1:6, "Lord is this the time you are going to restore the kingdom to Israel?"). The early community of believers is continually pictured as playing "catch-up" with what the Spirit is actually doing, rethinking the old story in the light of the new in such a way that it is continually being transformed. Luke's picture of the coming of the Spirit at Pentecost in Acts 2 and the pouring out on *all* flesh is significant in this context—breaking the old mold, and demanding a new one. The same is true of what happens at Caesarea in Acts 10, where following a dream about sheets and animals, Peter is being "converted" into a whole new way of seeing, which shatters his inherited traditions of Jewish thinking. He is just as much in the world-changing process of conversion as either Cornelius or his household. New understandings must arise in the light of these divine interventions. And these interventions demand new ways of understanding the tradition once more. Take the account of the Jerusalem Council in Acts 15 as a further example. John V. Taylor sums up the narrative with characteristic understatement: "The author of Acts makes it very clear that to live and be moved by the Spirit's guidance is to open oneself to the most unguessable options."[9]

It is precisely these responses by the early apostles to acts of divine intervention and guidance that re-create and rebuild the "tradition" in which they understood themselves to be standing. Here is the making of theology, understood as response to God's divine actions in an historical context. But the question of relationships to past, present, and future must inevitably go on being asked in relation to later traditions of systematics. Scripture—as Brad clearly points out—remains the touchstone within which we are called to discern truth from error. Historical context is never the a priori upon which the theological enterprise is determined. However, the biblical narrative (as I have tried to show) is always one in which tradition is to be understood as the faithful contextual response to the divine activity of

---

9. John V. Taylor, *The Go-Between God: The Holy Spirit and the Christian Mission* (London: SCM Press, 1972), 108.

God in history. And does not Scripture lead us to believe that this work of reappropriation will continue even as the church charts new courses under the guidance of the Spirit? As missiologist David Bosch put it: "the Christian faith must be rethought, reformulated and lived anew in each human culture."[10]

So, this second question relates to how theological traditions pay due and appropriate attention to both past and present, as well as to the future. In essence, how does the systematic enterprise stop itself from becoming a largely intrasystemic mode of theologizing, with little to contribute in terms of the church's future mission? On the contrary, to give a right place to the role of historical context in the genesis of doctrine—as we have seen—will always challenge "repositorial" understandings of tradition. It will also serve to underline the pervasive activity of the Spirit, both in terms of understanding God's actions in the past and applying them to the present, but also in pioneering the future for the sake of the kingdom.

### 3. In What Direction Do Our Theological Traditions Lead Us?

I have argued that historical context is a significant driver and catalyst in the formation of theological tradition, and that any proper understanding of biblical tradition carries both a present and a future orientation. The key question, therefore, arises as to what the future implications of this story are. In what direction is biblical tradition headed? Or to put it another way: what is the bigger story with which this (or any) theological tradition has to deal? Here seems to be an important area for potentially fruitful conversation between systematic theologians and missiologists.

We could begin by returning to Paul's letter to the Ephesians, where Paul expounds a message about Jesus that is both deeply theological, but at the same time, future-oriented, and indeed cosmic in its logic. It is a message that finds its ultimate fulfillment in the reconciliation of the entire cosmos in and through Jesus. God's purpose, says Paul, is

---

10. David Bosch, *Transforming Mission: Paradigm Shifts in Theology of Mission* (Maryknoll, NY: Orbis, 1991), 452.

nothing less than "to gather up all things in him, things in heaven and things on earth" (Eph 1:10). It is "in him" that the "dividing wall" of hostility between Jew and gentile has been broken down (2:14), and it is "in him" that God is now creating "one new humanity in place of the two, thus making peace" (2:15). The theological flow of the epistle is inescapably Christocentric, reinterpreting the tradition in the light of who Jesus is revealed to be. At the same time, the participation of the believer is never abstract, nor in any way removed from the dynamic power of the ongoing and missional flow. The path of discipleship is deeply and personally involving (note Paul's *mathétés* language in relation to the tradition about Jesus in Eph 4:20). The believer is grafted onto—and called into—an ever-deeper sense of being involved in this missional movement of God in Christ. Organizationally, the ethical and doctrinal elements of the epistle are both part of this wider missional vision for the world.

But the epistle to the Ephesians is no isolated instance of this wider vision. As both David Bosch and Chris Wright have helped us to see over the past twenty years, the underlying "grammar" of the biblical narrative is inescapably "missional" in its scope and orientation. Wright describes this as the matrix for hermeneutics and biblical theology,[11] arguing that "the writings that eventually came to comprise the collected canon now called 'the Bible' are themselves the product of, and witness to, the ultimate mission of God."[12]

What then of the relation between a systematic and a missiological approach to the theological enterprise? Are they related in a linear sense, in which the tradition of the past is now taken up for present purposes (much as a preexisting toolkit is used to accomplish a household task)? Or is the relationship of mission to theology much more integrated? Wright argues in relation to the biblical material that

a missiological reading of such texts is very definitely not a matter of (1) finding the "real" meaning by objective exegesis, and only then (2)

---

11. See Christopher J. H. Wright, "Mission as a Matrix for Hermeneutics and Biblical Theology," in *Out of Egypt: Biblical Theology and Biblical Interpretation*, ed. Craig Bartholomew, et al. (Grand Rapids: Zondervan, 1994), 102–43.

12. Ibid., 120.

cranking up some "missiological implications" as a homiletic supplement to the text itself. Rather, it is to see how a text often has its origin in some issue, need, controversy or threat that the people of God needed to address in the context of their mission. The text in itself is a product of mission in action.[13]

It is for this reason that Bosch can argue in relation to Paul's writings that his "theology and his mission do not simply relate to each other as 'theory' to 'practice' in the sense that his mission 'flows' from his theology, but rather in the sense that his theology is a missionary theology . . . and that mission is integrally related to his identity and thought."[14] He concludes that "Paul was the first Christian theologian precisely because he was the first Christian missionary."[15] His theology was derived—like that of faithful Israelites before him—from a "learner-disciple" engagement with the revealed purposes of God for the world.

This missional vision of the biblical narrative (past-embracing, future-oriented, and continually active in the present) is precisely that reality with which all theology has to do. In Bosch's words, it is "the 'synoptic discipline' within the wider encyclopaedia of theology. It is not the case of theology occupying itself with the missionary enterprise as and when it seems to it appropriate to do so; it is rather the case of mission being that subject with which theology is to deal."[16]

Perhaps this is the single most important point that systematic theologians and missiologists need to keep constantly in view as they develop in conversation with each other. After all, neither can exist without the other. In this response to Brad's article, I have tried to describe some of the dangers on the side of systematics as I see them, but the conversation has to go both ways. Perhaps some words of T. F. Torrance are apt as a way of concluding these remarks. "It is certainly clear," he writes,

---

13. Christopher J. H. Wright, *The Mission of God: Unlocking the Bible's Grand Narrative* (Nottingham, UK: Inter-Varsity Press, 2006), 49.
14. Bosch, *Transforming Mission*, 124.
15. Ibid.
16. Ibid., 494.

that in any serious theological study of the Holy Scriptures we cannot operate without concepts, but since they have to be natural to the material content of God's self-revelation to us in and through the Scriptures, we have to develop them as we go along and work them into an interpretative framework for continuously deepening exegesis and interpretation. As such, however, they must be constantly submitted to critical clarification and revision in the light of the realities that become disclosed to us through the Scriptures, so that they may retain their semantic function as conceptual signs and not become theological objects which terminate our understanding on themselves.[17]

Torrance lucidly catches here both the promise and the danger of a systematic approach to tradition. Paying attention, he says, to the underlying structure and purpose of the biblical narrative will help to keep systematic theologians—as well as missiologists—from eddying into intramural backwaters, and promises to open up exciting possibilities for the future. If Bosch and Wright are correct to identify the cosmic mission of God as that unifying purpose (and I think that they are), then today—as in Paul's day—God's mission continues to be (in Bosch's words) "that subject with which theology is to deal."[18] To take the enterprise forward, we will need all the help we can gather from every theological discipline, but most of all, we will need the continuing grace and guidance of God to take its theological vision seriously.

---

17. T. F. Torrance, Reality and Evangelical Theology: The Realism of Christian Revelation (Downers Grove, IL: InterVarsity Press, 1999), 70–71.
18. Bosch, Transforming Mission, 494.

5

---

# Doing Theology for the Church's Mission: The Appropriation of Culture

## Kirsteen Kim

### Introduction

*Culture* has become a pervasive term in the humanities and social sciences such that "theologians, no less than other intellectuals, have come to view human beings as historical creatures located within the complex matrices of particular cultures and social worlds."[1] By this definition, theology itself is part of culture: it is "a cultural production; theology is something shaped *by* concrete social practices."[2] This is

---

1. Sheila Greeve Davaney, "Theology and the Turn to Cultural Analysis," in *Converging on Culture: Theologians in Dialogue with Cultural Analysis and Criticism*, ed. Delwin Brown, Sheila Greeve Davaney, and Kathryn Tanner (Oxford: Oxford University Press, 2001), 5.
2. Kathryn Tanner, *Theories of Culture: A New Agenda for Theology* (Minneapolis: Fortress Press, 1997), 67.

partly because, as Stanley Skreslet points out, mission practice has raised and continues to raise important cultural questions for theology, including "how nascent communities of faith work out their own theologies in a variety of local circumstances."[3] Since the ethnographic sense of the word *culture* emerged in the late nineteenth century, missionaries and mission theologians have found the concept useful for understanding and practice. In this sense, it became widely used in theories of mission, such as inculturation, people groups, and contextualization and was also closely associated with communication and theologizing. The continuing importance of "culture" for mission theology is evident in the three recent statements on mission from global bodies: *The Cape Town Commitment* by the Lausanne Movement (2011), *Together towards Life* by the World Council of Churches (2013), and *The Joy of the Gospel* (*Evangelii Gaudium*) by Pope Francis (2013).

This chapter will interrogate the varied meanings of the word *culture* that have been appropriated in mission theology and ask how they have been used.[4] It will take a historical approach, beginning in 1910, considering evangelical, ecumenical, and Catholic discussions, concluding each section with an examination of one of the three recent statements. In so doing, it will raise some questions from mission history about the appropriation of culture in theology, and particularly, in theology of mission.

## Culture at Edinburgh 1910

Culture was not a topic for discussion at the World Missionary Conference (WMC) at Edinburgh in 1910. In fact, the conference did not, "by and large," use the language of "culture" to refer to the particularities of different societies. Instead, "race" was the primary means used to delineate different peoples and their ways of life.[5] When the word "culture" does appear in the reports, the predominant use is

3. Stanley H. Skreslet, *Comprehending Mission: The Questions, Methods, Themes, Problems, and Prospects of Missiology* (Maryknoll, NY: Orbis, 2012), 69.
4. I have discussed the relationship between "the Spirit and cultures" at some length in Kirsteen Kim, *Joining in with the Spirit: Connecting World Church and Local Mission* (London: SCM, 2012), 40–72.
5. Brian Stanley, *The World Missionary Conference, Edinburgh 1910* (Grand Rapids: Eerdmans, 2009), 308.

in the sense of "cultured" or "best culture,"[6] the product of individual intellectual, character, and moral formation such as endowed by a good education,[7] high social class,[8] Christian upbringing,[9] and preferably, a combination of these.[10] Culture, in this sense, was the end result of a process of human development.[11] So, in the Edinburgh reports, "culture" is also found in verb form[12] and is linked to education[13] and to moral "self-culture."[14] The term was applied to the growth of individuals, but also, by analogy, to the development of societies. In this sense, derived from the Enlightenment, culture was the aim of the process of civilization, which posited a universal human history.[15] It was par excellence the attribute of Western or European societies that were assumed to be leading that process and who had achieved a common culture that was considered manifestly superior even to the highest of the others. Such a process of human development suggested that there were "stages" and "levels" of culture[16] on which certain individuals or groups could be arranged. In this sense, "culture" was used of the more "civilized" nations, including Japan,[17] China,[18] India,[19] and Persia,[20] with which various achievements were associated in areas such as literature, material or physical culture, and religion. Although the Enlightenment tended to separate civilization and culture from

---

6. World Missionary Conference, *Report of Commission V: The Preparation of Missionaries* (Edinburgh: Oliphant, Anderson, and Ferrier, 1910), 17.

7. WMC, *Report of Commission V*, 36, 119, 248; World Missionary Conference, *Report of Commission I: Carrying the Gospel to All the Non-Christian World* (Edinburgh: Oliphant, Anderson, and Ferrier, 1910), 319.

8. WMC, *Report of Commission I*, 272.

9. Ibid., 300, 370.

10. Ibid., 105; WMC, *Report of Commission V*, 323.

11. Cf. T. J. Gorringe, *Furthering Humanity: A Theology of Culture* (Aldershot: Ashgate, 2004), 3.

12. For example, WMC, *Report of Commission V*, 17; World Missionary Conference, *Report of Commission VI: The Home Base of Missions* (Edinburgh: Oliphant, Anderson, and Ferrier, 1910), 36.

13. WMC, *Report of Commission I*, 319.

14. World Missionary Conference, *Report of Commission IV: The Missionary Message in Relation to Non-Christian Religions* (Edinburgh: Oliphant, Anderson, and Ferrier, 1910), 55, in the case of Confucianism.

15. Cf. Tanner, *Theories of Culture*, 10.

16. WMC, *Report of Commission I*, 435; World Missionary Conference, *The History and Records of the Conference* (IX) (Edinburgh: Oliphant, Anderson, and Ferrier, 1910), 174.

17. Ibid., 50.

18. Ibid., 81.

19. Ibid., 151.

20. Ibid., 182.

Christianity, for the Protestants at Edinburgh Christianization and civilization were combined in the primary aim of mission expressed in Edinburgh: "advancing the kingdom of Christ."[21]

At Edinburgh, E. B. Tylor's book *Primitive Culture* (1871) was cited to consolidate the perceived hierarchy of human cultural development. But Tylor's ethnographic definition of culture as a "complex whole which includes knowledge, belief, art, morals, law, custom, and any other capabilities and habits acquired by man as a member of society" was not cited.[22] Nevertheless, there are instances in which culture was used in a cultural-anthropological sense. For example, trainee missionaries were expected to know about "the people, their culture and their religion,"[23] or their "temper, culture, and political habits."[24] Since Christianity is "universally indigenous," missionaries were urged to "adapt" the gospel to people and not expect them to "follow in every respect the lines of European and American Christianity."[25] Since world evangelization was also "an Asiatic and African enterprise," as far as possible, church order should be "indigenous,"[26] and native leaders should use indigenous methods to train local staff.[27] But whereas "adaptation" to local conditions was regarded as obligatory in the cases of preaching the gospel, organizing churches, and translating the Bible, in other cases it was selectively applied. Education and medicine were not so adaptable, and there were many social customs such as caste and dispositions such as "intemperance, immorality," and a host of

21. See Kirsteen Kim, "Edinburgh 1910 to 2010: From Kingdom to Spirit," *Journal of the European Pentecostal Theological Association* 30 (2010): 3–20. What was meant by the kingdom and how its coming could be hastened was worked out in terms of strategies for "carrying the Gospel to all the non-Christian world," building up "the Church in the mission field," Christianizing societies by education, and fulfilling the "non-Christian religions" (Commissions I, II, III, and IV), and for facilitating this through preparation of missionaries, building up support from the home base, cooperation with governments, and the promotion of Christian unity (Commissions V, VI, VII, and VIII).

22. E. B. Tylor, *Primitive Culture: Researches into the Development of Mythology, Philosophy, Religion, Language, Art, and Custom* (London: John Murray: 1920 [1871]), 1.

23. WMC, *Report of Commission V*, 281.

24. WMC, *The History and Records of the Conference*, 197; cf. WMC, *Report of Commission V*, 284; WMC, *Report of Commission I*, 122; WMC, *Report of Commission V*, 248.

25. WMC, *Report of Commission I*, 35. Indigenization was the policy of most Protestant missions, although in practice the extent of it was limited. David J. Bosch, *Transforming Mission: Paradigm Shifts in Theology of Mission* (Maryknoll, NY: Orbis, 1991), 295.

26. WMC, *Report of Commission I*, 313.

27. WMC, *Report of Commission I*, 369.

others that should be confronted and "abolished."[28] At Edinburgh, the gospel appeared as a "prefabricated" whole to be transported from the West whereas indigenous cultures were not treated as wholes, but as made up of "elements" to be discarded, reshaped, or possibly baptized. Adaptation appeared as an optional concession to local Christians who were not yet ready to embrace the "universal" culture being exported.[29]

## German Protestant Missions and *Kultur*

There was a German contingent at the Edinburgh conference, but the event was conducted entirely in English and there was not much sign of the distinctive German approach to culture in the Edinburgh discussions.[30] In English (and in French, from which the word *culture* was derived), culture was either a synonym for, or the means of, civilization.[31] Yet, in the context of the search for a common German-ness to support nationalism and unification, the primary sense of the German *Kultur* became particular to a people (Volk) instead of universal.[32] The key philosophical foundation for this approach had been laid by Johann Gottfried Herder (1744–1803) in his theory of *Volksgeist*, which recognized a multiplicity of cultures of different peoples in various regions of the world. He partially relativized European culture in relation to these,[33] and since he regarded each culture as representing a different embodiment of the Spirit, he argued that each should be preserved and respected.[34]

In Germany, the Enlightenment separation between culture and

---

28. WMC, *Report of Commission I*, 310–16.
29. Cf. Bosch, *Transforming Mission*, 448–49. The commissioners preparing for the Edinburgh 1910 conference did not use the term *accommodation* to which Bosch refers.
30. Stanley, *World Missionary Conference*, 308.
31. Tanner, *Theories of Culture*, 6–8, 12–16.
32. Ibid., 9–12. Germans distinguished civilization and culture at Edinburgh (for example, WMC, *History and Records of the Conference*, 20).
33. See, for example, Johann Gottfried Herder, *Letters for the Advancement of Humanity*, tenth collection, [Letter] 117, in *Johann Gottfried Herder: Philosophical Writings*, trans. and ed. Michael N. Forster (Cambridge: Cambridge University Press, 2004), 393–97. Subsequently, a clear hierarchy of these cultures and an understanding of the history of culture was established in German philosophy, particularly by Gustav Friedrich Klemm, on which Tylor drew for his schema.
34. Herder, *Letters for the Advancement of Humanity* (1793–1797), tenth collection, [Letter] 116, in *Philosophical Writings*, 380–83. See also Gorringe, *Furthering Humanity*, 7–8.

Christianity was felt particularly keenly, and Friedrich Schleiermacher, among others, had famously responded to the "Cultured Despisers" of the religion.[35] The great German missiologist Gustav Warneck (1834–1919) also grappled with "culture-strife."[36] For Warneck, Christianity was the most powerful "culture-force" in the world,[37] especially because Christian culture had not only material and intellectual dimensions but also a moral one supported by a particular cult.[38] Mission would result in Christianization, but it was primarily about the salvation of sinners[39] and was to be sharply distinguished from the civilization brought by modern Western missionaries, which Warneck regarded as harmful, both for those primitives he called "nature peoples" and for the "civilized heathen peoples" of China, Japan, and other places.[40] So, according to Warneck, the relationship between Christian missions and culture was "a struggle against the heathenish uncultured," on the one hand, and "against the Christian overculture," on the other.[41] Warneck died in 1910 and was not able to attend the Edinburgh conference, but his emphasis on the Christianization of a whole people or ethnic group was to have continuing importance in German missiology.[42] German missionaries encouraged in different lands the development of *Volkskirche*, or a church of the people, which was indigenous in its expression and locally led. On the one hand, this fostered respect for local cultures and opposition to the link between mission and "expansion of the white race."[43] On the other hand, it encouraged the disastrous link between religion and nationalism, which, at home in Germany, produced the infamous "German Christian" movement that attempted "to fuse

35. Friedrich Schleiermacher, *On Religion. Speeches to Its Cultured Despisers*, trans. John Oman (London: Kegan Paul, Trench, Trubner, 1893 [1879]). Cf. Gorringe, *Furthering Humanity*, 6.
36. Gustav Warneck, *Modern Missions and Culture: Their Mutual Relations*, trans. Thomas Smith (Edinburgh: James Gemmell, 1883 [1879]), 2.
37. Ibid., 2.
38. Ibid., 6–7, 12.
39. Ibid., 15.
40. Ibid., 44, 106.
41. Ibid., 377.
42. Timothy Yates, *Christian Mission in the Twentieth Century* (Cambridge: Cambridge University Press, 1994), 34–56.
43. Julius Richter, quoted in John G. Flett, *The Witness of God: The Trinity, Missio Dei, Karl Barth, and the Nature of Christian Community* (Grand Rapids: Eerdmans, 2010), 81.

Christianity with Germanness and purge it of Jewish influence."[44] Whereas German missionaries continued to advocate the Christianization of other cultures, during the period of Nazi dominance, mission leaders did not avoid making use of the Nazi culture theories.[45] The chief exemplar of this compromise was Bruno Gutmann, a missionary and anthropologist in East Africa who stressed that the church as a community should revitalize the existing organic bonding of a people and resist Western "civilizing" individualism.[46] It was in this context of debate about mission and culture that Karl Barth made his 1932 speech to the Brandenburg Missionary Conference—an intervention later credited with originating the *missio Dei* paradigm of theology of mission.[47] In it, Barth rejected both Gutmann's Christianization and Anglo-American civilization on the grounds that they were secularizing mission and focusing on the human rather than on Christ.[48] Barth's intervention was, at the same time, a rejection of an absolute understanding of culture, which defined a people and determined their destiny, such as the Nazis were advancing. It denied any suggestion that membership of the church was determined by blood ties or race.[49]

The dangers of linking missionary discussion of culture too closely to race and ethnicity had become very clear, but the German concept of cultures (plural) as the distinct, self-contained way of life of different peoples was mediated to the United States from the 1920s by Franz Boaz, in particular, one of the founders of "cultural anthropology" there. Cultural anthropologists regarded culture as a mark of all human life, but recognized that it is plural. Cultures are human constructions,

---

44. Doris L. Bergen, *Twisted Cross: The German Christian Movement in the Third Reich* (London: University of Carolina Press, 1996), xi; Cornelia Füllkrug-Weitzel, "A German Perspective," in *Called to One Hope: The Gospel in Diverse Cultures: Report of the Conference of the CWME, Salvador, Brazil, 1996*, ed. Christopher Duraisingh (Geneva: WCC, 1998), 111–20.

45. Flett, *Witness of God*, 78–122, especially 80n3. See also, Werner Ustorf, *Sailing on the Next Tide: Missions, Missiology, and the Third Reich* (Oxford: Peter Lang, 2000).

46. Flett, *Witness of God*, 101; Yates, *Christian Mission*, 116.

47. Erroneously, according to Flett, *Witness of God*, 105–12.

48. Ibid., 110–12.

49. Defenders of Gutmann argue that these were not, in fact, views that he was holding and that he was the victim of the polarized theological situation in Germany at the time. See Yates, *Christian Mission*, 49–56; Flett, *Witness of God*, 101–5.

the result of social consensus and protected by censure and sanctions. Whether conscious of it or not, individuals exist and act within a cultural milieu and the surrounding culture acts upon them to form and even determine them. Cultural anthropologists tended to study isolated cultures in remote areas that they perceived as largely beyond the influence of civilization, and they treated them as distinct wholes. In addition to cultural holism, another feature that distinguished cultural anthropology from the earlier ethnographic approach of Tylor was that it treated culture as a shared worldview or mental map giving meaning through norms, values, beliefs, and dispositions, rather than as a collection of customs, rituals, and practices. Furthermore, in keeping with the emerging ideas of racial equality and human rights, cultural anthropology espoused a principle of cultural relativity or at least advocated that the ethnographer suspend any judgment of a culture according to preconceived notions of high culture or the norms of his or her own culture.[50] In sum, since Edinburgh "culture" had shifted from a normative to an empirical concept,[51] and instead of being used to rank different groups of humanity, it was used ostensibly to promote human equality.

### Cultural Anthropology and Evangelical Missiology

During the "Great Reversal,"[52] evangelicals set themselves over and against culture in the sense of Western civilization. But by the 1960s, partly as a result of the influence of figures such as Francis Schaeffer and C. S. Lewis, this attitude had changed significantly.[53] The cultural anthropology developed between the 1920s and the 1960s became dominant in Evangelical mission thinking in the United States.[54] It

---

50. For more detailed discussion, see Tanner, *Theories of Culture*, 25–37.
51. Neil J. Ormerod and Shane Clifton, *Globalization and the Mission of the Church* (London: T&T Clark, 2009), 123.
52. See George M. Marsden, *Fundamentalism and American Culture*, 2nd ed. (New York: Oxford University Press, 2006), 85–92.
53. William A. Dyrness, "Evangelical Theology and Culture," in *The Cambridge Companion to Evangelical Theology*, ed. Timothy Larsen and Daniel J. Treier (Cambridge: Cambridge University Press, 2007), 149–53.
54. Wilbert R. Shenk, *History of the American Society of Missiology, 1973–2013* (Elkhart, IN: Institute of Mennonite Studies, 2014), 55–56.

predominated in the American Society of Missiology (ASM), founded in 1973, and Fuller Theological Seminary's School of World Mission, which provided the base for ASM.[55] At Fuller, through the work of Donald McGavran, a close relationship was forged between cultural anthropology and church growth; the people-group approach of Ralph Winter—cofounder of ASM—owed much to the discipline; and Charles Kraft stressed the link with cross-cultural communication.[56] So central did cultural anthropology become as the key scholarly discipline to which missiology related that the society took over the journal *Practical Anthropology*, which had been edited by Alan Tippett at Fuller, and changed its name to *Missiology*.[57] Then, in the early 1990s, Fuller Theological Seminary renamed its MA program in missiology as MA intercultural studies, and later, its School of World Mission as School of Intercultural Studies, as if mission and cultural change were synonymous.[58]

The influence of the cultural-anthropological approach on evangelical missiology is seen clearly in the *Lausanne Covenant* (LC, 1974), the founding document of the Lausanne Movement (for world evangelization).[59] By this time, evangelicalism had developed a multicultural identity.[60] The document, as a whole, envisages the people of God existing in many different cultures, which are not necessarily identified with nations, but are local, and it regards this positively (LC, 2, 11). The central importance of cultural anthropology is demonstrated both by the fact that paragraph 10 of fourteen

55. Fuller anthropologists included Paul G. Hiebert, *Anthropological Insights for Missionaries* (Grand Rapids: Baker, 1985); Charles H. Kraft, *Anthropology for Christian Witness* (Maryknoll, NY: Orbis, 1996); and Alan R. Tippett, *Introduction to Missiology* (Pasadena, CA: William Carey Library, 1987).

56. Kraft drew particularly on the work of the Catholic anthropologist Louis B. Luzbetak.

57. Although the ASM and *Missiology* broadened to cover "mission history, . . . the religions, and mission spirituality" as well, the study of cultures—now under the heading of "contextualization"—continued to play a central role. Shenk, *History of the American Society of Missiology*, 32.

58. This decision was more a response to the difficulties posed for missionaries working in sensitive parts of the world posed by having a degree in mission studies than any considered attempt to redefine mission studies, but it was influenced by Fuller's strength at that time in cultural anthropology. See "Our History," Fuller Theological Seminary, http://www.fuller.edu/about/history-and-facts/our-history/ (accessed July 5, 2014) and below.

59. Lausanne Committee for World Evangelization, *The Lausanne Covenant*, http://www.lausanne.org/content/covenant/lausanne-covenant (accessed July 4, 2014).

60. Dyrness, "Evangelical Theology and Culture," 153–54.

paragraphs in the document is devoted to culture, and also that it is titled "Evangelism and Culture," evangelization being the main goal of the movement. In common with the German vision of Christianization, it declares that "under God, the result [of evangelization] will be the rise of churches deeply rooted in Christ and closely related to their culture." It continues in this Warneckian vein by condemning the export with the gospel of an alien culture. However, it also inserts a Barthian caveat that "culture must always be tested and judged by Scripture" (10). Following cultural anthropology's egalitarian approach to culture, the covenant asserts that the gospel "does not presuppose the superiority of any culture to another" (5). However, the basis for this is not human commonality, but rather, because the church transcends culture (6) and the gospel "evaluates all cultures according to its own criteria of truth and righteousness, and insists on moral absolutes in every culture" (10).

A cultural anthropological definition of culture is even more apparent in the *Willowbank Report* of the Lausanne consultation on Gospel and culture (1978; section 2).[61] There, the understanding of cultures as discrete and complete wholes encourages the under-standing of evangelism as a "cross-cultural" endeavor (section 5). Although this terminology tended, on the one hand, to highlight the presumed difference between the missionary and the local people, on the other hand, like the *Lausanne Covenant*, the *Willowbank Report* drew attention to the uniqueness and lordship of Christ, and therefore their common need of grace and the importance of missionary humility (section 6). Furthermore, the culture concept allowed evangelicals to consider whether differences in missiology or theology were cultural, rather than sinful in origin (see section 7), and thus paved the way not only for recognition of multiple expressions of Christian living and worship but also for recognition of multiple theologies.

Although the *Lausanne Covenant* denies that culture is absolute, its organic holism is susceptible to policies of separate development on

---

61. Lausanne Committee for World Evangelization, *The Willowbank Report: Consultation on Gospel and Culture*, Occasional Paper 2 (1978), http://www.lausanne.org/en/documents/lops/73-lop-2.html#2 (accessed July 5, 2014).

the basis that cultures so shape the lives of individuals that people of a particular culture think and reason differently from those in another. The South African missiologist David J. Bosch detected this danger in McGavran's "homogeneous unit principle," especially in light of his experience of the system of apartheid.[62] Seeing cultures as discrete wholes is also a tendency of the mission theology of translation that has been developed by Andrew Walls and Lamin Sanneh because of its reliance of the model of language.[63] Such an approach may also lead to pessimism regarding the possibility of human cooperation, such as expressed in Samuel P. Huntington's influential "clash of civilizations" theory, in which he painted a picture of a new division of the world into religio-cultural blocs, including Western, Chinese, Indian, and Islamic, which have irreconcilable differences.[64] This leads to a defeatist view that neglects common humanity and contributes to the rise of intersocietal conflict. Reflecting on Edinburgh 1910, Brian Stanley issues a more general warning about the appropriation of cultural anthropology in mission: "Modern concepts of plural cultures have emerged from the soil of concepts of plural races, and in principle are vulnerable to similar critique on the basis of either their tendencies to anthropological essentialism or an implicit moral relativism."[65]

From the early 1990s, culture again came into popular usage among evangelicals through the gospel and Our Culture Network and the missional church movement formed to take up "the Newbigin gauntlet"[66] of a truly missionary encounter of the Gospel and Western culture. Drawing on Michael Polanyi's view that all knowledge is personal, and therefore limited, and a Barthian insistence that the

62. David J. Bosch, *Witness to the World* (Atlanta: John Knox, 1980), 208. The Lausanne Movement also recognized the difficulty and held a conference on the topic in Pasadena in 1978. Lausanne Committee for World Evangelization, *The Pasadena Consultation—Homogeneous Unit Principle*, Occasional Paper 1, http://www.lausanne.org/en/documents/lops/71-lop-1.html (accessed July 5, 2014).

63. Lamin Sanneh, *Translating the Message: The Missionary Impact on Culture* (Maryknoll, NY: Orbis, 1989), 211–38.

64. Samuel P. Huntington, *The Clash of Civilizations and the Remaking of the World Order* (London: Free Press, 2002).

65. Stanley, *World Missionary Conference*, 309.

66. George R. Hunsberger, "The Newbigin Gauntlet: Developing a Domestic Missiology for North America," *Missiology: An International Review*, 19 (1991): 391–408.

gospel is not possessed by any culture but judges them all, Newbigin again turned the spotlight on the singular culture of the West, but at the same time, this returning missionary viewed it from the outside and with the benefit of experience of other cultures.[67] Since Newbigin's view of Western culture was, on the whole, a negative one, Stephen Bevans categorizes his approach as "counter-cultural."[68] However, Michael Goheen argues that this is to neglect Newbigin's emphasis on the permeation of the Gospel into culture, the mission of the laity to shape society, and the participation of the church in cultural development.[69]

## Cape Town Commitment (2010)

The 2010 *Cape Town Commitment* (CTC) of the Lausanne Movement,[70] especially in its theological first part (I), treats culture in the plural and uses the word as synonymous with peoples, languages, and nations, and as the assumed meaning of the *ethné* of the Great Commission (Matt 28:18; see, for example, CTC I 6–7, 25–26). So, as in the *Lausanne Covenant*, the predominant use is in the cultural-anthropological sense. Culture refers primarily to the shared worldview of a society, as distinct from "economic, social, political and religious life" (8a). Cultures are personified: they are the object of Christian love, to be treated with equal respect, exhibiting the image of God yet flawed, and they are redeemable (7–8, 25–26). The second part of the document, which treats the application of theological truth to mission realities, starts with a recognition that the old evangelical world defined by a patchwork of entrenched cultures is breaking down under the influence of postmodern relativism, according to which truth is merely a cultural construct (II A 2). Nevertheless, the *Cape Town Commitment* continues with the established usage. It is clear that world evangelization involves constructive engagement with cultures (II D),

---

67. Lesslie Newbigin, *Foolishness to the Greeks* (Grand Rapids: Eerdmans, 1986).
68. Stephen B. Bevans, *Models of Contextual Theology*, 2nd ed. (Maryknoll, NY: Orbis, 2002), 117–38.
69. Michael W. Goheen, *As the Father Has Sent Me* (Zoetermeer: Boekencentrum, 2000).
70. Lausanne Movement, *The Cape Town Commitment*, http://www.lausanne.org/content/ctc/ctcommitment (accessed July 5, 2014).

but on the whole, Christianity is seen as counter to and distinct from the "surrounding" culture or cultures (especially II E; also II F). The old absolute sense of "culture" is retained partly because it is closely linked to "religion" as the chief concern of evangelization (II A 2; II C). In this respect, the document resonates more with Edinburgh 1910 than with the *Lausanne Covenant*.

## Ecumenical Theology of Culture and Sociopolitical Context

In the postwar period, German experience and Barthian criticism discouraged use of the word *culture* in the International Missionary Council (IMC), the Ecumenical continuation of Edinburgh 1910. However, the North Americans at the IMC's conference at Willingen, Germany, in 1952 did not share the same reservation. H. Richard Niebuhr's trinitarian approach informed the development of the *missio Dei* theology that developed there and his typology of "Christ and culture" models both affirmed human culture and at the same time encouraged the relativization of Western culture and its disconnection from the kingdom of God.[71] In emphasizing the local nature of each church, including those in the West, the emerging paradigm advanced an egalitarian view of churches that was similar to cultural anthropology's impartiality toward cultures. However, going into the 1960s, under the influence of secularism and Marxism and in reaction to the *völkisch* approach, Johannes Hoekendijk's reformulation of *missio Dei* focused on common humanity and the world as a whole, rather than on its differentiation into cultures, and it supported the dominant international development agenda of the era.[72]

In the mid-twentieth century, Niebuhr used "culture" to refer to the beliefs and practices of wider society, or "the world,"[73] while, under the influence of existentialism, Paul Tillich and others treated culture

---

71. In John Flett's analysis, use of the Trinity as the starting point enabled Niebuhr and the IMC to affirm aspects of the creation theology of German Christianization, and at the same time to incorporate Barth's eschatologically oriented discontinuity between any particular culture and kingdom of God. See Flett, *Witness of God*, 141–49.

72. Ibid., 66–72, 101–3.

73. Cf. Tanner, *Theories of Culture*, 61–62.

as something expressive of common human experience.[74] Either way, "culture" was used most often in the singular and not clearly distinguished from Western or post-Enlightenment culture. Moreover, ecumenical theology tended to retain the elite understanding of culture as "cultured," to link it to the arts and to religion, and to see the furtherance of it as an, or even the, goal of mission.[75] The work of Tillich, which had a more explicitly evangelistic aim,[76] was particularly influential in mission circles in this regard. Whereas US evangelical cultural anthropologists such as Charles Kraft could see religion as a segment of culture that, when a society converted, could be removed and replaced by another,[77] ecumenicals who had a European understanding of church as closely integrated with society, like Tillich, regarded religion as at the heart of culture.[78] In this light, the discussion of religions that dominated the IMC meetings at Jerusalem (1928) and at Tambaram (1938) was a way of dealing with culture and cultures, as was more recent ecumenical discussion of religions and interreligious relations. In his promotion of dialogue in the World Council of Churches (WCC) from the 1970s, Stanley Samartha worked to separate it from mission. He found the "exclusive claims" and aim of conversion that were integral to the mission theology of the time incompatible with the mutual respect necessary for his roundtable vision of dialogue.[79] Although he received fierce criticism from missionaries, and Newbigin especially,[80] Samartha's approach prevailed, and religions, like cultures, were treated relativistically in the WCC *Guidelines for Dialogue* (1979).[81]

In order to address local beliefs and practices in general, rather

---

74. Paul Tillich, *Theology of Culture* (Oxford: Oxford University Press, 1959).

75. Ernst Troeltsch was the chief example of this approach. See Tanner, *Theories of Culture*, 62.

76. Tillich, *Theology of Culture*, 201–13.

77. Charles H. Kraft, *Christianity in Culture* (Maryknoll, NY: Orbis, 1979).

78. Confronted with the fact that, in Europe, religion had been displaced from that transcendent position, Tillich tried to reintegrate it as "the depth dimension of reality," the "fundamental level" of "being itself." Tillich, *Theology of Culture*, 59.

79. Stanley J. Samartha, *Courage for Dialogue: Ecumenical Issues in Inter-Religious Relationships* (Geneva: WCC, 1981).

80. See the record of the WCC Nairobi General Assembly in David M. Paton, ed., *Breaking Barriers: Nairobi 1975* (Geneva: WCC, 1976).

81. Stanley J. Samartha, *Guidelines on Dialogue* (Geneva: WCC, 1979).

than only religion, in the early 1970s, the Ecumenical Education Fund chose "context" rather than "culture." "Contextualization" replaced "indigenization," which tended to be used for "responding to the Gospel in terms of traditional culture" and was, therefore, "past-oriented." Furthermore, "context" was preferred over "culture" because it was seen to be a broader term that included questions of the socioeconomic forces of change, modernity, interethnic politics, intercultural relations, and globalization.[82] In ecumenical circles, the dialogue with Marxism and the influence of liberation theology meant that sociological perspectives and socioeconomic issues increasingly took precedence over the ritual, symbolic, and aesthetic aspects of human behavior. In the first official statement of the WCC Commission on World Mission and Evangelism—*Mission and Evangelism: An Ecumenical Affirmation* (EA 1982)[83] drafted by Emilio Castro—discussion of culture was subsumed under the liberation motif.[84]

"Contextualization" carried with it the historical sense that theology is influenced by the situation in which it is done, which was a view pioneered in theology by Schleiermacher. Partly because of this association, "contextual theology" was resisted by many evangelicals. The contextualization debate pitted Barth and Tillich against one another as starting from the (biblical) text and from the context, respectively. The *Willowbank Report* (1978), however, showed how evangelicals, steeped in cultural anthropology, were able to accommodate the influence of context, both within God's self-revelation and also in contemporary interpretation and application of that divine self-revelation. The difference between evangelical and ecumenical discussion at the time was about what was included under "context." So, for example, the *Willowbank Report* suggested that for

---

82. Shoki Coe, "Contextualizing Theology," in *Mission Trends 3: Third World Theologies*, ed. Gerald H. Anderson and Thomas F. Stransky (New York: Paulist, 1976), 19–24.
83. World Council of Churches, "Mission and Evangelism: An Ecumenical Affirmation," in *"You Are the Light of the World": Statements on Mission by the World Council of Churches 1980–2005*, ed. Jacques Matthey (Geneva: WCC, 2005), 4–38.
84. Even though a passage on "inculturation" was included (EA 26–27), which affirmed diversity of witness, it also stressed that *"the best way to stimulate the process of inculturation is to participate in the struggle of the less privileged for their liberation. Solidarity is the best teacher of common cultural values"* (EA 26; italics original).

the foreign missionary, contextualization should include mastering the local language, understanding, and empathizing with the people, and following local custom, but argued that economic identification (of Western missionaries with the poor) would not be authentic.[85] Whereas the *Ecumenical Affirmation* invited "those who announce Jesus as the servant king . . . to enter with him daily in identification and participation with the poor of the earth" (7).

From the 1970s, cultural anthropology was challenged by perspectives from history, "conflict" sociology, political science, and literary theory.[86] It was criticized for inattention to historical and global processes. Postcolonial perspectives especially exposed the representation of cultures as internally consistent wholes and the result of social consensus as the view of the privileged outsider who generalizes and caricatures, a form of the "orientalism" identified by Edward Said.[87] Neo-Marxist Antonio Gramsci drew attention to the controlling power of culture and its use by the ruling class to exercise power without the use of force.[88] The application of anthropological methods to Western cultures revealed even greater complexity of the concept. Globalization and social plurality drew attention to cultural interaction. Rather than *cross-cultural*, the terms *inter-cultural* and *multi-cultural* became preferred. With the rise of literary theory, much of the initiative in the study of cultures passed from anthropology to the disciplines of critical and cultural studies. This created a further shift from an emphasis on culture as an external system in which we live to culture as "constantly being constructed by those who participate in it," like a performance or a conversation.[89] In this case, the focus is on questions of identity, and culture is constructed and representational, rather than an expression of any objective reality.[90]

---

85. LCWE, *The Willowbank Report*, section 6 B.
86. Tanner, *Theories of Culture*, 38–56.
87. Edward Said, *Orientalism: Western Conceptions of the Orient*, 3rd ed. (London: Penguin, 1995).
88. T. J. Jackson Lears, "The Concept of Cultural Hegemony: Problems and Possibilities," in *Antonio Gramsci: Critical Assessments of Leading Political Philosophers*, vol. 4, *Contemporary Applications*, ed. James Martin (London: Routledge, 2002), 324–54.
89. Robert J. Schreiter, "Inculturation of Faith or Identification with Culture?" in *New Directions in Mission and Evangelization 3: Faith and Culture*, ed. James A. Scherer and Stephen B. Bevans (Maryknoll, NY: Orbis, 1999), 71.

Culture is not something monolithic and unchanging, but dynamic and fluid, and even "tradition" can be invented or reinvented for particular ends.[91] Instead of the individual being formed by culture, culture is more often seen as a tool to be used for creating and defining an identity. This new perspective refuses to see people as determined by their culture, but sees them as the shapers of it. In the 1990s, the "Gospel and Our Cultures" process of the WCC not only brought home to that constituency the anthropological principle of cultural relativism, but at the same time embraced cultural plurality and celebrated diversity. Moreover, the process went further to reflect on culture as the construction of identity and culture as a means of power or hegemony.[92]

### Together towards Life (2013)

The main theme of the WCC document *Together towards Life* (TTL), published in 2013,[93] is life in the sense of justice and peace for all. It sees the world as multicultural, and, in a way that is closely linked to that, multireligious (TTL 9). The document discusses multicultural and "intercultural engagement" positively (70). It refers to receiving "life-giving wisdoms" from different cultures (27) and to "cultural difference as a gift of the Spirit" (75). However, reflecting the older understanding of culture as what humanity aspires to, the document makes a broad distinction between cultures that are life-affirming and those that are not. It seeks to work with the former (27, 110), but takes a countercultural, confrontational approach to the latter (37, 49, 108), which is accused of degenerating and destroying life by sustaining "massive poverty, discrimination, and dehumanization" (37). So, it overlays the multicultural model with an opposition between "market

90. Chris Barker, *Cultural Studies: Theory and Practice* (London: Sage, 2000), 95, 166.
91. Anthony Giddens, *Runaway World: How Globalization Is Reshaping Our Lives*, 2nd ed. (London: Profile, 2002), 36–50.
92. Duraisingh, *Called to One Hope*, especially "Conference Message," 20–28.
93. World Council of Churches' Commission on World Mission and Evangelism, *Together towards Life: Mission and Evangelism in Changing Landscapes* (2013), http://www.oikoumene.org/en/resources/publications/together-towards-life-mission-and-evangelism-in-changing-landscapes (accessed July 5, 2014).

ideology" or mammon, on the one hand (98), and the Spirit of Life, on the other. As such the predominant understanding of culture appears neo-Marxist in that it is suspicious of all cultures as potentially harmful to human flourishing.

## Catholic Missions, the Second Vatican Council, and Culture as Symbolic

At the First Vatican Council (1870), the Roman Catholic Church positioned itself firmly against the contemporary culture of modernism. Nevertheless, on the mission field, many Jesuits persisted with the accommodation approach they had inherited from earlier pioneers, such as Roberto de Nobili and Matteo Ricci, who adopted the policy of "adaptation" conceived by Alessandro Valignano as a way of reaching the centers of power of the great cultures of Asia and gaining a foothold for the church.[94] In the process, Ricci in China deliberately withheld doctrines such as the crucifixion that he knew the Chinese literati would find unpalatable until they were able to appreciate them through the eyes of faith.[95] After the persecution of clergy during the French Revolution (1789–1799) and other attacks on the church in Europe, Catholic attitudes to culture—at least Enlightenment culture— became decidedly negative, and at the First Vatican Council (1870), the church firmly rejected modernism, while many Jesuits developed the practice of inculturation, reexpressing the gospel in local terms to win people for Christ.[96]

In the 1930s, the official position of the Catholic Church on the matter of accommodation to culture was forced to change significantly, first because, under pressure, it signed a concordat with militarist Japan, which allowed traditional ancestor rites, and second,

---

94. Stephen B. Bevans and Roger P. Schroeder, *Constants in Context: A Theology of Mission for Today* (Maryknoll, NY: Orbis, 2004), 183–91.
95. Douglas Lancashire and Peter Hu Kuo-chen, "Translators' Introduction," in *Matteo Ricci, the True Meaning of the Lord of Heaven (T'ien-chu Shih-i)*, ed. Edward Malatesta, trans. Douglas Lancashire and Peter Hu Kuo-chen (St. Louis: The Institute of Jesuit Sources, 1985), 3–53.
96. William R. Burrows, "A Seventh Paradigm? Catholics and Radical Inculturation," in *Mission in Bold Humility: David Bosch's Work Considered*, ed. Willem Saayman and Klippies Kritzinger (Maryknoll, NY: Orbis, 1996), 121–38.

because of the obvious need for the churches in Asia to appoint local bishops and clergy in order to distance themselves from the European colonial interests.[97] Furthermore, by the 1950s, the theological pressure on the church for a reengagement with European culture had become irresistible. The aim of the Second Vatican Council (1962–1965) was to open the church to the modern world. The council was optimistic that "seeds of the Word" may be present and active in various religions and in the hearts of all "men of good will."[98] *Gaudium et Spes* (GS, 1965), one of the four constitutions produced by the council, specifically addressed culture, but in its earlier sense of the medium of human education and development (53). *Gaudium et Spes* sought to establish "communion" between "the message of salvation" and "human culture" in its various expressions in order to purge and renew the latter (58) so that it would serve the higher purpose of the "integral perfection of the human person" (59). The term "inculturation" which came into common currency among Jesuits in the 1970s, built on their tradition of accommodation and on the dialogical approach established by Pope Paul VI (*Ecclesiam Suam*, 1964). Inculturation "denotes the presentation and re-expression of the gospel in forms and terms proper to a culture"—processes that result in the reinterpretation of the Gospel as well as the culture, but "without being unfaithful to either."[99] The aim was "synthesis" of faith and culture, but not syncretism.[100]

The 1975 exhortation of Paul VI on Evangelization, *Evangelii Nuntiandi* (EN), integrated culture in the older sense of "cultured" (70) into the plural anthropological sense and endorsed the concept of inculturation. It declared the independence of the gospel from cultures, but recognized that, in the building the kingdom of God, the church could not "avoid borrowing the elements of human culture

---

97. Cf. Bevans and Schroeder, *Constants in Context*, 244.
98. See the following documents of the council: *Ad Gentes*, paragraph 11; *Lumen Gentium*, paragraph 17; *Gaudium et Spes*, paragraphs 22, 26, and 57–58.
99. Aylward Shorter, "Inculturation: Win or Lose the Future," in Scherer and Bevans, *New Directions in Mission and Evangelization 3*, 55.
100. Shorter, "Inculturation," 55, 57; see also, Aylward Shorter, *Evangelization and Culture* (London: Geoffrey Chapman, 1994), 30–33. Bevans, *Models of Contextual Theology*, 88–102; Robert Schreiter, *Constructing Local Theologies* (Maryknoll, NY: Orbis, 1985), 144–58.

or cultures" (20). However, rather than changes in the church, the pope gave greater emphasis to the hope that, through suitably adapted proclamation and other activities, the gospel would "permeate" cultures so that each culture could be evangelized "in a vital way, in depth and right to its roots" (20). This approach was similar to the transformational approach of the *Lausanne Covenant* of a year before, although it was more positive about culture as a human construction. Paul VI stressed that the person, and human relations, was the starting point for evangelization (EN 20), not culture itself. This meant both that inculturation was intended to be personal, rather than systematic, and, that culture was not determinative of human beings. In this respect, the Catholic appropriation of culture is influenced by the "transcendental" approach of theologians such as Karl Rahner and Bernard Lonergan, which attends to self-understanding rather than to the externals of cultural behavior in the belief that our inner life is shaped by the culture in which we live.[101] By recognizing this, we can understand ourselves and ultimately transcend our cultural limitations to reach a new and authentic expression of gospel in culture. In other words, spiritual life leads culture, rather than the other way around.

However, the encouragement given by Vatican II and Paul VI to dialogue with the world became polarized in the 1970s and 1980s in two directions. Although "inculturation" was intended to include modernity and social change as well as culture in the sense of tradition,[102] it was claimed by those working with respect to traditional cultures, and "liberation" was used by those addressing contemporary socioeconomic realities. It was perhaps unavoidable in the context of the Cold War that advocates of liberation theology, who were dialoguing with Marxists and emphasizing how a common humanity was divided by poverty linked to social class, would challenge theologies of inculturation, which tended to reexpress the gospel in terms derived from the local high culture, and therefore insufficiently challenged the status quo.[103] A further problem for inculturation was

---

101. Bevans, *Models of Contextual Theology*, 103–16.
102. Shorter, *Evangelization and Culture*, 30.

that, despite the council's encouragement, under John Paul II, and even more so Benedict XVI, those putting inculturation into practice encountered many restrictions.[104] These popes erred on the side of proclamation and tended toward the countercultural model as described by Bevans.[105] In his encyclical *Redemptoris Missio* (1990), John Paul II affirmed this cautious approach when he described inculturation as a "slow journey," or "incubation," bringing about a new form of life that is marked by both "compatibility with the gospel and communion with the universal Church."[106]

The linguistic/literary approach to culture in the form of semiotics promoted by Clifford Geertz and others was mediated to Catholic mission theology in the late 1980s, particularly by Robert Schreiter in his widely known book *Constructing Local Theologies*, and by another Catholic, Louis Luzbetak.[107] In this view, culture is a complex web of symbols, signs, or signifiers, and these carry meaning when they are used according to shared rules. Semiotics is particularly appropriate in the context of the Catholic Church because of its sacramental theology. The Eucharist is a prime example of a sign that, having deep resonances with church culture, is only really understood from within.

### *Evangelii Gaudium* (2013)

The first encyclical of Pope Francis, *Evangelii Gaudium* or *The Joy of the Gospel: On the Proclamation of the Gospel in Today's World* (EG, 2013),[108] stresses "the importance of understanding evangelization as inculturation" (EG 122). It defines culture in the anthropological sense

---

103. Bosch, *Transforming Mission*, 421. For the case of India, see Paul F. Knitter, *One Earth Many Religions: Multifaith Dialogue and Global Responsibility* (Maryknoll, NY: Orbis, 1995), 163–66.

104. Shorter, *Evangelization and Culture*, 32. For example, the process for translation and adaptation of the liturgy is laborious and controlled in Rome; see Peter C. Phan, "Liturgical Inculturation," in *Liturgy in a Postmodern World*, ed. Keith Pecklers (London: Continuum, 2003), 55–91.

105. Bevans, *Models of Contextual Theology*, 117–38.

106. John Paul II, *Redemptoris Missio*, "On the Permanent Validity of the Church's Missionary Mandate" (1990), http://w2.vatican.va/content/john-paul-ii/en/encyclicals/documents/hf_jp-ii_enc_071 21990_redemptoris-missio.html (accessed July 5, 2014), 52–54.

107. Schreiter, *Constructing Local Theologies*; Luzbetak, *The Church and Cultures*.

108. Francis, *Evangelii Gaudium* or *The Joy of the Gospel: On the Proclamation of the Gospel in Today's World* (2013), http://w2.vatican.va/content/francesco/en/apost_exhortations/documents/papa-francesco _esortazione-ap_20131124_evangelii-gaudium.html (accessed July 5, 2014).

as that which "embraces the totality of a people's life" (115) and is positive about it as the receptacle of God's grace in which "God's gift [of grace] becomes flesh" (115). Evangelizers, the pope writes, should not be content merely to reach each person in the world or to proclaim the gospel to cultures as a whole, but, in line with the inculturation approach, should aim to "embed" the gospel in each culture. When this happens, the message is no longer transmitted solely from person to person, but through the culture itself through socialization and education (129, cf. 68–69). The pope recognized some cultures as evangelized because they exhibit a "Christian substratum," especially in the realm of values. Because of this, the culture has resources of faith, solidarity, and wisdom, which encourage the development of "a more just and believing society" (68). In such a situation, the people of God "by the constant inner working of the Holy Spirit, is constantly evangelizing itself" (139). But Francis also pointed out that culture is not static, but "a dynamic reality which a people constantly recreates," and therefore such embedding is an ongoing dialogical process (122). The pope envisages a "multicultural church"—"a people of many faces"—and, departing somewhat from his predecessor, insists that "cultural diversity is not a threat to Church unity" (117). However, although the faith must be inculturated, Pope Francis "insists on the existence of objective moral norms which are valid for everyone" (64). Chief among these, the pope reminds his flock, is "the option for the poor," which being "primarily a theological category rather than a cultural, sociological, political or philosophical one" (198), is a universal obligation that transcends local concerns. Instead of elite culture, the norm for human development is justice for the poor, and the pope criticizes the ideology—or culture—of capitalism because it denies that (53–57, 60, 69, 202, 204). Francis leans more toward liberation than inculturation, but he also brings the two together in his insistence that evangelization means (collective) "human advancement" (178), the kingdom of God (180), "a better world" (183).

## Doing Theology for the Church's Mission:
## The Appropriation of Culture

As we have seen from the documents of the global evangelical, ecumenical, and Catholic bodies, today, the appropriation of culture in mission theology is a given. But the question is, what understanding of culture has been appropriated? Each of these documents treats culture in a way that is in keeping with earlier usage in its constituency. The definition of culture that these mission bodies, working globally, find most useful is the cultural-anthropological view that culture is the shared values and beliefs of a people. However, in the last fifty years, earlier static understandings of culture have given way to analysis of cultural change, not least in conversion and evangelization itself, and also, the application of "culture" to all kinds of groups, including ways this has been done in the West. The sense of cultures as self-contained wholes prevalent in evangelical discussion, which tended to talk about "cross-cultural" mission, has given way to "multicultural" and "intercultural." The churches vary in the value they give to other cultures. Since the 1960s, the Catholic Church has become affirming of the potential of all cultures for good, whereas Evangelicals have tended to be more wary of them. The recent WCC document celebrates indigenous cultures, but, reflecting postcolonial and neo-Marxist cultural criticism, condemns market-driven global culture.

All three documents use "culture" to describe only one aspect of the shared life of a people, citing society, economy, politics, and religion as other aspects. In view of earlier uses of culture, I suggest some caution with regard to the way these are linked. First, associating culture too closely with religion seems to me to be a step backward toward a monolithic view of religions and incompatible with the vision of multicultural churches. Second, the origins of the word *culture*, its associations with the elite and its tendency to conservatism[109] continue, in my view, to leave open the danger that concern with culture leads to the neglect of social justice. Third, and related to

109. Cf. Tanner, *Theories of Culture*, 167–71.

the previous point, in dealing with culture primarily in relation to ethnicity and often from afar, mission bodies may not be alert to the multiple layers of culture, cultural subgroups, the power relations within culture, and the extent to which cultures can be manipulated as a means of social control. The WCC document draws attention to such power issues in the case of market capitalism, but neglects to mention the soft power that is exerted by dominant cultures through media, music, advertising, and other means. This does not always correspond with economic power,[110] but generally it does.

A further limitation in the use of *culture* in each of the documents, which is in keeping with the dominance of cultural-anthropological approaches, is that the primary reference of culture is to local cultures. However, as pointed out, the ecumenical document additionally applies "culture" to the global culture of capitalism. Although he uses "ideology" rather than "culture" to refer to the market economy, Pope Francis also recognizes a higher tier beyond the local by his references to common human culture. In contrast to the other documents, the CTC uses "culture" only to refer to local traditions. Although it does recognize the universal permeation of sin and evil (I 8 A) and the need for worldwide action to address issues such as media (II A 4), trafficking, and poverty (II B 3), there is little sense of the structural and systemic challenges at a global level or self-awareness of the culture of the Lausanne Movement itself. This is surprising, considering the evangelical participation in the development agenda and advocacy of holistic and integral mission.[111] On the contrary, considering that both a century ago at Edinburgh and in the WCC in the 1960s, the universal imperatives of the kingdom of God were interpreted without necessary sensitivity to local culture or religion, it is wise to be cautious about global solutions. Although "justice," for example, may be a value in many cultures, it is not absolutely defined; what is justice for one party is not necessarily so for the other. Whereas

---

110. See Roland Robertson, *Globalization: Social Theory and Global Culture* (London: Sage, 1992), 96.

111. For example, Vinay Samuel and Christopher Sugden, eds., *Mission as Transformation: A Theology of the Whole Gospel* (Oxford: Regnum, 1999); David Emmanuel Singh and Bernard Farr, eds., *Christianity and Cultures: Shaping Christian Thinking in Context* (Oxford: Regnum, 2008).

common humanity implies some problems are universal, justice means that the solutions must always take into account the particular.

A further concern is that culture tends to be treated in these documents as something that conditions human behavior even after conversion. The deconstructionist and postcolonial insight that culture may be defined, rather than defining, has not been taken on board. With increasing migration and other issues that present questions of identity, there is a need to give more freedom to others to determine themselves and their culture, rather than boxing them into stereotypical categories. When we hear how others define us, we soon realize the limitations of cultural definitions. The Catholic transcendentalist vision of overcoming cultural limitations by self-knowledge, although criticized as introspective, individual, and elitist,[112] may also be empowering and should be given further consideration. Last, in regard to the ambiguity of culture, the view of cultures as existing separate and distinct from one another should be challenged on several grounds. First, the world traveler knows that the point on a map where one culture becomes another may be hard to define. Second, cultures do not necessarily match religious adherence or belief systems because, for one thing, conversion from one faith to another does not necessarily mean significant cultural change, and for another, not only Christianity, but other world religions recognize their own cultural diversity. Third, cultural hybridity and mixing is increasing and is not only a recent phenomenon. As postcolonial and transcendental approaches show, culture is a constructed, human category and should not be absolutized or allowed to inhibit the freedom of the gospel or the expression of our common humanity.

Culture plays such a significant role in mission studies that in 2008, the "Religious Studies and Mission Studies" section of the Academic Association for Theology (WGTh) and the administrative board of the German Association for Mission Studies (DGMW) fixed on the culture concept as the best way "to define the function and position of the subject Mission Studies within the area of Theology as well as in its

---

112. Bevans, *Models of Contextual Theology*, 103–16.

interaction with Religious Studies" by giving it the alternative name of "Intercultural Theology."[113] The proposal was based on the following arguments. First, on a global level in the twenty-first century, culture and religion are closely related and mission is crossing cultural/ religious boundaries. Second, historically, the discipline of mission studies has always been partnered with ethnology, anthropology, and "non-European philology," and it has given rise to "intercultural theology" before the term "intercultural" was used in other disciplines.[114] However, in the view of the German missiologist Werner Ustorf, intercultural theology was little more than a rediscovery of Herder in the context of theology of mission, and, what is more, it redefined mission studies in the very European categories of culture and religion. So that, although it attacked "the privileges both the western academy and the western church had been enjoying for a long time," it did so "only by making sure that nobody else could ever have epistemological privileges again." "Paradoxically, intercultural theology challenged hegemonic thinking but, at the same time, it universalized the critique of it."[115] Furthermore, respondents from some other contexts were not impressed by the suggestion that intercultural theology should be another name for mission studies. Francis Oborji regarded it as a retrograde step toward parochial and ethnic theology in an era of globalization and self-defeating when its intention was global interaction and global theology.[116] Ken Miyamoto pointed out that in Asia, mission is primarily to people of the same culture, not a different one, and that mission is about social and political questions and not only religious ones.[117]

---

113. The "Religious Studies and Mission Studies" section of the Academic Association for Theology (WGTh) and the administrative board of the German Association for Mission Studies (DGMW), "Mission Studies as Intercultural Theology and Its Relationship to Religious Studies," *Mission Studies* 25 (2008): 103–8.

114. Werner Ustorf describes the emergence of "intercultural theology" in this German sense in 1975 from the work of the Lutheran Hans Jochen Margull, the Reformed theologian of Pentecostalism Walter Hollenweger, the Catholic missiologist Richard Friedli, the Reformed missiologist Theo Sundermeier, and Ustorf himself (Reformed). Werner Ustorf, "The Cultural Origins of 'Intercultural Theology,'" *Mission Studies* 25 (2008): 229–51.

115. Ustorf, "Cultural Origins," 242–43.

116. Francis Anekwe Oborji, "Missiology in Its Relation to Intercultural Theology and Religious Studies," *Mission Studies* 25 (2008): 113–14.

The discussion about the intercultural studies proposal highlighted just how much the appropriation of culture by mission, and also mission's contribution to defining the culture-concept, is bound up with a long European encounter with and perception of the world as divided into cultural blocs that are primarily religiously defined.

"Intercultural" preserves the sense that cultures are integral wholes. The dominance of culture in European mission studies is not a reason for continuing to privilege it. Culture has played an important place in theology of mission, and while it is so significant in theology and the humanities generally, it will continue to be relevant, but it is just one partner of mission studies and the subject is impoverished if it is allowed to become the only one. Furthermore, by its nature, mission studies is an international discipline. Culture should be given a proper place in it through a process of conversation with the concerns of mission theologians from other continents.[118] They may analyze the world differently and have other priorities for mission.

117. Ken Christoph Miyamoto, "A Response to 'Mission Studies as Intercultural Studies and Its Relationship to Religious Studies'," *Mission Studies* 25 (2008): 109–10.
118. See Kirsteen Kim, *The Holy Spirit in the World: A Global Conversation* (Maryknoll, NY: Orbis, 2007).

6

———

# A Theology of Culture for the Missionary Task: A Response to Kirsteen Kim

## Daniel Strange

### Introduction

Performed on the occasion of Adolf Hitler's birthday in 1933, it was Friedrich Thiemann, one of the protagonists in Hanns Johst's play *Schlageter* who utters the infamous, and now often both misattributed and misquoted lines, "Whenever I hear of culture . . . I unlock the safety on my Browning!"[1] If I may be permitted to engage in my own little misappropriation, even a cursory glance at the history of the definition of the word *culture* does not engender the most peaceful

---

1. A "Browning" being the make of a widely used revolver. Johst (1890–1978) was a Nazi poet laureate. The line seems to have been put in the mouths of many of the most infamous of the Nazi hierarchy.

of thoughts, but quite the opposite. Somewhat ironically, it is none other than Raymond Williams, the godfather of late twentieth-century cultural studies who notes that "culture is one of the two or three most complicated words in the English language. This is so partly because of its intricate historical development, in several European languages, but mainly because it has now come to be used for important concepts in several distinct intellectual disciplines and incompatible systems of thought."[2]

Given such a complex and, one might say, tumultuous background, Kirsteen Kim is to be highly praised for the way she has expertly navigated through these choppy waters, giving us an extremely lucid and helpful historical account of the way the term *culture* has been appropriated missiologically from 1910 to the present, and across three very different Christian traditions. At the end of this panoramic sweep, one might be left more convinced than ever of the truth of Williams's statement, but also, I think, clearer on the nature of the complexity and what this might mean as mission studies/intercultural theology goes forward. I found especially helpful the comparison of *The Cape Town Commitment, Together towards Life,* and *Evangelii Gaudium,* particularly because as they came onto the scene, we were able to trace how these three traditions had arrived at their respective definitions of culture. More challengingly, as one who teaches in an evangelical seminary where we have a mission stream in our curriculum titled "theology for crossing cultures," Kim's chapter has certainly given me pause for thought as to the suitability of such nomenclature.

In this short response, I wish to offer an explicitly *theological* definition and account of culture, which, I hope, will complement Kim's account but will also offer some further clarification and critique to some of her more evaluative comments toward the end of her chapter. Methodologically, one of the striking elements that comes out in her chapter is the importance of continuing the discussion as to the interrelationship between theology and missiology, on the one hand, and the humanities and social sciences, on the other. I hope

2. Raymond Williams, *Keywords* (New York: Oxford University Press, 1985), 87.

that comparing and contrasting a historical account of how missiology has appropriated culture with a more constructive biblical theology of culture will be helpful in this ongoing conversation.

## 1. Cultural Themes

In preparation for this theological analysis, I would like to reiterate a number of overlapping definitional "cultural tensions" and "cultural struggles," some explicitly described by Kim, others more implicit. The first concerns that of prescription versus description when it comes to definitions of culture. Kim notes the gradual transition from culture as normative concept to culture as empirical concept.[3] Apart from Matthew Arnold (arguably the most famous representative of the "culture as civilization" definition), all the major figures in the development of the history of the term *culture* are present and correct with some of their underlying philosophical and ideological commitments on display. Although a version of the cultural-anthropological view appears to have the won the day in terms of the wider definition in missiological studies, I do not want to discount the significance of a more normative and prescriptive definition of culture.[4]

My second observation is an instantiation of the perennial philosophical problem of the one and the many. In Kim's historical description, we see the human need to recognize and categorize cultural difference for noble purposes, but also, tragically, for nefarious ones. Classification and generalization are necessary human endeavors, as is education, since particulars cannot rule out universals. However, working with universals without particulars means inflexible, static, monolithic definitions of culture that do not account for nuance and subcultural distinctions and which can produce

---

3. See p. 80.
4. I recognize that all description is covertly prescriptive; thus we are not talking of being more or less normative, but more or less openly normative. If there is a fear that norms undermine human flourishing, the response is to try to reject normativity. However, this means there is no sure way of *human* flourishing (for such demands a single normative account of human culture). As I will indicate, God's norms provide a single account that allows for the diversity of human flourishing in different cultural expressions.

caricatures and stereotypes, not dealing with increasing fluidity and multiple belongings in our globalized world. Related to this, of course, is the long-standing battle between cultural definitions, which are more essentialist/primordialist, and those that are more constructivist/instrumentalist. Does culture produce us? Do we produce culture? Is it a mixture of both, and if so, in what proportion? On this point, Kim states, "Culture is a constructed, human category and should not be absolutized."[5] We will return to this later.

My final observation concerns the nebulous and knotty relationship between our concept of culture and another two terms that are notoriously slippery to define: *religion* and *worldview*. If each of these terms is difficult to define, then relating all three together would appear to increase the complexity exponentially. Both *worldview* and *culture* do crop up in Kim's chapter, the latter being especially associated with Paul Tillich in terms of religion being at the heart of culture.[6] However, one of Kim's concluding suggestions is that "associating culture too closely with religion seems to me to be a step backward toward a monolithic view of religions and incompatible with the vision of multicultural churches."[7] I would like to challenge this conclusion, and wish to argue that "religion" (properly defined) is the hermeneutical key to the definition, understanding, and the flourishing diversity of culture. It is to a theological explanation that I now turn.[8]

## 2. A Brief Theology of Culture

I approach a theology of culture from the confessional stance of Reformed evangelicalism. Methodologically, this warrants two preliminary comments that bear on our discussion of culture. The first is an epistemology that recognizes the key metaphysical building

---

5. See p. 97.
6. See pp. 80, 84.
7. See p. 95.
8. Although dealing primarily with theology of religions rather than theology of culture, much of the following is taken and adapted from Daniel Strange, *For Their Rock Is Not as Our Rock: An Evangelical Theology of Religions* (Nottingham, UK: Apollos, 2014); Strange, *Their Rock Is Not Like Our Rock: A Theology of Religions* (Grand Rapids: Zondervan, 2015).

block of the Creator-creature distinction. Human beings' finite and culturally located knowledge is dependent upon a totally independent Creator. This epistemology can be called "transcendent foundationalism"[9] and is able to sympathize with both modern and postmodern concerns concerning knowledge. With D. A. Carson, we are able to say that "no truth which human beings may articulate can ever be articulated in a culture-transcending way—but that does not mean that the truth thus articulated does not transcend culture."[10] It is only within this epistemological framing that I am happy to affirm with Kim that theology is "a cultural production."[11] On the one hand, culturally indigenous theologizing is inevitable, and this still needs to be recognized and appropriated by some Christian communities. Although now forty years old, Robert McAfee Brown's tale remains salutary:

> In 1975, I attended a conference of North and South Americans at which there were a number of theologians. After three or four days, one of the Latin-American theologians said to us, "Why is it when you talk about our position you always describe it as 'Latin American theology' but when you talk about your position you always describe it as 'theology'?"[12]

Put more positively, such cultural locatedness does not entail relativistic agnosticism, but is rather, a God-given blessing to the global church: "Not all of God's truth is vouchsafed to one particular interpretative community—and the result will be that we will be eager to learn from one another, to correct and to be corrected by the

---

9. I borrow this term from Mark Kreitzer, *The Concept of Ethnicity in the Bible: A Theological* Analysis (London: Edwin Mellen, 2008), 427. Kreitzer explains, "All true thought begins within a relationship with the invisible Creator, his comprehensive truth system, and his true data points. All true data that comes into human senses, thus, are not ordered by the human mind but by God's mind. . . . Humans can perceive some true data and can discover some aspects of their coherency within the divine truth system, but never comprehensively. However, sin and incautious perception can distort perceived information. The Holy Spirit unbends and heals the distortion caused by sin. The Spirit-led reading of Scripture in all groups and ethnicities of humanity together limit our human finiteness. Therefore, facts that exist are not first interpreted by human minds. God is the original Creator and interpreter. Humans must think God's thoughts after him to know certain truth and factuality."

10. D. A. Carson, "Maintaining Scientific and Christian Truth Claims in a Postmodern World," *Science and Christian Belief* 14 (2002): 107–222, 120.

11. See. p. 73.

12. Robert McAfee Brown, *Theology in a New Key: Responding to Liberation Themes* (Louisville: Westminster John Knox), 77.

other.... The truth may be one, but it sounds less like a single wavering note than like a symphony."[13]

On the other hand, because there is "oneness of truth," the arena in which we culturally construct our theologies has definite boundaries as we continue to recognize and deploy the categories of "orthodoxy" and "orthopraxis" (and so "heterodoxy" and "heresy"); of the apostolic "pattern of sound teaching"[14] (contrasted with gangrenous teaching);[15] of the ministerial "rule of faith," and what Carl Trueman calls the "creedal imperative."[16]

Second is the primacy of revelation enshrined in the doctrine of *sola Scriptura*.[17] The Bible is God's inerrant word, our ultimate[18] authority on all matters, and the lens through which we interpret the world, including historical and social-scientific definitions of culture. As William Edgar states, "Defining terms can be a tautological game, of course, but it can become the recognition of proper practical usage. But consensus is impossible when the basic framework is lacking."[19] The Bible does not use the words *culture*, *religion*, or *worldview*, but this might be a help, rather than a hindrance in our theological construction. I wish to argue that all three concepts are present in Scripture and give us that basic framework which we need to bring some much-needed clarity to the definitional morass, and so, help missiology's appropriation of the terms.

In speaking of culture from a theological perspective, I will base myself within the loci of theological anthropology and branch out as appropriate. In what follows, I would like to give a condensed biblical theology of culture in three familiar movements: culture and creation, culture and the fall, and culture and redemption.

---

13. D. A. Carson, *The Gagging of God: Christianity Confronts Pluralism* (Grand Rapids: Zondervan, 1996), 552.
14. 2 Tim 1:13.
15. 2 Tim 2:17.
16. Carl R. Trueman, *The Creedal Imperative* (Wheaton: Crossway, 2012).
17. See also chap. 3 of this vol. for Brad Green's exposition of this principle of *sola Scriptura* also as key to a Protestant theological appropriation of "tradition" in the task of doing theology for mission.
18. Not the "only" authority, of course.
19. William Edgar, "Cult and Culture," in *Creator, Redeemer, Consummator: A Festschrift for Meredith G. Kline*, ed. H. Griffith and J. R. Muether (Greenville, SC: Reformed Academic Press, 2000), 289.

## a) Cultural Rule

When we return to the beginning, the genesis of "culture" is the fruit of the relationship between three aspects or perspectives of the *imago Dei*: the revelational, the relational, and the representational. Created human beings *reveal* the Creator in that we are his "analogues" in every respect in which it is appropriate for created beings to be such. Not only are we created to be in *relationship* with God, with each other, and with the rest of creation, but "the image is to be understood . . . as an office or embassy, a covenantal commission with an eschatological orientation."[20] This leads us to the *representational* aspect. God reveals himself to be the archetypal Speaker and Maker, and our ectypal imaging of him is as speakers and makers. This had been called the "cultural mandate": to "fill," "subdue," and "have dominion" (Gen 1:28; cf. Ps 8:4–8) over the rest of creation, and to "work" (in the sense of "cultivate") and "take care of" (in the sense of "not exploit") the environment around them (Gen 2:15). Culture is a calling. Human beings have a delegated kingly authority and vicegerency to rule over creation, but crucially, this is under God's norms and with a telos: for God's glory.[21] Moreover, the relationship of God to creation means that this glory extends to creation too. God's norms are the way to the telos of humanity's glory and glorification. As Irenaeus famously stated: "the glory of God is man who is entirely alive."[22]

Given the nature of the triune Lord, God who reveals himself as both unity and diversity, one and many, our reflected lordship of cultural development does not imply a bland monochrome cultural uniformity, but wonderful creativity, and tremendous variety, while always displaying a God-centered unity.

At this point, we can add to the pot our other tricky terms, *worldview* and *religion*. As I have argued elsewhere, we might say that culture

---

20. Michael S. Horton, "Image and Office: Human Personhood and the Covenant," in *Personal Identity in Theological Perspective*, ed. Richard Lints, Michael Horton, and Mark R. Talbot (Grand Rapids: Eerdmans, 2006), 184.
21. It is not insignificant that Adam's first cultural task is the naming of the animals (Gen 2:19–20). The need for classification is a response to the "one and many" problem I outlined earlier.
22. Irenaeus, *Adversus Haereses* 4.20.

is worldview exteriorized and worldview is culture interiorized, both stemming from the religion of the human heart.[23] Cultures are dynamic "*lived* worldviews,"[24] which communicate, orientate, reproduce, and cultivate.[25] Culture is the "fruit" of our "root" covenantal heart relationship with God. John Frame makes this connection well.

> Culture is what a society has made of God's creation, together with its ideals of what it ought to make. Or maybe we should put the ideal first. People make things, because they already have a plan in view, a purpose, a goal, an ideal. The ideal comes first, then making things. First the norm, then the cultivation, the culture. So now we can see how culture is related to religion. When we talk of values and ideals, we are talking religion. In the broad sense a person's religion is what grips his heart most strongly, what motivates him most deeply. It is the value which transcends all other values. . . . It is interesting that the Latin term *colere* . . . also refers to religious service, and comes into English as *cult, cultic* and so on. Culture and cult go together. If a society worships idols, false gods, that worship will govern the culture of that society. If a society worships the true God, that worship will deeply influence, even pervade its culture. If like ours, a society is religiously divided, then it will reveal a mixture of religious influences.[26]

Returning to some of the descriptions of culture in Kim's paper, at this stage, we can say that a biblical definition takes (or has had taken from it) elements that appear in the major definitions of culture. Culture is *both* normative and empirical, both descriptive and prescriptive. Because all human beings are made in the *imago Dei*, culture has a functional aspect that describes in symbols all aspects of human life (in cultural anthropology definitions) including the economic, social, and political.[27] And yet, given that the cultural mandate is to conform to the norms of the Divine Ruler, there is a qualitative and ethical dimension that can be more evaluative (in the more Arnoldian definitions) when humans depart from God's norms. Perhaps most surprisingly, given

23. Strange, *For Their Rock Is Not as Our Rock*, 68–71.
24. Kevin Vanhoozer, "What Is Everyday Theology? How and Why Should Christians Read Culture?," in *Everyday Theology: How to Read Cultural Texts and Interpret Trends*, ed. Kevin J. Vanhoozer, Charles A. Anderson, and Michael J. Sleasman (Grand Rapids: Baker Academic, 2007), 26 (his italics).
25. Vanhoozer, "What Is Everyday Theology?," 27–32.
26. John M. Frame, *The Doctrine of the Christian Life* (Phillipsburg, NJ: P&R, 2008), 857.
27. And so encompasses areas of social and economic justice.

my confessional commitments, one can appreciate and appropriate Tillich's description that religion is at the heart of culture (although shorn of Tillich's existentialist framework). In Henry Van Til's oft-quoted aphorism, "Culture is religion externalized."[28]

## b) Cultural Ruin

What do sin and the fall do to culture makers and their products? From Gen 3:15 onward, where God puts enmity between the "seed of the woman" and the "seed of the Serpent," history shows two streams of humanity diametrically opposed to one another. Theologians have called this the "antithesis," which is captured in a wealth of biblical contrasts seen genealogically and typologically in the Old Testament (seen immediately in the Cain-Lamech line, as opposed to the Adam-Seth line), and described in the New Testament as the stark difference between death and life, darkness and light, being in Adam and in Christ, goats and sheep, as covenant-keepers and covenant-breakers. The antithesis is comprehensive and extends to all areas of human life, noetically and ethically. Once again, *religion* as defined "kardioptically"[29] dwells at the root of this antithesis. If the *imago Dei* means we are metaphysically *homo adorans* (worshiping people), then there is an ineradicable spiritual core to humans beings, which means we either worship the living triune God or we worship a counterfeit idol. There are no additional options or alternatives. Colossians 2:6–8 describes these two forms of existence when it speaks of those "rooted and built up in Christ" and those captive to "hollow and deceptive philosophy, which depends on human tradition and the elemental spiritual forces, and not according to Christ."

How then does the religious root affect cultural fruit? As sin does not obliterate the *imago Dei*, and because of God's providential restraint exercised by an external work of the Spirit,[30] in a structural sense, all

---

28. Henry Van Til, *The Calvinistic Concept of Culture* (Grand Rapids: Baker Academic, 2001), 200.
29. David K. Naugle, *Worldview: The History of A Concept* (Grand Rapids: Eerdmans, 2002), 291.
30. What Reformed theologians call "common grace," to be compared and contrasted to, say, a Wesleyan understanding of "prevenient grace." "External" here means a "nonsalvific" work, as opposed to an internal regenerating work.

human beings, however sinful, continue their prophetic, priestly, and kingly functions; in this sense they produce "culture." Hence, the more descriptive, functional definition of culture stands. However, such forms of "culture" can only be the vestiges or remnants of true culture since they are made for and in the captivity of an idol and not explicitly for the triune God. Hence, the more prescriptive, normative definition of culture also stands.[31] In Adam, we have lost true dominion. As such, our making a home for ourselves after the fall cannot properly be called "culture" because the norms and telos are so radically different from those established in the original creation.

This kind of harmartiology enables us to further comment on Kirsteen Kim's study. First, the theological anthropology I have just described makes sense of some of the differences between evangelical and Catholic cultural engagement, which Kim helpfully delineates.[32] In Roman Catholic theology, "wounded" nature (as opposed to totally depraved nature in antithesis) generally allows for a superficially more positive engagement with human cultures.[33] Second, given the religious root of culture and the reality of the antithesis, Samuel P. Huntington's "clash of civilizations" theory is not so much "defeatist"

---

31. See John Barber, *The Road from Eden: Studies in Christianity and Culture* (Dublin: Academia Press, 2008), 493–96. Commenting on 1 Tim 4:4–5, Calvin writes: "Now Paul's doctrine proceeds on this principle, that there is no good thing, the possession of which is lawful, unless conscience testify that it is lawfully our own. And which of us would venture to claim for himself a single grain of wheat, if he were not taught by the word of God that he is the heir of the world? Common sense, indeed, pronounces, that the wealth of the world is naturally intended for our use; but, since dominion over the world was taken from us in Adam, everything that we touch of the gifts of God is defiled by our pollution; and, on the other hand, it is unclean to us, till God graciously comes to our aid, and by ingrafting us into his Son, constitutes us anew to be lords of the world, that we may lawfully use as our own all the wealth with which he supplies us. Justly, therefore, does Paul connect lawful enjoyment with 'the word,' by which alone we regain what was lost in Adam; for we must acknowledge God as our Father, that we may be his heirs, and Christ as our Head, that those things which are his may become ours. Hence it ought to be inferred that the use of all the gifts of God is unclean, unless it be accompanied by true knowledge and calling on the name of God; and that it is a beastly way of eating, when we sit down at table without any prayer; and, when we have eaten to the full, depart in utter forgetfulness of God." John Calvin, *Commentaries on the Epistles to Timothy, Titus, and Philemon*, trans. William Pringle (Edinburgh: Calvin Translation Society, 1856), 105.

32. See pp. 80–95.

33. This difference came out in my dialogue on the "theology of religions" with Roman Catholic theologians in Gavin D'Costa, Paul Knitter, and Daniel Strange, *Only One Way? Three Christian Responses to the Uniqueness of Christ in a Religiously Pluralist World* (London: SCM, 2011). I say "superficially positive" because the Roman Catholic position falsely limits the extent of sin. In reality, a Reformed view is ultimately a more positive engagement with culture as it confronts sin more deeply and shows the way to redemption.

and "pessimistic," as theologically accurate and realistic. Third, if culture construction post-fall is inextricably related to idolatry, then in a dialectic relationship, we *both* make and are made by culture. The Bible testifies in numerous places that idols are the "work of human hands"[34] and "nothing"[35] (compared to the transcendent uniqueness of Yahweh), but end up controlling the worshiper, who "becomes like them."[36] Generalizing, rather than caricaturing, there are connections between the doctrine of god in Islam (Allah is a monad and not triune) and the tendency toward unitary culture that many schools of Islam would like to construct.[37]

### c) Cultural Renewal

When we come to the subject of redemption, we can affirm the Christocentric heart of culture. Jesus Christ is the Alpha and Omega of creation, and his redemptive work in the gospel is cosmic in scope (Col 1:15–20; Rom 11:36; Eph 1:21). As Isaac Watts poetically put it, "He comes to make his blessings flow / Far as the curse is found." As the recapitulating second Adam, Jesus Christ, the image of the invisible God (Col 1:15), is the man of culture par excellence, anointed by the Spirit, demonstrating his perfect dominion over creation (being the fulfilment of Ps 8 in Heb 2:5–9), his propitiatory death reversing the curse, and his resurrection being the firstfruits of the new creation. How do we to describe the relationship between the gospel of Christ and human culture?

I am not convinced that the language of "incarnation" is appropriate or helpful here.[38] More promising is a trip back to the missionary

---

34. For example, Deut 4:28; 2 Kgs 19:18; Isa 37:19; Ps 115:4; 135:15; 2 Chr 32:19.
35. 1 Cor 8:4.
36. Ps 115:8.
37. See Robert Letham, *The Holy Trinity: In Scripture, History, Theology, and Worship* (Phillipsburg, NJ: P&R, 2004), 442–46. Letham focuses on the *ummah, dhimmitude,* and lack of differentiation between church and state.
38. As Horton puts it, "Jesus is a Savior, not a symbol. His incarnation is unique and unrepeatable. It cannot be extended, augmented, furthered, or realized by us. It happened . . . [Jesus] did not come to show us how to incarnate ourselves, but to be our incarnate Redeemer. . . . But nowhere, not even in Philippians 2, are we told to imitate, repeat, or extend Christ's incarnation. . . . The qualitative difference between the person and work of Jesus Christ and the person and work of believers makes it impossible to see the incarnation as a paradigm for our ministry. Rather,

council of Tambaram in 1938, and Hendrik Kraemer's term "subversive fulfilment."[39] I have used this term elsewhere to construct my own theology of religions, but I think it is equally appropriate in constructing a theology of culture, given my thesis that culture is religion externalized. Both the antithetical and counterfeit nature of idolatry means that the gospel both confronts and connects with every culture, therefore subverting and fulfilling it at the same time. Paul's encounter at the Areopagus in Acts 17 is narratively the locus classicus of this dynamic. The same apostle describes subversive fulfillment more didactically in 1 Cor 1:18–25. The preaching of the cross of Christ is the supreme contradiction and confrontation of the world's wisdom ("a stumbling block to Jews, and foolishness to Gentiles" [v. 23]), and yet, in a way that still fulfills the baseline cultural narratives of both Jews who look for power, and Greeks who look for wisdom: "Christ the power of God and the wisdom of God" (v. 24b).

## 3. Culture and Mission

What does the "subversive fulfilment" of culture mean for missiology and the mission of the church? First, just as the apex of God's good creation is seen in his "very good" image-bearers, at the center of Christ's redemptive work is the salvation of a people who have turned from idols to the living God and who have been adopted through the propitiatory work of Christ.[40]

Second, how do we describe the gospel and culture when it comes to both missional theology in terms of gospel communication and ecclesial theology in terms of gospel discipleship? While one can recognize *in practice* a certain degree of inconsistency and "messiness," *in principle,* the inextricable link between religious root and cultural fruit means that I think Kim's statement goes somewhat awry, saying

Christ's incarnation is the reason that a ministry exists at all in the first place." Michael Horton, "Does Anybody Really Know What Time it is?," *Modern Reformation* 18 (2009): 15.

39. Hendrik Kraemer, "Continuity or Discontinuity," in *The Authority of Faith: International Missionary Council Meeting at Tambaram, Madras* (London: Oxford University Press, 1939), 5. This is the only occasion Kraemer uses the term.

40. To use J. I. Packer's summary of the New Testament in *Knowing God* (London: Hodder and Stoughton, 2004), 214.

that "conversion from one faith to another does not necessarily mean significant cultural change."[41] Certainly, cultural "forms" may stay the same, but in terms of "content," there is literally a world of difference. J. H. Bavinck describes what takes place here in his critique of the term of the gospel "adapting to" or "accommodating culture." He writes:

> The term "accommodation" is not really appropriate as a description of what actually ought to take place. It points to an adaptation to customs and practices essentially foreign to the gospel. Such an adaptation can scarcely lead to anything other than a syncretistic entity, a conglomeration of customs that can never form an essential unity. "Accommodation" connotes something of a denial, of a mutilation. We would, therefore prefer to use the term *possessio*, to take in possession. The Christian life does not accommodate or adapt itself to heathen forms of life, but it takes the latter in possession and therefore makes them new. Whoever is in Christ is a new creature. Within the framework of the non-Christian life, customs and practices serve idolatrous tendencies and drive a person away from God. The Christian life takes them in hand and turns them in an entirely different direction; they acquire an entirely different content. Even though in external form there is much that resembles past practices, in reality everything has become new, the old in essence has passed away and the new has come. Christ takes the life of a people in his hands, he renews and re-establishes the distorted and deteriorated; he fills each thing, each word, each practice with a new meaning and gives it a new direction. Such is neither "adaptation" nor "accommodation"; it is in essence the legitimate taking possession of something by him to whom all power is given in heaven and on earth.[42]

As Kim recognizes, we can and must acknowledge increasing cultural complexity and hybridity. We must be ready to utilize the findings within the disciplines of anthropology and ethnography. As Kim notes, we must "alert to the multiple layers of culture, cultural subgroups, the power relations within culture, and the extent to which cultures can be manipulated as a means of social control."[43] However, this recognition must not be at the expense of religious antithesis. Multiple cultural belongings and cultural diversity can never legitimate multiple religious belongings.[44]

---

41. See p. 97.
42. J. H. Bavinck, *An Introduction to the Science of Missions* (Phillipsburg, NJ: P&R, 1960), 179.
43. See p. 96.

Finally, I wish to return to the idea culture as "calling." While the gospel both confronts and reforms existing cultures, there is a normative aspect of culture creation and culture building that can manifest in a wonderful multiplicity of ways, but which all conforms to God's norms and for his glory. Given the decreational devastation of sin, the summons to repentance and faith in Christ means we must speak of the "ultimacy"[45] and "radicalness"[46] of evangelism, *but in a way that is congruent with our cultural calling.* As Frame notes:

> The Great Commission is the republication of the cultural mandate for the semi-eschatological age. Unlike the original cultural mandate, it presupposes the existence of sin and the accomplishment of redemption. It recognizes that if the world is to be filled with worshippers of God, subduing the earth as his vassal kings, they must first be converted to Christ through the preaching of the gospel.[47]

If "incarnation" language is inappropriate, a better "imitation" model is expressed in the New Testament in terms of union with Christ (being the body of Christ in relation to him as our head). We are those united to Christ (body to head), and his story of relating to culture becomes ours: death (subversion) and resurrection (fulfillment). Christians are those who are anointed by the Spirit of Christ, and who, in their adoption as sons and daughters, are restored to take up the cultural mandate originally given to Adam. Our "good works"/"fruit of righteousness," which cover every aspect of our individual, social, and political lives while *never* redeeming are part of the redemptive kingdom and as they are done in Christ and by the Spirit, are the instrumental cause of God extending his kingdom in the present. As faithfully present ambassadors of Christ, we actively proclaim his lordship, taking every thought captive for him in anticipatory foretaste of the final consummation.[48] And however mission/intercultural

---

44. See Daniel Strange, "'There Can Be Only One': The Impossibility and Idolatry of 'Dual Belonging,'" in *Buddhist-Christian Dual Belonging: Affirmations, Objections, Explorations*, ed. Gavin D'Costa and Ross Thompson (New York: Routledge, 2016), 71–88.
45. Christopher J. H. Wright, *The Mission of God: Unlocking the Bible's Grand Narrative* (Nottingham, UK: Inter-Varsity Press, 2006), 319.
46. Timothy Keller, *Ministries of Mercy* (Grand Rapids: Zondervan, 1989), 114.
47. Frame, *Doctrine of the Christian Life*, 310.
48. I concur with Klaas Schilder (1890–1952), that the mission of the institutional church is to be

theologians appropriate the concept, when *they* hear the word *culture*, they must not forget this transformative vision.

distinguished from the mission of Christians in the world, each with their own specific tasks. This distinction and to an extent "protection" of the former is not to diminish the cultural task but to enable its flourishing: "The Church should not be even in the smallest direct center of culture, but she *must* be the greatest indirect cultural *force*." Klaas Schilder, *Christ and Culture* (Winnipeg: Premier Printing, 1977), 107 (available at http://www.reformed.org/webfiles/cc/christ_and_culture.pdf). For more on this distinction, see Daniel Strange, "Rooted and Grounded? The Legitimacy of Abraham Kuyper's Distinction between Church as Institute and Church as Organism, and Its Usefulness in Constructing an Evangelical Public Theology," *Themelios* 40 (2015): 429–44.

# PART II

# Assessing the Shape of Theology and Mission in Dialogue

# 7

## Theology, Bible, and Mission

### Mark W. Elliott

Mission is the vehicle that delivers the product of reconciliation with God and new life in Christ. Yet, if today we continue to be captivated by the notion that the medium is the message,[1] the danger is that our gaze shifts from the gift to its packaging and delivery operation. Moreover, the church of this age is all about what we do, what we are, and who we are as a church. Concomitantly, churches look for success stories and try to imitate them, or take the five steps to ensure growth and health through looking outward to those with signs of fresh spiritual life, or who are worse off than we are. Part of the benefit accrued is that when one does this, one does not dwell on things that might cause division, but rather one participates in the God who moves out in trinitarian fashion, with centrifugal force. "As the Father

---

1. See Marshall McLuhan, *Understanding Media: The Extensions of Man* (New York: McGraw Hill, 1964; reissued by MIT Press, 1994).

has sent me, so I send you" (John 20:21). This might seem to be the answer to Jesus's own prayer a few days and chapters earlier in the Gospel that "they all may be one as you [Father] and I are one" (John 17:21). Therefore, the ecumenical movement long ago stopped trying to agree on the wording of doctrine, and looked outward, being unified in the common task of outreach, inviting the really unchurched to the messianic banquet (Luke 14:23). And as this happens, the themes of identity, ecclesiology in movement, living and serving, all seem to fall into place. Jesus saves, yes, but the only hands he has are ours, to paraphrase Teresa of Avila. We reach out to help, to bless, to transform, just as he did and we receive blessing to share on the way.

There is, in all this, something very healthy and upbeat in dark days of conflict and confusion. Those who have the energy left over to worry about the souls and bodies of people they have never met, and otherwise would not meet, are, through God's grace, stimulated to take care of them and are, surely, happy people. Andrew Walls relates the story of Alexander Duff, a product of the St. Andrew's Missionary Society, a student influenced by Thomas Chalmers. His contemporaries thought Hinduism in India was too hard to take on, and so one should avoid conflict with the higher castes and simply seek out the poor and evangelize them only. Duff insisted on the importance of attacking the foundations or worldview of the other religion, hence debate with the Brahmins. Walls's only criticism of Duff's modus operandi consists in his observation that our task is not to judge worldviews, but to introduce Christ into them. Yet, he applauds Duff's speech at the 1839 General Assembly of the Church of Scotland, "*Missions as the Chief End of the Christian Church.*" This was at a time when the Church of Scotland was nearing the waterfall of schism, of self-destruction. After the Disruption of 1843, Duff persuaded the resultant Free Church of Scotland's New College to integrate missions into theological teaching, with a chair of evangelistic theology. For all the supposed hyper-Calvinism, as Walls comments: "Certainly the Free Church did produce marked and regular liberality for missions even when Duff was not present; the Church of Scotland had more difficulty raising missionary income,"[2] even after the inspiring death of David Livingstone. The chair was frozen before the century was out, but its legacy continued. Not least in the shape of the story of John Mackay, who in the early twentieth century, went from Scotland to South America, and then on to a distinguished position at Princeton Theological Seminary: a veritable triumph for world Christianity and mission informing theology.[3]

This might be approved by Mike Goheen, who comments: "David Bosch says of the theological curriculum: 'A major problem is that the present division of theological subjects was canonized in a period when the church in Europe was completely introverted.'"[4] Bosch seemed prophetic when he claimed that "unless we develop a missionary theology, not just a theology of mission, we will not achieve more than merely patch up the church."[5] So, mission is what the Bible is all about and should be the hermeneutical lens for reading the Scriptures, because it is anti-individualizing. Positively put, its message is cosmic, communal, and only then, individual. Correspondingly, Chris Wright notes that "a missional hermeneutic will work hard to read any text in the [scriptural] canon within this overarching narrative framework."[6]

One might want to respond: Should one try to "work hard" if that really means reading against the plain sense of a scriptural text? Goheen invokes Richard Bauckham to support his argument, who actually (and rightly) says that a missional hermeneutic "could and should only be one way of reading Scripture among others, since mission itself is not the comprehensive subject of the whole Bible."[7] That is a welcome qualification, but rather than talk of "ways of

---

2. Andrew F. Walls, "Missions," in *Dictionary of Scottish Church History and Theology*, Nigel M. de S. Cameron (Edinburgh: T&T Clark, 1993), 567–94, 572.

3. John A. Mackay, *The Other Spanish Christ: A Study in the Spiritual History of Spain and South America* (London: SCM, 1932). This work was brought to my attention by David Kirkpatrick.

4. David J. Bosch, "Theological Education in Missional Perspective," *Missiology: An International Review* 10 (1982): 26.

5. David J. Bosch, *Believing in the Future: Toward a Missiology of Western Culture* (Valley Forge, PA: Trinity Press International, 1995), 32.

6. Christopher J. H. Wright, "Mission and Old Testament Interpretation," in *Hearing the Old Testament: Listening for God's Address*, ed. Craig G. Bartholomew and David J. H. Beldman (Grand Rapids: Eerdmans, 2012), 184.

7. Richard Bauckham, "Mission as Hermeneutic for Scriptural Interpretation" (Currents in World Christianity Position Paper, 106 [1999]), 1.

reading Scripture," it is perhaps better to think that some parts of Scripture speak about mission, other bits about politics, other bits about ecology, and other things.[8]

However, one can understand why Western believers want to look outward and see what God is doing "in the mission field." The world has become bigger again. Looking overseas to the growing church makes one more encouraged about "church," while theology in the West remains almost inevitably "negative" and critical (evaluating rather than doing, or inspiring). Holistic mission looks to the Gospels as well as Paul: the kingdom includes justice, and this theme should be added on or added alongside Pauline soteriology. Darrell Guder's *Missional Church*[9] calls for the *notae ecclesiae* to be worship, discipleship, community, and mission.

Indeed, a socially engaged church (in Andrew Kirk's phrase) is called to link with the nonchurched. As always, the gospel is about transformation: salvation means "creation healed" (I think the phrase goes back to Hans Küng and was a favorite of David Watson), that is: "transformed into wholeness." Although overseas churches in the majority world are full and there are now many Christians in those societies, there is no commensurate political transformation, which the festschrift for Andrew Kirk complains.[10] This needs to change, even as so many evangelicals have returned to the holistic approach to outreach they had in the early nineteenth century, the age of Shaftesbury and Wilberforce. A key figure for contemporary evangelical, N. T. Wright insists that Christianity offers not some spiritualized heaven, but a transformed world.[11] The covenant climaxes in blessing for "the other." And with every breath of proclamation, there is love enacted in service. There are no longer "two mandates" of

8. Andreas J. Köstenberger and P. T. O'Brien, *Salvation to the Ends of the Earth: A Biblical Theology of Mission*, New Studies in Biblical Theology 11 (Downers Grove, IL: InterVarsity Press, 2001); J. P. Dickson, *Mission-Commitment in Ancient Judaism and in the Pauline Communities: The Shape, Extent and Background of Early Christian Mission*, WUNT II 159 (Tübingen: Mohr Siebeck, 2003).

9. Darrell Guder, *Missional Church: A Vision for the Sending of the Church in North America*, Gospel & Our Culture (Grand Rapids: Eerdmans, 1998).

10. John Corrie and Cathy Ross, eds. *Mission in Context: Explorations Inspired by J. Andrew Kirk* (Farnham, UK: Ashgate, 2012).

11. See, for instance, N. T. Wright, *The Resurrection of the Son of God* (London: SPCK, 2004).

preaching and social outreach, but an integral one, as with René Padilla or David Bosch.[12]

The concept of "mission" implies "intention from the beginning," something planned and even demonstrable in a "mission statement." So, is there mission in the Bible from the start? Is the Old Testament the story of God? I'm not so sure. The subject of the Pentateuch is more "law" than narrative. Thereafter, accounts of a nation that fails to honor God and is punished: is that really "God's story"? (Although, admittedly, much of God is indeed revealed.) Israel was not very missionary most of the time, with Jonah perhaps an exception, although he did not have "good news" to preach. In Jonah's case, Nineveh is spared rather than converted to or by good news, and Nahum rather curbs our enthusiasm about the long-term effectiveness of Jonah's preaching. Isaiah points to the future inclusion of the gentiles, but it seems like some way off. I am not convinced that God wanted Israel to be very missionary. The most inclusive story, Ruth, is just that—it is about drawing-in, not outreach. Perhaps when we are uncomfortable about something, we tend to give it higher importance. A preexisting mission of God for New Testament believers to participate in sounds good, but I do not see it in the Old Testament, nor is it unproblematic to posit it as the view of the New Testament.

We preach not ourselves, but Christ Jesus the Lord and ourselves your servants (2 Cor 4:5). Christ crucified is also Christ the Lord, so we should have confidence to preach. But "our mission," even if we call it *missio Dei* rather than "proclamation of Christ," implies we have more to offer than this message, even expectations to deliver on. It then becomes hard not to "preach ourselves." This is the theme of justification by faith transposed into another key. We have been sent by someone, with their derived authority, and yet, sometimes that just gives us confidence to make it all up and leave the original message behind. We train people to be trainers to train others without evangelizing their hearts or "making disciples" of *them*. Of course, the

---

12. See chap. 11 of this volume, and also David J. Bosch, *Transforming Mission: Paradigm Shifts in Theology of Mission* (Maryknoll, NY: Orbis, 1991).

New Testament has something to say about church and its running; Paul has an ecclesiology, a profound one. Yet it is not at the center of his preaching. He mentions his apostolate at the start of letters and sometimes returns to the topic (for example, 2 Corinthians) and how it relates to his mission. But it is hardly the central message: *that* is rather the identity of the Messiah and what he means. The Truth sets free, but we go on wanting to preach methods. Methods, organization, institutions, authority dominate, at the expense of the content of the message. Modernist questions of authority are more our concern than before.

The charismatic movement has not always helped. One would imagine it would. Lively experience of grace, the presence of Jesus, power rather than words (1 Corinthians 2), all come to the fore in this experience. Doctrine seems something stuck in the past, the stuff of overnice scholastic definitions and rhetoric whereby false objectivity of truth could serve the will to power, atonement and "Christ crucified" theology seems part of that, with the atonement viewed as a debate, not a reality. So it seems better to preach about the Spirit of Jesus, what God is *doing*. A down-to-earth but up-to-date God, as it were, who makes all things new and so is always future, always one step ahead. To proof text Isa 43:18: "Forget the former things; do not dwell on the past. See, I am doing a new thing! Now it springs up; do you not perceive it?"

One response might be to focus on God as he is, and to develop a concern with the Trinity. Of course, this means a God of personhood, of some amount of mystery (if persons are mysterious?), but not too much. More is then made of a family to join in, some energies to participate in, a house for belonging. The reluctance to distinguish between primary and secondary causes, and the theme of participation in the mission of God comes at a price, that of not knowing our place and our responsibility. In fact, in the New Testament, the Spirit gets portrayed more as the mind of God communicated to the apostles and other believers (1 Cor 2:11), rather than some force field or river to swim in. This leaves believers with the agency, even if the power comes from God.

Is the heart of the faith "mission," and is the medium the message? Now, paying more attention to a neglected thread is more than praiseworthy, but to promote it to the status of "hermeneutical lens" seems peculiar. Even if one accepts that mission should be "integral," is it still not the case that preaching and service are two different types of activity? The question is not, are they mutually related? Of course, they are, but the question is rather: how?

Moreover, the feature of mission studies designated as "the history of mission" too often becomes self-referential in telling stories about heroes of missiology (those of David Bosch and Andrew Walls come to mind), rather than about heroes of mission, usually because the former at least were writers who were located "out there in the real world" (attractively) having left behind their ivory towers. There is also a playing down of many *missionaries* for their suspect colonialist values, despite Brian Stanley's robust defense.[13] No doubt their academic careers were full of risk and virtue, yet not in the way of saintliness that marked the life of a Francis Xavier or a Henry Martyn. To call the church of the Middle Ages and Reformation "inward-looking" at the time it forged the paradigm for Western ecclesiology seems anachronistic and silly. The Reformations, Protestant and Catholic, were enthusiastic about spreading the gospel along with their interpretation of it wherever they could: whether in Scandinavia, Scotland, Bohemia, or Brazil.

N. T. Wright has observed that however one interprets Jesus's reply to the question about his restoring the kingdom to Israel (Acts 1:6), it should be understood as something that is real in terms of space–time coordinates, and not merely spiritual. The kingdom exists in the world, and that should encourage a positive mood as befits those who are on the "winning team," a team whose membership is wide open and inclusive. However, a good dose of Lutheranism tells us to get actual,

13. Brian Stanley, *The Bible and the Flag: Protestant Missions and British Imperialism in the Nineteenth and Twentieth Centuries* (Trowbridge, UK: Apollos, 1990).

then real, then actual again. The actuality is that we are selfish people who often get excited because we are professionals who want more people to support us. The reality is that we are forgiven and empowered, and the new actuality that can result from this is cheerful "mission." This needs to happen in the right order. Mission can well be a demonstration of faith, but it needs repentance and faith to drive it. The *missio Dei* in Christopher J. H. Wright's theology works through the participation therein of disciple makers—passing on teaching without it going through us at a terribly deep or problematizing level. We spend more time on the culture of others rather than the cultures within us and can be awkwardly unaware of ourselves. Prayer for the world and troubled regions sometimes seems abstract (at best) and dishonest (at worst) as we list and lament the sins of others far away, but remain vague about those closest to home. Fine, if our missionary efforts are first about resourcing the local church to evangelize as it repents; but there is something about mission theology that hovers at a distance from the action: it is meta-evangelism just as it is meta-holistic help. Why call that combination "mission," rather than "evangelism and holiness"? Now, of course, part of the gift is passing it on. But what is it? Is it a witness? The language of witness is more to God and Christ than to their mission,[14] even God's mission. One may speak of our being sent by the Risen Christ to meet God. Is that a *missio Dei*? Is there a "wave"? Or is there a witness to the wave? I am not sure how much talk there is of waves in the Bible or whether it fits its pattern of call and response.

To arrive at last at the well-known Gospel passages that relate to our topic. Along with the famous Matt 28:19–20, there is Luke 24:47, where Jesus speaks about his messiahship in connection with the forgiveness of sins to be preached to all nations. The emphasis here is to all nations other than Israel. It is not about ticking off a checklist, when he commands that every nation must be reached. "To the end of the earth:

---

14. See Alison A. Trites, *The New Testament Concept of Witness* (Cambridge: Cambridge University Press, 2004).

you will be witnesses," as the risen Jesus puts it in Acts 1:8. Or in Mark 16:20—"going out they proclaimed everywhere wherever [*pantachou*]." Calvin in his Gospel synopsis is worth hearing here:

> *Teach all nations.* Here Christ, by removing the distinction, makes the Gentiles equal to the Jews, and admits both, indiscriminately to a participation in the covenant. Such is also the import of the term: go out; for the prophets under the law had limits assigned to them, but now, the wall of partition having been broken down (Eph. 2:14), the Lord commands the ministers of the gospel to go to a distance, in order to spread the doctrine of salvation in every part of the world. For though, as we have lately suggested, the right of the first-born at the very commencement of the gospel, remained among the Jews, still the inheritance of life was common to the Gentiles. Thus was fulfilled that prediction of Isaiah (Isa. 49:6) and others of a similar nature, that Christ was given for a light of the Gentiles, that he might be the salvation of God to the end of the earth.

There is no application of this to present-day church, unlike that which immediately follows Jesus's statement on baptism:

> Accordingly, it is said in Mark, He that shall believe and be baptized shall be saved. By these words Christ not only excludes from the hope of salvation hypocrites who, though destitute of faith, are puffed up only by the outward sign; but by a sacred bond he connects baptism with doctrine, so that the latter is nothing more than an appendage of the former. But as Christ enjoins them to teach before baptizing, and desires that none but believers shall be admitted to baptism, it would appear that baptism is not properly administered unless when it is preceded by faith. On this pretense, the Anabaptists have stormed greatly against infant baptism. But the reply is not difficult, if we attend to the reason of the command. Christ orders them to convey to all nations the message of eternal salvation, and confirms it by adding the seal of baptism. Now it was proper that faith in the word should be placed before baptism, since the Gentiles were altogether alienated from God, and had nothing in common with the chosen people; for otherwise it would have been a false figure, which offered forgiveness and the gift of the Spirit to unbelievers, who were not yet members of Christ. But we know that by faith those who were formerly despised are united to the people of God.

> It is now asked, on what condition does God adopt as children those who formerly were aliens? It cannot, indeed, be denied that, when he has once received them into his favor, he continues to bestow it on their children

127

and their children's children. By the coming of Christ God manifested himself as a Father equally to the Gentiles and to the Jews; and, therefore, that promise, which was formerly given to the Jews, must now be in force towards the Gentiles, I will be thy God, and the God of thy seed after thee (Gen. 17:7.) Thus we see that they who entered by faith into the Church of God are reckoned, along with their posterity, among the members of Christ, and, at the same time, called to the inheritance of salvation. And yet this does not involve the separation of baptism from faith and doctrine; because, though infants are not yet of such an age as to be capable of receiving the grace of God by faith, still God, when addressing their parents, includes them also. I maintain, therefore, that it is not rash to administer baptism to infants, to which God invites them, when he promises that he will be their God.

Teaching them to observe all things. By these words, as I have formerly suggested, Christ shows that, in sending the apostles, he does not entirely resign his office, as if he ceased to be the Teacher of his Church; for he sends away the apostles with this reservation, that they shall not bring forward their own inventions, but shall purely and faithfully deliver from hand to hand (as we say) what he has entrusted to them.[15]

No doubt, because of the Anabaptist threat at the time, Calvin spends much longer on baptism than mission. That does not mean he did not believe in evangelism, as his sermon on Micah 2 makes clear. Yet the thrust of Calvin's message is that the church is to focus on its duty to baptize and to teach more than to "do mission." We are to baptize in a meaningful way and teach in an imaginative, relevant way. Can there at least be winsome preaching and administration of the sacraments? If believers and churchgoers are being bored by repetitive and thin sermons, what chance is there nonbelievers are going to be convinced?

Finally, the difference between mission theology and intercultural theology needs to be mentioned. Being prepared to read theology from different parts of the world, and learning from it, is not the same thing as a theology that exists to take a message—in action—to the unreached. The two might be connected and even practiced by the same people. However, their aims seem different. In a way, intercultural theology is at least trying to say things about God by

---

15. John Calvin, *Commentary on a Harmony of the Evangelists, Matthew, Mark, and Luke*, trans. William Pringle (Edinburgh: Calvin Translation Society, 1843; repr., Grand Rapids: Baker, 2003), 384.

taking into considerations perspectives that are "fresh" to most in the Western church and Western academy. It remains to be seen whether there truly is a "Chinese theology" that does this, rather than one that ends up addressing the same old identity questions of being human, of common spirituality, and transcendental longings, as have been rife in Western liberal departments for the last generation. The challenge to keep one's eyes on God's self-revelation in Christ even while addressing the fundamental issues of values and political life will be the challenge for both mission theology and intercultural theology. A theology that begins and ends with worship will include a lot of things in the middle: but they will be penultimate, and seen clearly in the glory reflected on them by the Alpha and Omega.

8

———

# Doing Theology for the Church's Mission: A Historian's Perspective

## Brian Stanley

The divorce between theology and the other human sciences is perhaps the most profound and far-reaching consequence of the European Enlightenment. It is not a divorce that theology itself has ever willingly accepted, but theology has found the other party to the marriage obstinately opposed to any recourse to the marriage guidance counselor, and increasingly finds itself thrown out of the marital home. I first became fully aware of the implications of this divorce when I read a review of my first book, *The Bible and the Flag: Protestant Missions and British Imperialism in the Nineteenth and Twentieth Centuries*,[1] published in the *Journal of Religion in Africa* in 1992. The

---

1. Brian Stanley, *The Bible and the Flag: Protestant Missions and British Imperialism in the Nineteenth and Twentieth Centuries* (Leicester, UK: Apollos, 1990).

review was, in fact, a remarkably favorable one, but the reviewer nevertheless felt bound to add, with reference to chapter 8 of the book, which had attempted a theological evaluation of the historical evidence it had surveyed:

> By examining the whole question at the end "from a specifically Christian perspective," the author weakens the book's effectiveness as an historical work. It might have been better if he had put his "theological evaluation" in a separate volume, thus avoiding predictable accusations of religious bias.[2]

Historical analysis of the record of the church is one thing. Theological evaluation of that record is quite another, and the prevailing wisdom is that the two should not be combined. Those who attempt to do so are liable to attract secularist gunfire. It will be interesting to see how reviewers react to a more recent historical book from an openly Christian author, which similarly makes bold to close its superb historical analysis of the Catholic politics of Rwanda before the genocide of 1994 with an epilogue that draws profound and explicitly theological "lessons" from that narrative of Christian failure.[3]

The World Missionary Conference held at Edinburgh in 1910 was intended by its architects, especially its secretary, J. H. Oldham, to cultivate the study of Christian mission as an empirical science, an academic subject that could take its rightful place in the academy alongside the other human sciences.[4] While the conference did lead to the founding of chairs in Christian mission in a number of universities and seminaries in North America,[5] in Britain, "missiology" generally failed to establish a permanent place in British academic life; for nearly a century, the Selly Oak Colleges in Birmingham represented a notable attempt at the task. At New College, Edinburgh, the chair of evangelistic theology (the first academic chair in mission studies anywhere in the world) created for Alexander Duff had lapsed as early

---

2. Review by Hugh Cecil, *Journal of Religion in Africa* 22 (1992): 269–70.
3. J. J. Carney, *Rwanda before the Genocide: Catholic Politics and Ethnic Discourse in the Late Colonial Era* (New York: Oxford University Press, 2014), 201–8.
4. Brian Stanley, *The World Missionary Conference, Edinburgh 1910* (Grand Rapids: Eerdmans, 2009), 3–5.
5. Ibid., 316–17.

as 1892. In the University of Birmingham, the only British university to have committed itself to the academic study of Christian mission at professorial level (an indirect legacy of the World Missionary Conference), the chair in mission formerly held by Werner Ustorf lapsed on his retirement in 2010, although Professor Allan Anderson's post in the university is still denominated as a chair in mission and Pentecostal studies. One suspects that the title will not outlive his impending retirement.

Although the academic study of Christian mission has generally failed to gain a secure foothold in British universities, the last two decades have witnessed the growth, modest in Britain and Europe, but much more expansive in North America, of the new multidisciplinary field of "world Christianity." It is appropriate to ask whether what is now termed world Christianity is, in fact, mission studies by another name. There is some evidence in favor of this suggestion. The historian of missions and world Christianity Andrew F. Walls, the second librarian of Tyndale House from 1952 to 1957, who was appointed professor of world Christianity in the University of Edinburgh in 1987, saw himself as inheritor of the Alexander Duff tradition, teaching a form of theology and Christian history that had reflection on the remarkable expansion of southern Christianity at its heart.[6] The subsequent development of the field of world Christianity owes an enormous amount to his influence, exercised through his numerous articles and the many research students whom he has supervised. Kirsteen Kim, another of the contributors to this volume, is, more explicitly than Walls, a theologian with primarily non-Western interests, but also a strong commitment to mission studies; her chair at Leeds Trinity University is, however, denominated as a post in theology and world christianity, with no explicit mention of mission.

By and large, world Christianity can only secure a place in the modern secular academy if it rigorously eschews any overt missional agenda. Academic theologians are perennially concerned to watch

---

6. See Brian Stanley, "Founding the Centre for the Study of Christianity in the Non-Western World," in *Understanding World Christianity: The Vision and Work of Andrew F. Walls*, ed. William R. Burrows, Mark R. Gornik, and Janice A. McLean (Maryknoll, NY: Orbis, 2011), 54.

their own backs against secular accusations that theology is an antiquated confessional subject that has no place in the ideologically plural university, and hence tend to be very wary of missiology as a polite name for the sanctioned study of religious proselytism, one of the great "No-No" words of contemporary intellectual discourse. Hence, a second divorce has opened up between the academic study of theology and the study of Christian mission. Where theology departments have retained posts that used to contain the mission "word" in their titles, they have tended, as Professor Kim points out in her chapter, to be redenominated as posts in "intercultural theology." The absolute value previously ascribed to the propagation of the Christian revelation has been transferred to the social-scientific concept of "culture": intercultural theology conjures up a picture of the theological task faced by Christians as they have to negotiate their way and their message between the supposedly fixed points of at least two given "cultures."

The recent expansion of studies in world Christianity is indeed very welcome, but only exceptionally have such studies included specifically theological perspectives. The field is populated over-whelmingly by historians and social scientists, rather than theologians. Because the rapid growth and high visibility of southern Christianity is simply *there*, it provides its own legitimation for historians and social scientists engaged in the explanation and interpretation of observable phenomena. However, with a few exceptions, they do not see their task as in any way serving the mission of the church. The University of Cambridge is a good example of both the welcome expansion in the study of world Christianity (in marked contrast to Oxford, which remains in deep denial of the very existence of the field) and the continuing regrettable theological lacuna at the heart of the field. The Dixie Professor of Ecclesiastical History, David Maxwell, is a scholar of African Christianity, particularly of Pentecostalism; he is the first holder of that chair to work on non-European Christianity. The Sigrid Rausing Chair of Social Anthropology at Cambridge has been occupied since October 2013 by Joel Robbins, who is best known for his book

*Becoming Sinners*, which is an anthropological treatment of the theme of revival among the Urapmin, a small people group in Papua New Guinea.[7] Even the Faculty of Divinity appointed, in 2013, its first lecturer in world christianities in the person of Dr. Joel Cabrita. Once again, however, she would not describe herself primarily as a theologian, but as a social scientist who studies African Christianity. Between 2011 and 2012 the editorial board of Cambridge University Press's *Journal of Ecclesiastical History* took on three new members in David Maxwell, the sociologist of Yoruba Christianity Professor John D. Y. Peel,[8] and myself in welcome recognition that Christian history embraces more than the history of Christian Europe, but the yawning gulf remains between the preoccupations of *theology* in the Western academy and anything directly related to Christian mission.

Yet, the study of world Christianity is continually throwing up questions that demand theological answers if the church is to engage with these questions in ways that will bear fruit for the church's mission. I wish to identify what seem to me three of the most pressing of these. I shall spend most time on the first, which relates most closely to the other chapters in this volume. The second and the third represent issues that I should like to see placed firmly on the agenda of evangelical theological reflection in the service of the mission of God, and I shall mention them more as a postscript to my remarks.

**How can we forward the mission entrusted to the church by reflecting theologically, on the basis of Scripture, about the relationship between the observable diversity of humanity and the Christian claim that human beings are intended to find their true meaning and deepest satisfaction in being united in and with Christ?**

Initially, I had in mind phrasing this first question simply as, "How can we forward the mission entrusted to the church by reflecting

---

7. Joel Robbins, *Becoming Sinners: Christianity and Moral Torment in a Papua New Guinea Society* (Berkeley: University of California Press, 2004).
8. Sadly, Professor Peel pass away on November 10, 2015.

theologically about the issue of the plurality of human *cultures?*" However, I rapidly came to the conclusion that to frame the question in this way would be to skew the discussion from the outset, for three reasons:

1. It too easily invites us to accept the normativity and fixity of the idea of culture, a concept that attained its present meaning through the impact of the new science of functional anthropology only a century ago. Such a view of culture was at its most plausible when anthropologists were studying isolated "tribal" societies. It is decreasingly plausible in today's highly mobile and interconnected global village.

2. To frame the question in these terms would be tacitly to assume that the issue of cultural plurality can neatly be separated from the wider issue of religious plurality. Kirsteen Kim first drew my attention to the remarkable way in which the Lausanne Covenant of 1974 makes this separation, seeing all *cultures* as manifesting something of the beauty and goodness of God as well as the flaw of sin, but being much more reluctant to concede the same point in relation to *religions.*[9] I am not unsympathetic to that distinction, but the boundaries cannot be drawn quite so neatly. Both the notion of culture and the notion of religion are artificial constructs shaped in the factory of Western post-Enlightenment thought, and the idea that the two terms describe two essentially different things owes a good deal to the idea at the heart of the Enlightenment project—namely, that the socially destructive power of religious antagonism can be neutralized by confining "religion" to a sealed box of its own, located in the private sphere. To take one obvious example, we cannot treat the question of how Christian truth relates to Hindu culture as separable from the question of how Christian truth relates to the "religion" that we call "Hinduism," even if we accept the contested point that there

---

9. "The Lausanne Covenant," http://www.lausanne.org/en/documents/lausanne-covenant.html. Compare paragraph 10, "Evangelism and Culture," with paragraph 3, "The Uniqueness and Universality of Christ."

is a single religious entity that we may term "Hinduism," a term that only becomes commonly employed from the early nineteenth century. Protestants, and especially, evangelical Protestants, have tended to regard theological reflection about the issue of Christian responses to what we have come to term "world religions" as an entirely separate matter from the supposedly more practical missiological issue of how to respond to particular cultural practices. These two fields of reflection need to be brought together. Adherence to particular beliefs that we term "religious" results in certain practices and social attitudes that we tend to label as "cultural." Conversely, certain cultural practices that Christians have traditionally regarded as unacceptable (for example, what used to be called female circumcision, now FGM) are rooted in certain convictions about how things are and always should be, that cannot be separated from beliefs of a cosmological or religious kind.

3. Third, we should note that there has, in fact, been very deep theological reflection on the notion of human culture before. This is clearly no reason for not doing more of the same, but the precedents should give us pause for thought. As Kirsteen Kim has reminded us, such reflection was first done by German Lutheran missiologists in the early twentieth century, though it was soon echoed by Dutch Reformed mission theorists in South Africa. It was, in many ways, a necessary reaction to the unthinking export of European patterns of thought by so many Western missions in the nineteenth century. But we also know that German Protestant missiology premised on ideas of the sacred ethnic ties of *Blut und Boden* proved fertile soil for the germination of abhorrent racial ideology, just as Dutch Reformed evangelical mission theory contributed many of the theoretical principles underpinning apartheid ideology.[10] It was not so much that German mission leaders, to cite Kirsteen's chapter, were content "making use of

---

10. See Richard Elphick, *The Equality of Believers: Protestant Missionaries and the Racial Politics of South Africa* (Charlottesville, VA: University of Virginia Press, 2012).

the Nazi culture theories." Rather, recent scholarship on Germany in the Weimar and Nazi periods has emphasized how widespread and deeply rooted racial ideologies were in popular sentiment, including among Christian thinkers.[11] The Nazis drew their theories of culture from the prevailing intellectual environment of a formally Christian nation. Perhaps the most disturbing conclusion for Christians suggested by the story of the church in Nazi Germany is that neither the widespread profession of Christian belief nor even the acquisition of an ostensibly high level of theological scholarship provided an effective firewall against the virus of ethnic hostility. With reference to Bradley Green's chapter, I would comment that German missiology *was* deeply and self-consciously embedded in the Protestant tradition, or, to be more precise, it was embedded in *one particular* Protestant tradition—that of confessional Lutheranism refracted through the lens of the nationalistic theology of the German *Volk*.

The uncomfortable truth is that adherence to received Protestant tradition does not, in itself, guarantee fidelity to the demands of the biblical gospel, which, as David Kirkpatrick's chapter shows, was also René Padilla's point in his outspoken critiques in the 1970s of the prevailing American evangelical understanding of mission, as expressed in Latin America and elsewhere. For evangelicals, the discomfort becomes more acute when we take note of the parallels between early twentieth-century German *völkisch* mission theories of culture and those later promulgated by missiologists of the Donald McGavran church-growth school. Church-growth theory draws maxims for mission practice from the simple and apparently obvious empirical observation that conversions are more numerous when no cultural frontiers have to be crossed—a maxim that McGavran drew, reasonably enough, from his observation of people movements in India. But at a deeper level of philosophical assumptions, we have

---

11. See, in particular, Susannah Heschel, *The Aryan Jesus: Christian Theologians and the Bible in Nazi Germany* (Princeton: Princeton University Press, 2008).

to recognize its retrospective affinity with the German Romantic *Volkskirche* missiology of the interwar period. The classic work by the German missionary to northern New Guinea and onetime Nazi sympathizer Christian Keysser, *Eine Papuagemeinde* (1929), was republished in English by McGavran in 1980 under the title *A People Reborn*; McGavran's foreword makes clear that he became aware of Keysser's work in about 1958, three years after the publication of his pioneering work of church-growth theory, *The Bridges of God*.[12]

It is, of course, much easier to identify the problems and deficiencies of an essentialist and fixed notion of culture, especially in our culturally fluid globalized contemporary context, than it is to suggest what ought to be put in its place. Early twentieth-century missiologies of culture were a response to a nineteenth-century post-Enlightenment tradition in which partial Western values were confused with essential Christian ones. Nobody wishes to return to that syncretistic confusion. What is needed is a theology of human community that takes both the common grace of divine creation and the universality of sinful despoliation of that created image seriously. Evangelical mission thought has been rather less inclined than Catholic traditions to take seriously the vision of Revelation 21 of the gentile kings of the earth bringing the glory and honor of their respective nations as gifts into the holy city of the new Jerusalem—a text that speaks of the unity of the eschatological community as being made up of a mixture of the distinctive insights and riches of different ethnic and cultural traditions.[13] Yet the theological optimism of this vision of cultural inclusivity has to be balanced by a hard-edged Reformed realism about the depressing capacity of all Christian traditions to absorb elements of the surrounding intellectual environment that are, in principle, deeply subversive of Christian truth. Let me cite a Catholic voice to make

12. Christian Keysser, *A People Reborn* (Pasadena: William Carey Library, 1980), ix; see Timothy Yates, *Christian Mission in the Twentieth Century* (Cambridge: Cambridge University Press, 1994), 54–55; Donald A. McGavran, *The Bridges of God: A Study in the Strategy of Missions* (New York: Friendship Press, 1955).

13. I have investigated use of this text, particularly by Anglo-Catholic theorists in the early twentieth century, in my article, "From 'the Poor Heathen' to 'the Glory and Honour of All Nations': Vocabularies of Race and Custom in Protestant Missions, 1844–1928," *International Bulletin of Missionary Research* 34 (2010): 3–10.

this Protestant point: the late Catholic historian and theologian Adrian Hastings commented in 1993 in the context of the Bosnian genocide, but also with earlier German examples in mind, that "without a very strong sense of the power of sin, of evil in the world, it is impossible to formulate a theology of politics or of history, or to defend the ground out of which effective prophecy can come."[14] We could substitute for "effective prophecy" the phrase "faithful mission." In short, without a very strong sense of the power of sin, of evil in the world, it is impossible to formulate a theology of politics or of history, or to defend the ground out of which faithful mission can come.

**How can we reflect theologically about what the New Testament describes as conversion in ways that connect meaningfully with the wider phenomenon of religious conversion as studied by historians and social scientists?**

My second priority for the theological agenda of evangelical mission thinking would be to urge that we try to grapple with how to bring together an evangelical understanding of conversion to God in Christ with a recognition that turning to God never takes place in a social or cultural vacuum. Scholars of world Christianity spend much of their time analyzing and explaining the social processes of religious conversion to Christianity, or, less commonly, episodes of religious resistance to conversion to Christianity. Their explanations necessarily are couched in terms of social, material, and cultural dynamics. However, many, though not all, of these scholars are also themselves Christians who, in a confessional context, will profess that authentic conversion to *Christ* (not the same thing as conversion to Christianity, though there must be *some* relationship between the two) is never merely a matter of human persuasion and decision. Rather, it is ultimately a pneumatological event, a matter of divine agency through the working of the Spirit. The rules of the academic game dictate that such convictions cannot be brought into the arena of public

---

14. Adrian Hastings, *The Shaping of Prophecy: Passion, Perception and Practicality* (London: Geoffrey Chapman, 1995), 29.

intellectual discourse, but nonetheless Christian scholarship cannot rest content with a total bifurcation of interpretative schema. At the very least, Christian scholars ought to avoid statements which imply that missionaries convert anybody—I get out my red pen whenever students write in these terms, as they often do. Authentic conversion to Christ must be more than just another example of religious proselytism. I explored some of these issues—which are very admittedly difficult ones—in an earlier Tyndale Fellowship paper published in the *International Review of Mission* in 2003, and subsequently republished in Chris Partridge's edited collection, *Finding and Losing Faith: Studies in Conversion*.[15] I am still waiting for someone to take up the challenge of exploring these issues further.

**What contribution can biblical theology make by its reflection on the nature of divine blessing or salvation to the controversial issues raised by contemporary neo-Pentecostal understandings of divine blessing as a tangible, present, and even material phenomenon?**

My third priority for the theological agenda of evangelical mission thinking arises from the near-universal phenomenon of the explosion of neo-Pentecostal forms of Christianity. This trend is often interpreted by sympathetic observers as a form of restoration of evangelical holism to a truncated gospel that restricted salvation to the soul and the life to come, and that interpretation has much to commend it. Just as Padilla urged that the quest for justice should be seen as integral to the gospel, and not simply a logical deduction from it, so Pentecostals have reminded us that wholeness for the whole person, including the physical body, is integral to God's saving purpose, and not ancillary to it.

But there is an undeniable tendency in sections of neo-Pentecostalism, especially in Africa, so to emphasize the this-worldly

15. Brian Stanley, "Conversion to Christianity: The Colonization of the Mind?," *International Review of Mission* 92 (2003): 315–31, reprinted in Chris Partridge and Helen Reid, eds., *Finding and Losing Faith: Studies in Conversion* (Milton Keynes, UK: Paternoster, 2006), 150–74.

dimension of salvation that the old charge, famously articulated in 1971 by the Kenyan theologian John Mbiti in his *New Testament Eschatology in an African Background*, that missionary Protestantism taught African people an escapist and callous "pie in the sky when you die" message, is now being turned on its head.[16] Paul Gifford, one of the most influential current historians of neo-Pentecostalism in Africa, has, in fact, accused the movement of forgetting the pie in the sky altogether by collapsing the Christian concept of salvation entirely into the pursuit of material blessing here and now. African Christianity, warns Gifford,[17] is in danger of losing the future dimension of Christian eschatology completely, and hence of severing the direct correlation identified by Miroslav Volf, of which Andrew Marin's chapter reminds us, between eschatological hope and a reshaped temporal identity. According to many African Pentecostals, divine blessing is bestowed in response to faithfulness in Christian living, prayer, and above all in stewardship. Theologically, that emphasis can be defended as no more than an application of a biblical principle that is, for example, found in the Deuteronomistic tradition. However, in the Old Testament, the principle is primarily about the corporate well-being of the people of God, not about the self-promotion or accumulation of wealth of individuals. In the Hebrew Bible, the principle also insists on the priority of divine grace: it only operates within the context of the prior initiative of Yahweh in graciously calling and redeeming his people—a purpose that has the blessing of *all* nations as its ultimate goal. Where the prosperity gospel combines Western individualism with a belief that God gives to us *only* because we have first given to him, the result is the seductive teaching that the way for an individual to get rich is to maximize his or her giving to the church, which has obvious benefits for the pastor's income. The need for African Christians—and equally,

16. John S. Mbiti, *New Testament Eschatology in an African Background: A Study of the Encounter between New Testament Theology and African Traditional Concepts* (London: Oxford University Press, 1971), 57, 74, 80.
17. Paul Gifford, "African Christianity and the Eclipse of the Afterlife," in *The Church, the Afterlife and the Fate of the Soul: Papers Read at the 2007 Summer Meeting and the 2008 Winter Meeting of the Ecclesiastical History Society*, ed. Peter D. Clarke and Tony Claydon, Studies in Church History 45 (Woodbridge, UK: The Boydell Press for the Ecclesiastical History Society, 2009), 413–29.

Asian, Latin American, indeed *all* Christians—to articulate theologies of divine blessing that are *genuinely* holistic, authentically biblical, and transparently indigenous can hardly be overemphasized.

# 9

## Seeing and Believing

### Pete Ward

Belief is illusive. It might be mistaken or even misplaced. In fact, it is hard to know when it is present and when it is not. Belief is illusive because it is only really present when it is God breathed as a work of the Holy Spirit. Likewise, the church is the church because of the presence of Jesus Christ. So the clue to seeing the church lies in Jesus Christ, the way the truth and life (John 14:6). The church "is" because of Jesus Christ. "Wherever Jesus Christ is," says Ignatius, "there is the universal church."[1] It is the presence of Christ that constitutes the church. This presence, however, is mediated by the actions of the community. The church, in a sense, is present at its own making. It is in this making that through the work of the Holy Spirit, Christ's presence

---

1. Ignatius, *Epistle to the Smyrnaeans* 8, in the *Ante-Nicene Fathers*, ed. Alexander Roberts and James Donaldson, rev. A. Cleveland Coxe (Buffalo, NY: Christian Literature Company, 1885), 1:90, as quoted in Miroslav Volf, *After Our Likeness: The Church as the Image of the Trinity* (Grand Rapids: Eerdmans, 1998), 129.

is real. Hence, Irenaeus can speak in a very similar way of the Spirit constituting the being of the church. "For where the Church is there is the Spirit of God; and where the Spirit of God is there is the Church; and every kind of grace; but the Spirit is truth." The Spirit works to vivify and to keep the church youthful. Faith has been received and preserved in the church and "by the Spirit of God, renewing its youth, as if it were some precious deposit in an excellent vessel, causes the vessel itself containing it to renew its youth also."[2] Ignatius and Irenaeus demonstrate that from the earliest times it has been fundamental to the theology of the church that the social and the historical are seen as having their being (what they are) in the being of God. This being, however, is moving, made ever youthful by the work of the Holy Spirit. "Being," therefore, is not static, but fluid in nature.

Inspiration (the breath of God) is always carried in the cultural practice of fallible human communities. This means that it is never possible to filter out the work of God from the actions of individual believers because the two are interdependent and contingent on each other. The Spirit works in and with communities and their expression to make Jesus Christ present. The reference to communities here is not abstract. The presence of Christ makes the church the church in the particular and in the local. This means the everyday neighborhood congregation. There are implications for a theology of the church here and for the methods of inquiry and analysis that are most appropriate for ecclesiology. For while it is relatively easy to make distinctions between different concepts of believing at the level of the ideal, these judgments become much more problematic in relation to the actual practices of communities and the ways that individuals believe. As a result, some means of taking account of (or seeing) the lived complexity of communities is precisely what is required because the church does not inhabit the ideal of the academic text; it exists in the cultural and historical, and in this context, it seeks to fulfill its calling. So there will always be moments where it will be necessary to take stock and come to judgment, but discernment is far from

---

2. Irenaeus of Lyons, *Adversus haereses* 3.24, in *The Ante-Nicene Fathers*, 1:458.

straightforward because of the mixture of divine life and cultural expression that is part of the "being" of the church. Hence, to talk in solely theological ways, or in solely cultural and historical terms, runs the risk of not really seeing the church. The task of seeing requires that these elements are, in some way, combined.

## The True Church

Ecclesiology is keen to acknowledge the historical reality of the church, but it often does not know quite what to do with it. Part of the reason for this is that the church has always been subject to imperfections and divisions. Theological accounts of the church have been deeply aware of the faults in the historical church and yet also concerned to find ways to preserve the church as place of divine encounter and grace. This has led to somewhat idealized ecclesiologies. For example, when faced with the problems that arose from the Donatist schism, Augustine sought to make a distinction between the imperfect and divided community of the church and those whom God had truly called to himself. This church within a church was the precious and beloved whom he called the "dove" of God. There are some who even though they are baptized, says Augustine, still continue to live contrary to the commandments. These ones cannot be seen as part of the church that Christ purifies and presents "without spot or wrinkle." The churches of Christ are the ones of whom it is said, "'My dove is but one; she is the only one of her mother'; for she herself is without spot or wrinkle."[3] The notion of "the dove" solves the problem of the imperfection of the church by imagining a church within a church. This "true" church exists alongside and within the historical and social with all of its divisions and schisms, but this solution leaves a question mark around the exact status of this church. The "real" church, therefore, remains something of a mystery that is inaccessible and somewhat inexpressible. In other words, largely discounting or discrediting the

3. Augustine of Hippo, *On Baptism, against the Donatists*, 4.3.5, in *St. Augustin: The Writings against the Manichaeans and against the Donatists*, ed. Philip Schaff, trans. J. R. King, vol. 4 of *A Select Library of the Nicene and Post-Nicene Fathers of the Christian Church, First Series* (Buffalo, NY: Christian Literature Company, 1887), 448. Quote from Song of Sol. 6:9.

historical and cultural, or at least, seeing them as marginal to the being of the church has solved the problem of ecclesiology. Augustine's understanding of the church as somehow hidden within the social expression is also seen in the Reformation notions of ecclesial visibility and invisibility.

## Luther's Marks of the Church

In the *Schmalkald Articles*, Martin Luther says that the church is obvious that even a child can see it: "For thank God today a child of seven years knows what the Church is namely the holy believers and lambs who hear the voice of their shepherd."[4] Hearing the voice of the shepherd is not exactly straightforward, for while there is an assumed social form here, preaching in the context of the gathered congregation, actual hearing, or "faith" as Luther would put it, is hard to discern. So, for Luther, the preaching of the Word and the celebration of the sacraments are external signs of the church, pointing to the invisible faith of believers.[5]

The church, through human agency, takes a form in history. It acts and constructs "signs." These signs point to a deeper process that is taking place between the believer and Christ. This is a call and response. Luther, therefore, draws a distinction between the church visible and the church invisible. The visible church consists of the material and the social, while the invisible points to the inward response of the faithful.[6] Central to this idea is the sense that the outward aspects of the church carries but also conceals the presence of Christ. Action, agency, and materiality, therefore, are fundamental, but they are not everything that "is." As Luther puts it, "The Church must appear in the world. But it can only appear in a covering, a veil, a shell or some kind of clothes, which a man can grasp. Otherwise it can never be found."[7]

---

4. Martin Luther, *Schmalkald Articles*, part 3, article 12, 1537.
5. Martin Luther, *On the Councils of the Church*, 1539.
6. Ibid.
7. Martin Luther, *Letters* 9.608, 1542.

## The Concrete Church

Luther's understanding of the church draws attention to the central dilemma in ecclesiology. The church is constituted by the presence of Christ and the work of the Spirit, but it is "clothed" in forms. These forms are both the means of making the church visible and also a means of "veiling" the true nature of the church. Believing in the church itself is self-evident—a child can see it—but the true nature of the church is also hidden from sight. Seeing the church, therefore, is far from straightforward. This dynamic between the necessity of acknowledging the historical and the contingent, and the sense that this "reality" both reveals and veils the work of God, runs throughout theological discussions of the church. Karl Barth uses the phrase, later picked up by Nicholas Healy, "the concrete Church," to speak about the historical and social reality of the Christian community.[8] Yet, despite this affirmation of the "concrete," Barth seeks to find ways to locate theological authenticity in ways that subtly create a distance between the historical and social reality of the church and its Lord. The church is a community of believers present in history, says Barth, but it is only the church because of God. "The Church is, of course, a human earthly-historical construct, whose history involves from the very first and always will involve human action. But it is this human construct, the Christian Church, because and as God is at work in it by his Spirit."[9] There is a human "action" that builds the church, but what makes this "truly" the church is the work of God. In commenting on the Apostles' Creed, Barth rejects notions of the invisibility of the church. The church is visible, we believe in its existence. This means that each congregation is a congregation of Christ. "Take good note, that a parson who does not believe that in this congregation of his, including those men and women, old wives and children, Christ's congregation exists, does not believe at all in the existence of the Church. *Credo*

8. Nicholas Healy, *Church, World and the Christian Life: Practical-Prophetic Ecclesiology* (Cambridge: Cambridge University Press, 2000).
9. Karl Barth, Church *Dogmatics*, vol. IV, *The Doctrine of Reconciliation*, pt. 2, ed. Geoffrey W. Bromiley and T. F. Torrance (Edinburgh: T&T Clark, 1958), 616 (hereafter *CD*).

*ecclesiam* means that I believe that here at this place, in this visible assembly, the work of the Holy Spirit takes place."[10] In the "concrete" and particular congregation, the Holy Spirit, says Barth, becomes "event." Yet there is always a struggle between the empirical church and the "true" church. The "true" church is, for Barth, an event or a happening that comes through the "act of God." It emerges as a quickening of the Spirit as human work to build up the community into the true church.[11] Barth affirms the necessity of the social agency of the church, but by speaking of the true church as an event, he is concerned to emphasize the freedom of God as revelation. So, despite his affirmation of the fundamental necessity of the social and the historical, Barth effectively seeks to limit the "true" church to a moment, and hence he appears to simultaneously both affirm and downplay the significance of the social and the historical.

Barth's ecclesiology in effect brackets out the everyday in favor of a theological moment. The implication is clear: the historical and the lived are of the essence of the church, but they are also problematic. Barth's ecclesiology, therefore, develops an ideal or hermetically sealed event where church takes place. This is distinct from Augustine's dove, the church within the church, and Luther's visible and invisible church, but essentially sets out to achieve the same thing—how to account for the imperfections of communities and the divine within the human. In contrast to this, a number of contemporary theologians have sought to rediscover the theological significance of the everyday and the lived. Nicholas Healy criticizes idealized theologies of the church as "blueprint ecclesiologies." A theological blueprint is an attempt to reason abstractly about the "perfect" shape of ecclesial life. The pursuit of a shape for the church that is constructed as an ideal, Healy says, carries significant problems because it fails to account for the "concrete" church. "Blueprint ecclesiologies," he argues, "foster a disjunction . . . between . . . ideal ecclesiology and the realities of the concrete church."[12] So, in failing

---

10. Karl Barth, *Dogmatics in Outline* (London: SCM, 1949), 143.
11. Karl Barth, *CD* IV/2, 617.
12. Healy, *Church, World and the Christian Life.* 37.

to deal with the "lived" nature of the church, blueprint ecclesiology tends to overlook the theological importance of the struggles that are involved in being Christian disciples and the frustrations of dealing with a church that is not at all "perfect" in many respects.[13] This is an interesting point because Healy hints that theological learning and discernment require the ability to take account of the tensions and problems in communities. If the church is to move forward, then attention needs to be focused on the lived and the empirical as well as the theological or as the place where the drama of the theological is played out in history.

Harald Hegstad takes this argument further. In the creed, he says, we affirm that we "believe in the Church." Notions of visibility and invisibility are problematic to this believing. There are not two churches, but one. "My thesis," he says, "is that there is only one church, namely the church as visible and one that can be experienced in the world."[14] The imperfections in the church, however, need to be seen in a wider theological context. Believing in the church requires that this real community is viewed eschatologically. In other words, understanding the historical church depends on viewing it not simply in terms of empirical study of the present but also in relation to its future. The church we experience is a "sign and an anticipation" of the fellowship between God and humanity that is to come in the kingdom of God.[15] This theological perspective should not be taken as an excuse to construct ideal theological models; rather, it should encourage a particular theological focus on the visible. The theological vision of the church perfected becomes a corrective or a relativizing impulse in the present, but this is only possible if time and attention are paid to actual churches. Hegstad argues strongly that this kind of attention requires the theologian to take account of empirical methods to do ecclesiology correctly. His suggestion is helpful in that it indicates that the historical should be valued as the "being" of the church, but it is always in the making. Although he does not use the term, this

13. Ibid.
14. Harald Hegstad, *The Real Church: An Ecclesiology of the Visible* (OR: Wipf & Stock 2013), 2.
15. Ibid.

introduces a more fluid notion of ecclesiology. The problems that Augustine, Luther, and Barth find with the historical are that they are concerned with being, but this being is perhaps seen as essential, and hence static in nature. If, however, being is movement and flow, then change is part of what makes the church truly the church. So fluidity allows for correction and also deviation as part of an ecclesial movement over time and in culture. This notion gathers significance when cultural forms are themselves seen as generating meaning and identity that are themselves moving and liquid. It is in the liquid church that Jesus Christ the living water is to be found.

## Seeing as Wisdom

Seeing the church in the lived is a theological discipline of attention and contemplation. This situates empirical work in a theological epistemology. Such an approach is necessary because, as has been said, the church "is" the church because of the presence of Jesus Christ through the power of the Holy Spirit. It is also because "seeing" in this empirical/theological context should be regarded as an act of reaching out toward God through the use of human observation and reason. Seeing is sharing in a divine vision. Seeing the church, therefore, requires a spiritual methodology. Such a methodology also needs to be God breathed because it is an act of seeing Jesus Christ in the social and the historical.

Paul Fiddes defines seeing as Wisdom. Wisdom, he argues, does not locate the one seeing as above or beyond what is seen, but embraces embodied forms of knowing. These forms of knowing do not repeat the problems associated with the distance between the object and the subject and the consequent issues of power and claims to "comprehend" that characterize Enlightenment forms of knowing. So Wisdom is a discipline of reflection and a kind of knowing, but also transcends both of these. Through reason and knowledge, *seeing* the world "can be a means of knowing others in a truly relational way, and finally knowing God."[16] In the biblical tradition, Wisdom is personified in female form. Thus to see is to respond to the call of Lady Wisdom.

"Does not wisdom call, and does not understanding raise her voice? On the heights, beside the way, at the crossroads she takes her stand; beside the gates in front of the town, at the entrance of the portals she cries out" (Prov 8:1–3). The figure of Lady Wisdom represents the dancing and traveling of divine self-giving (Prov 8:22–31). This understanding of Lady Wisdom transforms the act of seeing (knowing and rationalizing) from the distanced gaze of the detached but powerful modern observer that has been problematized in more recent thought into an additional relational movement within the life of God. The call of Wisdom, says Fiddes, is to see the world and thereby know God.[17] Yet for Wisdom, there is a paradox that combines transcendence and immanence. As the Wisdom of Solomon says, "For wisdom is a kindly spirit, but will not free blasphemers from the guilt of their words; because God is witness of their inmost feelings, and a true observer of their hearts, and a hearer of their tongues. Because the spirit of the Lord has filled the world, and that which holds all things together knows what is said" (Wis 1:6–7). Here, says Fiddes, Wisdom is identified as the Spirit of Yahweh, and this identification contains both the notion of observer and wisdom as the means of coherence in the world. These two are held in paradox. Wisdom is therefore both a "faculty of mind and the field of investigation that lies outside in the world."[18] "Wisdom as the faculty of God is also there in the world, drawing near to her devotees on the path of daily life; she offers them communion with her, inviting them to walk with her on her own circuit through the cosmos. This is observation that it is also sympathetic participation."[19] Such Wisdom, however, cannot be pinned down. It is not to be found in a particular location. Wisdom is, rather, a riddle that points to a journey. Wisdom is not hidden away in a place where, if we knew the secret, she might be found. "Wisdom," says Fiddes, "transcends or 'goes beyond' the grasp of the

---

16. Paul Fiddes, *Seeing the World and Knowing God: Hebrew Wisdom and Christian Doctrine in a Late-Modern Context* (Oxford: Oxford University Press, 2013).
17. Ibid., 188.
18. Ibid., 199.
19. Ibid.

human mind" because God alone grasps the complexity of inexhaustible Wisdom.[20] So the personification of Wisdom is an invitation to participation in a kind of investigation and knowing that is shared with God. Seeing, even seeing in God, is not entirely straightforward. The Wisdom tradition speaks of the immensity of creation and the unknowability of the created world, which in turn invokes the "elusive" quality that exists alongside the possibility of exploration. Wisdom is there to be enjoyed, but she can never be possessed.[21] What Fiddes terms the "no place" of Wisdom represents a check on the assertion that to be "wise" is to have control over the world as "it affirms a hiddenness at the heart of reality."[22]

The figure of Lady Wisdom, the personification in the tradition, is picked up in John's Gospel in the person of Jesus Christ. In the prologue of John's Gospel, Jesus is introduced as the *logos*. "In the beginning was the word and the word was with God and the word was God" (John 1:1). The *logos* terminology in John's Gospel, Fiddes points out, echoes the personification of Wisdom. The implication is that Wisdom is made manifest in the person of Jesus Christ. The divine "wisdom" or *logos* is incarnate in Christ, and this is the "glory" that is seen by believers. "And the Word became flesh and lived among us, and we have seen his glory, the glory as of a Father's only Son, full of grace and truth" (John 1:14). The revealing of Wisdom in Jesus Christ, the *logos,* does not, however, lead to an escape from complexity and ambiguity. The plethora of names for Christ in the New Testament, even in this opening passage of John's Gospel (light, life, son, lamb, word), is an indication that in Jesus Christ there is the "fullness" of God. This personification (or incarnation) is the revelation of complexity. It is precisely for this reason that the Christ of the Gospels is elusive even as he is revealed.[23]

For Fiddes, "seeing" is not confined to the church. Seeing encompasses the ways of God in the world. Discerning Jesus Christ

20. Ibid., 239.
21. Ibid.
22. Ibid., 250.
23. Ibid., 345.

and the work of the Spirit, therefore, becomes a more fluid notion where the presence of Christ passes between the church and the wider culture. This fluidity challenges a solid notion of the church as containing the work of God and defining by its actions all that God might be and do. The presence of Christ in the church is, rather, a clue to the further discernment of the work of the Spirit beyond the solid meetings and worship activities of the community. This fluid nature of the work of the Spirit is a call to reach beyond the church that is, to some extent, embodied in the concern to express faith and connect, but it is also a continual challenge to the church to be drawn into and participate in the work of the Spirit beyond the solid boundaries of the church. Such fluidity is a parallel to the cultural adoption and adaption that mark the life of the contemporary Christian community. The contextualizing of worship and ways of experiencing faith through the use of the forms and ways of communicating of popular culture is a further clue that the Spirit, the world, and the church have porous boundaries. This is what I call Liquid Church.[24]

## The Trinity as Relations

God is seen by Fiddes as a complexity that matches the complexity of the world. The trinitarian God for Fiddes subsists as persons in relation. The Trinity, he argues, is "not a mathematical puzzle. It is all about a God who lives in relationship and is in movement."[25] The persons of the Trinity are not to be seen as formed by relations, but as actually being relations. "The Trinity, then is a vision of God as three interweaving relationships of ecstatic, outward-going love, giving and receiving."[26] The persons in relation move within and between each other in movements suggestive of a dance. This movement is expressed in the term *perichoresis,* where the persons in the Trinity "co-inhere" with each other without "confusion."[27] This is a development of the words of Jesus in the Fourth Gospel: "Believe me that I am in the Father

24. Pete Ward, *Liquid Church* (Peabody, MA: Hendrickson, 2002).
25. Fiddes, *Seeing the World*, 256–57.
26. Ibid., 150.
27. Ibid., 151.

and the Father is in me" (John 14:11). So, for Fiddes, "The hypostases are 'distinct' realities as relations and the *perichoresis* is an interweaving of relations."[28] This language about God is not generated out of the position of the distanced "observer" because to see in these terms is to share in the relations of God. God "makes" sense as we are "involved" in God's life. "Talk of God as Trinity is not the language of spectator, but the language of a participant."[29] To see God in this sense is to be taken up in movements of being glorified, being sent, and being breath. As Fiddes puts it, "Talk about God begins from encounter with God."[30] It is this God that opens a space in the interweaving and dancing movement for relations with human beings. "In creation and in redemption God opens a space within the interweaving movements of relation, so that the created universe exists 'in God,'"[31] and to speak of God in this way is not to "describe God" or to claim to see God. The language of relations "describes what it is like to engage in God."[32] Relation with God is like the intermingling flow of water. The Trinity is the fount, the spring, and the stream, "three currents or movements of 'delight,' which intermingle and can nevertheless be distinguished from each other."[33] The Trinity, seen as relations, opens the space for understanding the world as being within the movement of God. So, to see is to share in the divine movement, to see "in God." This form of knowing is particularly appropriate for ecclesiology, where cultural forms and theological expression are seen as being that is in movement. The liquidity of the church is, therefore, to be seen as arising from the being of God, but just as God is being in relation and movement, so is the church. Yet, in so saying, it is always acknowledged that the ability to "see" this movement and hence to discern the church arises from relation. Seeing is participatory, rather than being structured by modern notions of subject and object. There is then an appropriateness to this approach to epistemology as the

28. Ibid., 151.
29. Ibid., 152.
30. Ibid., 153.
31. Ibid.
32. Ibid., 257.
33. Ibid. 259.

basis for an ecclesiology that takes account of the lived in coming to discernment and also construction.

## Discerning the Body

The investigation of believing in the contemporary church requires the "wisdom" of God. But seeing is complex and discernment is not straightforward. The "reality" of believing is to be found in the work of the Spirit and in the presence of Jesus Christ. To see the church, therefore, is to see God. At the same time, this "seeing" requires the ability to discern Christ within the particularity of lived expression. Seeing, therefore, is problematic, and it equates to the Wisdom that Fiddes describes. To see, however, is not simply an academic exercise. Seeing and the attempt to develop discernment are responsibilities for every believer in the church. Christians are called, says Claire Watkins, to continually be attentive to the presence of Christ in the practices of the church. She calls this "discerning the body."[34] Her starting point for understanding what it means to discern the body is found in the eucharistic passage in 1 Cor 11:27–29: "Whoever, therefore, eats the bread or drinks the cup of the Lord in an unworthy manner will be answerable for the body and blood of the Lord. Examine yourselves, and only then eat of the bread and drink of the cup. For all who eat and drink without discerning the body, eat and drink judgment against themselves."

This passage has traditionally been interpreted in Catholic circles as concerning eucharistic reception, says Watkins, but the passage might also be seen in the light of the wider argument of the letter as a commentary on the life of the church. In particular, 1 Corinthians 10 and 11, she points out, are an extended discussion of the ethical behavior of the church, and particularly, the way that worship is conditioned by communal life. Verses 27–29 come, therefore, at the conclusion of some of these arguments. Discerning the body as a result becomes an admonition about what it means to be the church—the

34. Claire Watkins lecture at King's College, London, 2014.

body of Christ—and how, by not discerning the body, individuals may effectively put themselves outside the community by taking part in meals in inappropriate ways. The appeal to the words of the Lord and the discerning of the body, says Watkins, thus takes on a particular meaning. Believers are called to pay attention to the practice of the church and to be aware of their own participation in the practices because to share is to partake in the "body." There is, then, says Watkins, for all members of the church, a constant task of discerning the body of Christ, not simply in the sacraments but also in those practices and ways of living together that form communal life. Discerning the body means paying attention to Christ in and through the practices of the church, seeking out and being conditioned by the presence of Christ in the community. Discernment, however, is also a task that involves an ability to be self-critical and reflexive about the life of the church. Seeing in this sense involves a call to share in the life of the church while being attentive to the possibility that practices and communal expression may be less than the "body." This kind of discernment is a call to take responsibility for the imperfections of expression and the social forms that constitute the church. Such attentiveness does not mean separating oneself from the church to be "objective," or indeed, adopting the role of the "critic," but accepting that participation in the church always involves the contingency of cultural expression, and as such, discernment remains necessary even as Christ might be made present, be it in the sacrament or in preaching, or indeed, through singing contemporary worship songs.

The significance of Watkins's approach to discernment is that all Christians are called to be continually attentive to the life of the church. Discerning the body is an ongoing responsibility, a call to faithfulness. It is in this context that the work of the theologian should be understood. Theologians, says Watkins, are seeking to discern the body of Christ when they start to take seriously what is taking place on the ground. Such attention is a demand on theologians, but this kind of discernment is itself complex because there are different layers of meaning within communities. She calls these "Christ's various and layered presences in the practices of communities."[35] Discernment is, therefore, a human activity that is spiritual, pastoral, and intellectual. Discerning the body needs each of these areas if it is to be possible to encounter what she calls the mysteries of Christ's presences in practices. Discernment, therefore, requires an empirical engagement with ecclesial communities and the ways in which they express faith in cultural forms. So, for Watkins, the Spirit is out there, doing the work of God, and the task of the theologian is to catch up with what God is doing. An ecclesial practice is a response to the work of God in the world. The theologian articulates what is taking place. The role of the theologian is to articulate in relation to the empirical how God might be at work. This approach rests ultimately for Watkins on a particular understanding of the work of God in the world drawn from Catholic theology. Vatican II, she points out, argues that Scripture makes "progress" in the church with the movement of the Spirit. This includes all of the work and teaching of bishops and priests, but it is also concerned with the believing of individuals. As rendered in the Second Vatican Council's 1965 statement *Dei Verbum*:

> This tradition which comes from the Apostles, develops in the Church with the help of the Holy Spirit. For there is a growth in the understanding of the realities and the words which have been handed down. This happens through the contemplation and study made by believers, who treasure these things in their hearts (see Luke 2:19, 51) through a penetrating understanding of the spiritual realities which they experience, and through the preaching of those who have received through Episcopal succession the sure gift of truth. . . . The words of the holy fathers witness to the presence of this living tradition, whose wealth is poured into the practice and life of the believing and praying Church. Through the same tradition the Church's full canon of the sacred books is known, and the sacred writings themselves are more profoundly understood and unceasingly made active in her; and thus God, who spoke of old, uninterruptedly converses with the bride of His beloved Son.[36]

Here, from the view of the Catholic Church, revelation is seen as

---

35. Ibid.
36. Second Vatican Council, *Dei Verbum* 8, http://www.vatican.va/archive/hist_councils/ ii_vatican_council/documents/vat-ii_const_19651118_dei-verbum_en.html (accessed December 26, 2015).

developing both through official teaching and through the ways in which individual believers take up the words of Scripture and inhabit them as part of who they are. Seeing the church involves paying attention in order to "see" the work of Christ in communities and in practices. This process of discernment is likened to the revelation that comes upon the apostle Peter in the book of Acts when he sees the Holy Spirit descend upon the gentile Cornelius and the members of his household. Peter expresses his own transformation to Cornelius with these words. "I truly understand that God shows no partiality but in every nation anyone who fears him and does what is right is acceptable to him."[37] But even though he says these words of acceptance and welcome, it is only when he witnesses the Holy Spirit descending on these gentiles that he "discerns" Christ at work. Astonishment then quickly turns to acceptance, and these new believers are welcomed into the community through baptism.[38] Discernment, in this context, is complex. Peter is a participant in the events that are unfolding, but his understanding seems to grow as he "sees" the work of the Spirit.

This kind of participative discernment, Watkins argues, is the responsibility of every member of the church. The call is to seek to discern where and how God is at work. And in order that the work of God might be discerned, it becomes essential to engage with practice. In order to know what God is doing in the world, it is imperative to engage in attentiveness. This means that there is a requirement that theologians who study the church seek to develop the skills and ways of paying attention that are found in empirical work. It is important to stress that such attention is not a reduction of the theological to the social and cultural, but precisely the opposite. The point Watkins is making here is that these theological insights generate an approach to seeing and discernment that means that empirical methods are not simply an option; they are necessary. Seeing, in these terms, is participation in the complex and layered nature of the church.

37. Acts 10:34–35.
38. Acts 10:44–48.

## Introducing the Four Theological Voices

The contemporary church is a complex—a contradictory mix of theology and experience, individual spirituality, and corporate expression. Making sense of this rich and varied mix requires the ability to pay attention to a range of different ways of sharing faith. It is these different "ways" that take us deeper into the state of believing. In *Talking about God in Practice*,[39] the authors introduce what they call the different theological "voices" that become evident through a careful examination of the practice of the church. These voices are mixed together in the everyday speech and action of communities, and as such, they form a rich and living "whole." In seeking to understand how theology is intertwined in action, they have developed an interpretative typology that helps them to identify the different strands of theological communication in the life of the church. The authors are clear, however, that their typology is at risk of oversimplifying the organic and interconnected nature of the lived situation. They see the voices typology is a "working tool." The tool is developed around the notion that in the lived practice of the church, there are four theological voices: operant theology, espoused theology, normative theology, and formal theology.[40]

## Operant Theology

Cameron and company argue that the fundamental starting point needs to be the realization that the practice of the church is "theological." As Clare Watkins puts it, "practices are bearers of theology."[41] This means that "theology" is somehow embodied in the practice of the church. Embodied theology is not generally something that is easily explained or described, they argue; rather, it needs to be uncovered and discovered by believers themselves. This is because

---

39. Helen Cameron et al., *Talking about God in Practice: Theological Action Research and Practical Theology* (London: SCM, 2010).
40. Ibid., 49–56.
41. Clare Watkins et al., "Practical Ecclesiology: What Counts as Theology in Studying the Church?," in *Perspectives on Ecclesiology and Ethnography*, ed. Pete Ward (Grand Rapids: Eerdmans, 2012), 167–81.

"operant theologies" are often slightly hidden from view, or taken as "just the thing that we do." It is only when they are subjected to attention and reflection that these everyday ways of believing reveal their theological nature. This observation echoes the work of John Swinton and Harriet Mowat, who suggest that the theology that lies embedded in practice can be illusive and hard to find. "Practices," they argue, "contain values, beliefs, theologies and other assumptions which, for the most part, go unnoticed until they are complexified and brought to our notice through theological reflection."[42] "Complexifying" might suggest creating an elaborate theory around practices. This is not exactly what is meant here. Swinton and Mowat are talking about the way that focused attention on action and belief in the life of the church can reveal the layers of interaction and entwined meanings. This, in a sense, is exactly what T. M. Luhrmann's work does so successfully. By spending time in getting underneath the skin of the everyday, she reveals its depth, and also its many contradictions. The four-voices method of analysis has come about because the researchers have found in their work with churches a particular tendency for there to be differences between the theology that is evident in practice and the theology that people articulate. The first is operant theology, and the second is what the group call espoused theology.

## Espoused Theology

"Complexifying" is one of the most common issues that qualitative empirical research brings to the surface. Very often, when churches are studied, belief and believing appears to operate in a way that enables and occasionally supports subtle and at times confusing differences that coexist between what is stated and the underlying operant theology that works out in practice. Watkins gives the example of a Catholic diocesan agency for evangelization, where the espoused theological position may emphasize the responsibility of the church for the wider society, and yet the practice might actually be much more

---

42. John Swinton and Harriet Mowat, *Practical Theology and Qualitative Research* (London: SCM, 2006), 2.

orientated toward catechesis and adult education within the church. So the operant theology that lies behind these work patterns and strategies does not quite ring true with the theological position that the workers espouse or speak about as their theology.[43] This example serves to show how espoused theology is always connected to the other voices. It exists alongside operant theologies, but it is also drawn from formal and normative voices.

Espoused theology has its roots in the wider tradition and expression of the church. As Cameron and company put it, "Espoused theologies come from somewhere." Churches and believers develop their espoused theological understandings in relation to the ongoing teaching and theological understanding of their churches. So the theology that people speak about in relation to their practice is drawn from Scripture or liturgy or other theological and spiritual writings as well as experience.[44] The normative theological voice is introduced to show how these varied sources are often utilized as a guide and a corrective alongside practice both by communities and by believers; here again, it is possible to observe quite interesting and "complexified" relationships between the normative voice in a community and the espoused theology of individual believers.

## Normative Theology

In his study of an evangelical church in the North of England, the sociologist Mathew Guest traces the way that members of the congregation negotiate the official teaching of the church in different ways. From his extensive observation and interviews made over a period of seven years, Guest was able to identify the different theological positions that coexisted in the church.[45] Perhaps surprisingly, given its reputation as a leading Anglican evangelical church, Guest found that a great many people in the congregation appeared to hold quite liberal views. This liberalism extended to what

43. Watkins et al., "Practical Ecclesiology," 177.
44. Cameron et al., *Talking about God in Practice*, 53.
45. For methods, see Mathew Guest, *Evangelical Identity and Contemporary Culture: A Congregational Study in Innovation* (Aldershot: Ashgate, 2007), 231.

he identifies as key issues for this section of the church: namely, the kind of "truth" and authority that is to be found in Scripture, and the place of women in the ministry of the church. He also saw evidence that some were in the process of redrawing the boundaries of an evangelical worldview. Guest found that there was a move toward tolerance, universalism, and a general openness to spiritual exploration. This more open and experimental mind-set brought with it a sense that it was possible, and even desirable, to engage in rethinking the Christian tradition. The result was that congregation appeared to support more individualistic forms of believing.

The shift toward more open and exploratory forms of evangelicalism, however, was not universally welcomed in the congregation. Alongside the "liberals," Guest uncovered a number of conservatives who advocated a more traditional approach to evangelical theology. Interestingly, some of the leaders in the church welcomed the way that people with different perspectives were all able to be part of the congregation. Diversity, in this sense, became a value that they sought for the church. Yet this shift toward a more open theology that overtly welcomes diversity is kept in check by the conservative members of the congregation and the sense that a move toward more liberal theology would result in censure from the wider evangelical world. As a result, the more open theological approach of some of the leaders and some in the congregation does not find itself reflected in the official theological statements of the church. What appears to take place is a complex set of checks and balances between the public voice of the church and the more veiled private beliefs and convictions.[46] In the terms of Cameron and others, these correspond to the formal voice and the espoused voice, respectively. Guest traces this accommodation through a study of the sermons at the church.

From his study of just under fifty sermons, Guest concluded that the preaching served to minimize conflict between the conservatives and the liberals in the church.[47] They did this by charting a middle

46. Ibid., 95–97.
47. Ibid., 98–102.

path between the two groups, at times supporting one, and then the other. So the public discourse of the church, Guest argues, "appeared to function as a unifying force by keeping these two 'narratives' in tension. It did this by avoiding the open endorsement of extreme positions and evading issues likely to provoke disagreement."[48] Guest found that within the congregation, there were quite different perceptions of what it meant to be evangelical. The size of the congregation enabled different microclimates of theological understanding to coexist. In this context, the formal theology of the church as seen in the public preaching on the face of it offered a point of unity, but this is not really the whole story.

What Guest found was that individuals in the congregation heard and understood different things in what was being said by the leaders from the front of the church. "Conversations with individual parishioners revealed a vast diversity of responses to sermons, from boredom to incredulity, enthusiasm, emotion, deep reflection and an experience of being inspired to make life-changing decisions."[49] They found ways, therefore, to negotiate the space for their own particular forms of espoused theology. This space, it appears, is in part supported by the preaching, and in part worked out as a mild form of resistance to what is seen as the party line. Guest sees these dynamics as the collective mechanism that enables the church to maintain an evangelical identity while avoiding significant conflict, but they give a particular insight into how there are layers of theology that work together in the church. Read through the interpretative lens of the four-voices approach to theology, what becomes apparent is that an evangelical identity might encapsulate significant contradictions between formal theological utterances and more individual espoused theological positions. This contradiction may even extend to leaders who, consciously or unconsciously, reproduce a party line in public while holding different views themselves. Normative theological

48. Ibid., 102.
49. Ibid., 103.

speech and espoused speech in this way may be stretching in different directions when attention is paid to the lived expression of the church.

## Formal Theology

The final voice identified by Cameron et al. is that of formal theology. This refers to the contribution that might be brought to understanding practice and the life of the church by academic or "professional" theologians. This voice, however, is deeply entwined with the other three theological voices. Espoused and normative theology may draw to varying degrees on formal theology.[50] A good example of this is the way that ministers may continue to find inspiration from their studies at college when they preach or how the extent to which believers may engage with academic theology when they attend Christian festivals and events. The normative theology contained in the liturgy of the church is often influenced by the wider academic conversations that make up the formal theological voice. Alongside this embedded formal voice, there is a particular role that Cameron and company see for academic engagement with practice. Academic theology can offer a critical perspective on the lived expression of the church. It is able, when it is at its best, to "shine a light" on the actions of the church and the state of believing.

## The Four Voices and the State of Believing

The state of believing forms a part of the formal voice of academic theology. This means that by writing, I am adding my voice to other voices around, both operant and espoused, in the hope that I can help the church by shedding light and developing new perspectives. In other words, I understand the process of writing as part of the ecclesial conversation, rather than as something that is set apart from the conversation. Throughout the book, I make use of the idea of espoused and operant theologies to highlight the central problematic of the disconnection between the evangelical gospel and the lived expression

---

50. Cameron et al., *Talking about God in Practice*, 55.

of faith. So I adopt the term *espoused theology* as a reference to the gospel and operant theology as a shorthand for personal and communal lived believing. The use of espoused and operant in this way does have its problems. As Guest's work shows, there is a complex link between espoused theology in, for instance, a sermon and lived believing. It is a misunderstanding to treat one as entirely distinct from the other. The same is true of the kind of lived believing that we have seen in Luhrmann's *When God Talks Back*.[51] The vibrant lived faith of those who converse with God is constructed in relation to the wider discourse (or voice) of the community. In fact, operant theology is always and already espoused, and the same is very often the case for espoused theology that finds its life in what is lived or operant.

Despite these caveats, the terminology creates a distinction that is helpful in that it allows for an examination of a specific kind of doctrinal expression in relation to how this is habituated believing. This leaves the question of the normative voice. It is important to note that "normative" within the four-voices typology refers to those sources that are judged by those within the community as being authoritative. It therefore speaks of the way that churches self-regulate and seek affirmation and correction in their own lived expression. This is quite distinct from the notion of normativity that operates more widely in practical theology, where theological sources are used to develop a corrective or a transformed way forward for the church. Normativity here is a kind of judgment that the practical theologian offers to the community, rather than a reference to how sources are used authoritatively within the everyday. Normativity, in the way it is understood in practical theology, is probably best seen as part of the formal theological voice. Formal theology inevitably carries within it moments of choice and evaluation. I have referred to this as discerning the body and seeing the work of God in the church and in the world. The basis for such discernment, however, lies in rational

51. T. M. Luhrmann, *When God Talks Back: Understanding the American Evangelical Relationship with God* (New York: Vintage, 2012).

and considered intellectual work, but I am arguing that this finds its orientation in the call to abide in Jesus Christ.

The four-voices understanding of theology in the lived practice of the church offers a nuanced and attentive way into the questions that surround the state of believing. As we have seen, there is a tendency for theologians to express deep concern over the spiritual health and vitality of the church, but they generally fail to take the time to examine in detail what is actually happening in communities. The result of this lack of attention to the lived, which comes from a failure to value or make use of empirical methods, is that the problems are described in rather sweeping and broad-brush terms. The empirical study of the church that I am taking up requires attention to the lived through the four voices, but this is simultaneously a discerning of the body. Making sense of believing and discerning whether believing might need correction is not simply the exercise of reason. This is a journey toward seeing as the Wisdom of God. Seeing is the practice of abiding in Jesus Christ. Abiding, I suggest, has two aspects: the first is contemplation of Jesus Christ in the Scriptures; the second is reflection on the presence of Christ in the life of the Christian community. Reflection proceeds from contemplation because it is the discerning of Jesus Christ revealed in the Scriptures in the ongoing life of the church. Reflection is seeking the face of Jesus Christ in the practices of the church, but it is also a way to explore how the cultural forms of the church do not just "veil" the divine, but occasionally how they might obscure it. This kind of discernment is complex and needs a particular kind of attention.

The Four-Voices and other empirical methodologies offer tools to pay attention, but alongside them, there is a need to locate inquiry in the movement of God. This kind of work is impossible if sufficient time has not been taken to attend to the lived and the embodied theology of believers and how this is enacted in the context of the communal theological expression of their churches. This has particular implications for the way that theological insight might be offered to build the church in its journey toward faithfulness in the state of believing. Methodologically, this requires adopting a range of different empirical studies and methods that will explore the disconnection of espoused theology, which evangelical churches regard as the gospel, and lived theology. An approach to discourse analysis leads to drawing on insights from cultural studies. With a focus on diverse forms of communication, discourse analysis connects well with the idea that there are multiple voices in the church. I start by looking at the processes of communication that have generated the view that the gospel is "unchanging." This attention to the espoused and the lived is an exercise in seeing or discerning the body of Christ. Its research is analytical in nature, but it is also a critique that is seeking the presence of Christ and the work of the Spirit in the hope that by so doing, any problems that may be uncovered can be transformed as the church learns how to abide in Jesus and thereby share in the relational life of the Trinity.

# 10

Confessing Evangelical Theology in
Dynamic Public Spaces

Jason S. Sexton

## The Nature of Western Public Space

The ongoing and increasingly lively debate about the nature of
Western society highlights both the fluidity and the limitations of our
problematic context in the West. We have a difficult time locating
precisely where we are in light of our various competing histories
and whatever may be the precise nature of our "public." Whatever
charge may be placed on the Reformation, and whatever the American
contribution to this current situation,[1] the definitive statement is yet

---

1. Brad S. Gregory, *The Unintended Reformation: How a Religious Revolution Secularized Society*
(Cambridge, MA: Harvard University Press, 2012); Christian Smith, *The Secular Revolution: Power,
Interests, and Conflict in the Secularization of American Public Life* (Berkeley: University of California
Press, 2003).

to be made about whether the West is largely secular or religious, and also, regardless of what situation we find ourselves in, what might be decisively said about the relative goodness of either structure and situation.[2] What constitutes our public in the West, and how do we effectively live out Christianity in the Western public space?

As seen from the twentieth century, the West has boasted little significance, apart from its various forms of capital (esp. financial). These have often been reduced to supposed scientifically derived equations crunched by mathematically savvy economists found throughout the wider globalized society. As Thomas Piketty notes, the problem with this is that "there is often very little analysis of the relation between observed economic changes and the political and social history of the period under study. Instead one gets a meticulous description of the sources and raw data, information that is more naturally presented nowadays in spreadsheets and online databases."[3] A further question might be raised about whether this dominant form of economic governance—capitalism—is best for sustainability and flourishing, or even (and especially!) whether it is compatible with evangelical Christianity.[4]

Not just the West, but most of the globalized world is run by capital

2. See Peter Berger, *The Sacred Canopy* (New York: Doubleday, 1967) and, on the contrary, most recently Steve Bruce, *Secularization: In Defence of an Unfashionable Theory* (Oxford: Oxford University Press, 2011); and Jonathan Rauch, "The Great Secession," *The Atlantic*, June 25 2014, http://www.theatlantic.com/magazine/archive/2014/07/the-great-secession/372288/ (accessed January 1, 2015). See also the agenda-setting essay for an American public theology in Linell E. Cady, "Public Theology and the Postsecular Turn," *International Journal of Public Theology* 8 (2014): 292–312, and the critical conversation about postsecularism's relationship to politics and civic discourse in Luke Bretherton, "A Postsecular Politics? Inter-faith Relations as a Civic Practice," *Journal of the American Academy of Religion* 79 (2011): 346–77. Finally, see responses of the impulse to move beyond secularism: Khaled Furani, "Is There a Postsecular?," *Journal of the American Academy of Religion* 83 (2015): 1–26; and Atalia Omer, "Modernists Despite Themselves: The Phenomenology of the Secular and the Limits of Critique as an Instrument of Change," *Journal of the American Academy of Religion* 83 (2015): 27–71.

3. Thomas Piketty, *Capital in the Twenty-First Century* (Cambridge, MA: Belknap Press of Harvard University Press, 2013), 576–77. For a serious response to Piketty, more open to theological reflection and also with a view of the dynamic exchange of ideas that is conducive with Christian missionary activity, see Deirdre N. McCloskey, *Bourgeois Equality: How Ideas, Not Capital or Institutions, Enriched the World* (Chicago: University of Chicago Press, 2016).

4. This latter question was recently raised in a *New York Times* debate column, "Has Capitalism Become Incompatible with Christianity?," *New York Times*, June 25, 2014, http://www.nytimes.com/roomfordebate/2014/06/25/has-capitalism-become-incompatible-with-christianity (accessed January 1, 2015).

in one form or another that generates classisms with all of their fears of medieval to the gentry-peasantry paradigm, which both intimidates and distances the wider public from commencing any genuine public debate, and thus abandons the interpretive discourse to the "experts." But regardless of who's counting and interpreting the data, the identity of people is affected by such configurations whether they possess significant capital or not. And these people are *both* secular and religious, although with far more religious than not.[5]

From a Christian perspective, these numbers are seen in religious megachurch attendance, even as the smaller churches (which make up the majority) ebb and flow in size and existence. The matter is complicated and further complexified with the situation of the self-identifying religious "nones" and their relation to traditional religious institutions.[6] Religious adherents constitute a large number of the non-affluent "99%," whose identity as such we saw when the occupy movement emerged throughout our Western world. These occupants also consist of the many un- or underemployed (impoverished?), yet savvy, well-networked first- and second-generation immigrants. It seems like the variegated and dynamic culture that we are in—or better, constantly entering into—looks less like any monolithic notion of Christendom and much more like the pluralistic melting pot of, say, California, with its extravagantly polarized and radically contradictory forms of hospitality and ostracism, which have been well-documented. World-changing innovation that arises from the intense exchange of ideas in dynamic cultural centers also affords potential for unprecedented forms of irresponsibility, abuse, exploitation, and

5. The religious boast significantly higher numbers. "Worldwide, more than eight-in-ten people identify with a religious group. A comprehensive demographic study of more than 230 countries and territories conducted by the Pew Research Center's Forum on Religion & Public Life estimates that there are 5.8 billion religiously affiliated adults and children around the globe, representing 84% of the 2010 world population of 6.9 billion" ("The Global Religious Landscape," December 8, 2012, http://www.pewforum.org/2012/12/18/global-religious-landscape-exec/ [accessed January 1, 2015]).

6. See the recent Pew report, "America's Changing Religious Landscape," May 12, 2015, http://www.pewforum.org/2015/05/12/americas-changing-religious-landscape/ (accessed July 11, 2015), which highlights the declining religious population in America, perhaps enhanced by the "nones" who do not self-identify with any religion, largely struggling to reckon and reconcile beliefs and behaviors from the traditions and institutions they may have been much more closely related to early in life.

failure. There are winners and losers. Yet even losers remain present in public space, making meaningful life in the city.

Perhaps our public space is really a lot like the global city of Los Angeles, which searches in vain for a center that can never be found. Although there are many points of contact and convergence throughout the sprawl, where the narratives and renarrations intertwine in ways that highlight place as more like the content of a frequently tossed salad bowl instead of a melting pot. In similar fashion, the future of Christianity will also have no center, other than the sprawled communities of the faithful following Jesus in their dynamic particularities, which duly continues with its rise in the global South. This does not require an utterly displaced church,[7] finding no embedded expression in culture. But it moves with, in response to, and sometimes in opposition to, our dynamic culture. With culture constantly flowing both outward and inward, one of the few sure things in it is the fixed beauty instilled by the Creator's design in the peoples (*ta ethnē*), preserved in their languages and distinct ways, a virtue often not extolled in the totalizing Western juggernaut.

Locating a helpful public theology for this setting needs to acknowledge conversations that have not yet borne much fruit in our churches, many of which are paying very little attention to their contexts at all. Public theology must grapple with the driving features of the entire Western, and indeed, globalized civilization, especially capital and how it works, along with the social histories of the particular cultures the church finds itself in. Piketty invites participants with their own cultural histories to participate in the discourse of the development and usage of capital. As such, he invites citizens of various kinds to be not merely passive recipients of their own markets but to actively interpret data and its implications. In significant ways, this corresponds to the communitarian Christian vision of the kingdom and of the reality of our common life together

---

7. See Jonathan R. Wilson, "Aesthetics of the Kingdom: Apocalypsis, Eschatos, and Vision for Christian Mission," in *Revisioning, Renewing, and Rediscovering the Triune Center: Essays in Honor of Stanley J. Grenz*, ed. Derek J. Tidball, Brian S. Harris, and Jason S. Sexton (Eugene, OR: Cascade, 2014), 157–74.

in the present ecclesial situation and how it offers much for the wider societal common good—for the poor and the rich, for workers and shareholders.[8] This highlights the need for investigating how Christians confess their hope in an ever-changing world. And thus, instead of saying that theology is done from the church to the world, perhaps it is best acknowledged that theology is done within the setting of common dynamic and shared societal structures, in particular locations and situations where believers confess the hope within them.

Accordingly, and having framed the ensuing with this introduction, this chapter sets out to argue that dynamic and changing public space requires dynamic witness dependent on the dynamic Holy Spirit for meaningful witness today. This is the kind of theology most befitting the public space, accounting for conversion and eschatological hope in light of God's work in Christ. Within this article's purview is an attempt to address a number of evangelical sensibilities with a better evangelical public theology, reflecting on the overall shape of Western public space, and how Christianity and theology are best done in these public spaces.

## The Nature of Theology Confessed in Public

With the correlationist methodologies of leading twentieth-century theologians such as Gordon Kaufman, Paul Tillich, and David Tracy, theology was understood as operating in such a way that cultural questions and descriptions are given equal weight in biblical theological descriptions.[9] Under a different rationale, a similar approach was advocated by Wolfhart Pannenberg, who viewed theological claims as contestable on the same grounds as all other

---

8. See James K. A. Smith, "Christian Principles Hold Steady as the System Worsens," *New York Times*, June 25, 2014, http://www.nytimes.com/roomfordebate/2014/06/25/has-capitalism-become-incompatible-with-christianity/christian-principles-hold-steady-as-the-system-worsens (accessed January 1, 2015).
9. For a critique of the methodology, see Fred Sanders, "California, Localized Theology, and Theological Localism," in *Theology and California: Theological Refractions on California's Culture*, ed. Fred Sanders and Jason S. Sexton (New York: Routledge, 2014), 20–22; and also, Kathryn Tanner, *Theories of Culture: A New Agenda for Theology* (Minneapolis: Fortress Press, 1997), 65–69.

claims, on the grounds of history, and thereby subjecting the claims of theology to other scientific disciplines.[10] Working with a commitment to a correspondence theory of truth, such an approach proceeds in concomitance with the church's fundamental message, maintaining an internal (and external) coherence that stands in conflict with the present world order, giving way to proclamation power in any context, highlighting its external coherence with reality.

As such, the way Christian theology is best properly *confessed* is in light of public action—primarily of the triune God, and instrumentally, through the public missionary activity of the regenerated and redeemed community constituted as the new humanity. On an Augustinian account, this testifies to the reality of the present public situation in culture as one where sin and evil exist, and where conflict, cruelty, and suffering abound. All is not lost on such problems. Richard Mouw has tersely opined in public debate with John Howard Yoder that while culture is indeed fallen, it is still *created*.[11] Present human history then is really part of a much bigger story—the divine one—which highlights that God encompasses all. Avoiding any notion of what civil rights leader John Perkins calls cheap evangelism and cheap social action, the Christian confession that is suitable for a sin-riddled public displays an ongoing commitment to problems that are "in between,"[12] down here in the real world, and finds their healing through the cross and resurrection.

## Initiating Confession: Public Conversion

Confession begins as a matter of public conversion, which is the shape Christianity has always taken. This ran contrary to the Greco-Roman duality, where religious devotion was a personal, voluntary matter that affected the individual, the family, and small units, but with no

---

10. See the effort of Wolfhart Pannenberg, *Systematic Theology*, 3 vols. (Grand Rapids: Eerdmans, 1991–1998).
11. Richard J. Mouw, "The Enigma of California: Reflections on a Theological Subject," in Sanders and Sexton, *Theology and California: Theological Refractions on California's Culture*, 12.
12. John Perkins, *A Quiet Revolution: The Christian Response to Human Need . . . A Strategy for Today* (Waco: Word, 1976), 99–102.

attempts to address society and its broader concerns. In contrast, Christianity's emergence "spurned this dualism by laying claim to the heart without abandoning the public realm."[13] It rejected the private/public paradigm, opting instead for the integrity of faith lived out in public, where everything was open.

Throughout Scripture, this public nature of conversion is displayed, none of which is ever private. Reflecting on the wounds Jesus showed his disciples after the resurrection, Jean Vanier observes that they speak of Jesus's love for his followers; but they also tell that similarly through the wounds of Jesus's followers, God will give his strength, calling them not to live in a cocoon, but to live forward as instruments of peace in a world of war, being instruments of love amid hate and indifference.[14] Vanier describes the ensuing holiness as "not hiding ourself and saying prayers. Holiness is becoming like Jesus and taking our place in the world to reveal that God is mercy; God is love, God has come to bring us together and wants us to be a people filled with hope, and also with joy."[15] Christianity herein shows itself as distinct, in friendship with others (even with other religions and cultures), showing it for what it truly is and does. Indeed, the leper and another who couldn't speak or hear—the disabled—whom Jesus healed and then commanded *not* to tell anyone about his miracles were the very ones who simply found it impossible to remain in repressed isolation, and this in spite of Jesus's humility, self-effacement, and desired anonymity with which he forbade them to speak (Mark 7:36–7; Luke 5:14–15). Converted followers of Christ possessed a kind of power that was individual, corporate (Acts 1:8), and public (Rom 8:9).

Lesslie Newbigin observed that the early form of the Christian confession as properly trinitarian confession developed *in the very midst of* missionary activity. It was "right in the midst of the struggle between the Church and the pagan world" that the great ecumenical doctrines were publicly articulated, especially with regard to the features of central importance to the gospel, namely, the articulation

---

13. Duncan B. Forrester, *Theology and Politics* (Oxford: Basil Blackwell, 1988), 27–29.
14. Jean Vanier, *Encountering "the Other"* (Mahwah, NJ: Paulist Press, 2005), 45.
15. Ibid., 47.

of the relations between the Father and the Son. The church confessed this theology, chief among truths related to the gospel and the divine nature: the *homoousios* of the Son and Father. It confessed this as it was sent out to engage the intellectual struggle "to state the Gospel in terms of Graeco-Roman culture without thereby compromising its central affirmation."[16] Still functioning this way today, among other things, the gospel continually subverts what Oliver O'Donovan calls "Western place-denial,"[17] with its various cultural concepts at play that Christianity still makes use of for its ongoing task of confessing the trinitarian hope in our present world, offering particular forms of grace for the life of the church, its members, and for the world.

As such, amid the modest and still anemic vision of what he refers to as "new city commons," the faithful-presence model articulated by James Davison Hunter offers little more than the ideology of the US religious right against which it is defined.[18] His proposal, something of an anonymous or perhaps even private Christianity (which is advocated, perhaps unknowingly, by at least one contributor to this volume), knows little of the transformation narrative the gospel invokes nor the power it endues. It forsakes any self-conscious explication of the gospel message in plain view, which feature remains critical insofar as genuine transformation wrought by the divine saving action, and how this changes everything for the believer (2 Cor 5:17) is a crucial feature of the gospel. This transformation of the believer happens in plain public view, yielding ontological change, the verbal acknowledgment that "we will have lost power,"[19] or in the words of John the Baptist: he must increase and we must decrease. This new reality then sends believers into the world, "prepared to enter into

---

16. Lesslie Newbigin, *Trinitarian Doctrine for Today's Mission* (Eugene, OR: Wipf & Stock, 2006; first published as *The Relevance of Trinitarian Doctrine for Today's Mission* [London: Edinburgh House, 1963]), 34.

17. Oliver O'Donovan, "The Loss of a Sense of Place," in Oliver O'Donovan and Joan Lockwood O'Donovan, *Bonds of Imperfection: Christian Politics, Past and Present* (Grand Rapids: Eerdmans, 2004), 296–320.

18. See Damon Linker, "The Hobby Lobby Decision Is One More Sign of the Religious Right's Decline," *The Week*, July 2, 2014, http://theweek.com/article/index/264102/the-hobby-lobby-decision-is-one-more-sign-of-the-religious-rightrsquos-decline?utm_source=links&utm_medium=website &utm_campaign=twitter (accessed January 1, 2015).

19. Vanier, *Encountering "the Other,"* 13.

places of conflict . . . aware that we are vulnerable and can be hurt."[20] Having been birthed amid the hurting world as a subversive form of healing, believers then enter further into society's problems to help others be truly and fully themselves, appreciating the difficulties so that in particular ways, Christians can enter into the long journey of a relationship, with forgiveness and growth in community, toward holiness and wholeness, by virtue of the *energeia* and *dynamis* resulting from faith in God and empowerment of the Holy Spirit.[21]

In order to approach the reality of brokenness, points of pain and tension in the world (the situation of everything in this present postlapsarian reality), theological propositions resulting from active Christian witness in public spaces function as demonstrations that afford acknowledgment by the widest group of people when all things have come to light as the ontological priority of the eschaton comes into view, yielding ultimate public acknowledgment.[22] This confessed reality highlights something like what the microscope reveals, showing that the same world we interact with every day is of far greater significance—a far different world—than we had realized. Although oriented toward the future at every point, it is also oriented to revelation—a reality confessed amid a world with which it is variously at odds.

The nature of particular culturally embedded structures resistant to the Christian confession highlight the difficulty of the conflict. Public education serves as an example, itself hardly able to sustain any meaningful form of neutrality. None of the situations there are ever static. They are always being revised and reconfigured. All cultures, especially those more significantly affected by globalization, are being negotiated so that the endless exploration of their rhythms, objects, and values remains a requirement, even as these things change over time. While such study could be justified as time well spent, especially

---

20. Ibid., 41.
21. For example, see Rom 1:16; 1 Cor 12:11; 2 Cor 4:12; Eph 1:15–23; 3:6–7; 4:15–16; Phil 2: 12–13; 3:21; Col 1:29; 2:12–15; 1 Thess 2:13.
22. See Wolfhart Pannenberg's methodology in *Faith and Reality* (London: Search Press, 1977), and an exposition of this essential feature of Pannenberg's theology in Jason S. Sexton, *The Trinitarian Theology of Stanley Grenz* (London: T&T Clark, 2013), 26–29.

for the Christian missionary task, a commitment to genuinely liberal plurality is hard to come by.[23]

The mission of the church in the present world embodied by its core confession of Jesus as "Lord" often means coming against opposing forces in the unlikeliest forms. It bears the task of displaying not a braced, but an open and vulnerable display of charity throughout its own various forms of difficulty, being sent out into some even dangerous settings by the very one who, by nature, is love.

## Culture as Locally Located and on the Move

Culture, of course, while located "in a specific time and place," is also on the move. One may talk of "intercultural" in order to preserve "the sense that cultures are integral wholes,"[24] possessing their own integrity. Analogous to a genome, culture is also transmissible from one generation to another even as it is subject to a selection process, which, for culture, is negotiated in intercultural exchange with particular dialogue partners. As with genetic material, sometimes things go dreadfully wrong. To affirm these possibilities is to further assume that there is such a thing as "theology," and also that there are particular ways the exposition of the gospel will take shape in various cultural contexts, to speak to and labor to bring about real healing.

To assume that culture is located and on the move also assumes that there is also such a thing as "public" space, or reality. This is more than just where theology is done. Although it is that, it is also a place where theology (the true kind) may be found present and at work, shedding light on cultural realities in light of the personal action of the triune God. Here is where the dynamic negotiability, durability, and contingency of culture is also freely seen. There is no culture that has been "once and for all delivered to the saints," but

---

23. It is often thought that Lesslie Newbigin envisioned such a situation, but for a careful critique of Newbigin's vison of a Christian society, see Jeppe Bach Nikolajsen, *The Distinctive Identity of the Church: A Constructive Study of the Post-Christendom Theologies of Lesslie Newbigin and John Howard Yoder* (Eugene, OR: Pickwick, 2015), 87–91.
24. For this, see Kirsteen Kim, "Doing Theology for the Church's Mission: The Appropriation of Culture," chap. 5 of the current volume, pp. 73–99.

when God does a special work within a culture, this work is often specially acknowledged. Cultures still, however, exude powerful forces inseparable from some of their moods and objects, some of which may be beyond redemption. Bearers of the transcendent gospel are susceptible to these cultural wooings, especially when building institutions that mimic the structures of society.[25] It seems that Jesus's indictment, "Woe! when people speak well of you" (Luke 6:26–27) carries significant implications for institutions, especially religious and "confessional" ones.

Jesus and the gospel message are, at times, critical of established religion and confessional institutions that attempt to establish the kingdom city in this world on their terms. Even Jesus's high priestly prayer finds him praying for the disciples who are in the world. Taken as a petition to keep them in the world (John 17:15), this is precisely the remedy to their proneness to want to leave the world that they are drawn to for various reasons that are counterintuitive to coherent gospel exposition, or the consistency of belief and living. In this context, they must remain as those who are not of the world while being those who have the word (John 17:14).

Here is where vocation plays a part in public theology, which can never be inseparably linked to one's employment/occupation, but is inseparably tied to what one chooses to do with a particular occupation, tied to the manner in which believers attest to the gospel's reality. Such a confessional approach to vocation simultaneously embraces and throws off cultural structures, reading them for what they are, in a similar way to how the apostle Paul was provoked by idols one moment (Acts 17:16), and at another regards them as nothing (1 Cor 8:4). He carried on with his public missionary work, sometimes casting out demons and other times ignoring them (Acts 16:16–18). He participated in bringing healing through prayer (Acts 28:8), and

25. One recent example, however, of a secular co-opting of so-called Christian cultural creation is with Katy Perry's alleged infringement of copyright law by taking Grammy-winner Lecrae's beat for her popular song "Dark Horse." See Carey Lodge, "'Katy Perry Stole My Song' Say Christian Rappers about Dark Horse," *Christian Today*, July 3, 2014, http://www.christiantoday.com/article/katy.perry.stole.my.song.say.christian.rappers.about.dark.horse/38593.htm (accessed January 1, 2015).

elsewhere prescribed it through drinking wine (1 Tim 5:23). Similarly, today it might work from a theology as a vocation, or from other academic disciplines outwith the more traditional purview.[26]

All of this corresponds to the indicative nature of Christian witness (see Acts 1:8), which takes worship and prayer as its form of politics, and the act of being the church as the way witness is lived out in the world,[27] as the body of Christ broken for the sake of the world.[28] Such an ecclesiology may provide a way forward for contemporary evangelical disputes over the kingdom and church,[29] when the church as a whole, and Christians in particular, give themselves to the centrifugal witness the gospel propels them on; led by the Spirit they must not and cannot be confined to the internal and boundaried life of the ecclesial community. As James K. A. Smith has shown, some examples of this end up blurring the distinction between Augustine's earthly city and the eternal, heavenly city. It thus risks replacing the eschatological orientation of the present penultimate world with the eschaton itself in a kind of realized eschatology. The eschaton, of course, is something only God alone will bring about.

It is quite unfortunate that particular ways of confessing the gospel in different contexts end up emerging as epistemologies of theology that do all the work that the Spirit is shown in Scripture to do—illumining realities, converting souls, structuring ecclesial and common life, empowering mission and public service away from other things. Most of these things have, at points, been movements (of the Spirit), but evolved at various junctures into self-governing systems that branded themselves as all-encompassing. Inevitably, they became driving systems for complex movements and institutions that themselves need more careful assessment, especially regarding the

---

26. For example, see Jake Andrews, "Farewell to Theology?," *Anglican Theological Review* 96 (2014): 715–25.

27. For one strong proposal on this kind of ecclesiology, see Stanley Hauerwas's view of the church/world relationship in *The Peaceable Kingdom: A Primer in Christian Ethics* (Notre Dame: University of Notre Dame Press, 1991), 100.

28. See this ecclesiology developed further in Paul S. Fiddes, *Tracks and Traces: Baptist Identity in Church and Theology* (Carlisle, UK: Paternoster, 2003).

29. See the critical response to two-kingdoms advocates in James K. A. Smith, "Reforming Public Theology: Two Kingdoms, or Two Cities?," *Calvin Theological Journal* 47 (2012): 122–37.

nature of their confession and a bit more sober reflection and social-located acknowledgment of "place acceptance," to borrow O'Donovan's term. That is, it needs more localized self-awareness if the church is to confess a theology that is properly suited for the public sphere, where it lives out its life and where it may, prayerfully and in faithfulness to Christ, live a quiet, meaningful, and peaceable life in public (1 Tim 2:2).

## Public Theology Spreading into Public Spaces

California is often perceived as the land of the fruits, nuts, and flakes—the United States' left (or "party") coast—yet much of the place's history has been the ordinary experience of the working class.[30] Sought thrills repressed or somehow not obtained are just as easily carried off (like California's many convicts) to the desert—Las Vegas to be precise—where what happens there *stays there*, so it is sold. And yet, as the British tabloids and Prince Harry found out in August 2012, what happens in Vegas does not always stay there. It sometimes goes very public indeed.

### The Nature of Public Space

What is "public"? This is not the question of "what *is* public?" as in what actually exists in the public realm. We know what *goes* public, for Christian theology acknowledges that all things indeed *are* public insofar as action (with motive) is observed by noncorporeal beings, including, most importantly, a divine one; insofar as the consequences of every action have indeterminate and unknown but nonetheless sure consequences, having been enacted in a process carrying those consequences.[31] All things are already public insofar as all things now will one day be disclosed and are currently done before the eye of the

---

30. On Los Angeles, in particular, although with implications for wider California, see Hector Tobar's comment in the panel, "Exile and Place: Who Gets to Speak for L.A.?" (panel discussion, Tales from Two Cities: Writing from California–L.A., Los Angeles Public Library, February 21, 2014), http://library.fora.tv/2014/02/21/exile_and_place_who_gets_to_speak_for_la (accessed January 1, 2015).
31. For this account of human action, see Hannah Arendt, *The Human Condition*, 2nd ed. (Chicago: University of Chicago Press, 1998), 230–47.

Maker and Judge of all. This one will judge all things, including every careless word spoken (Matt 12:36).

The *Oxford English Dictionary* defines "public" as "open to general observation, view, or knowledge; existing, performed, or carried out without concealment, so that all may see or hear."[32] Applying this definition to the action of the church's theology, and thus public theology in something of an expansive form that points to but can never reduce the kinds of things that happen in public (which will include things that are creaturely and divine), highlights this as a Christianity that is universally verifiable, revealed, and experienced. It is Yahweh's movement to create and work through Israel's story; it is the incarnation and Jesus's crucifixion, burial, and resurrection; it is the Spirit's public action in the life the church; it is conversion narratives of the apostle Paul and those living with burned-out postcolonial guilt, for immigrant communities, and the weak and vulnerable in society.

But we want to know how theology matters in public spaces. Is democracy the best "public" state for theology to flourish? Whatever answer we give to this question must not betray our own eschatological orientation and aim to live with integrity in whatever "present age" and series of governance structures we find ourselves situated in, knowing that these too are being constantly negotiated and cannot remain fixed. Whatever the gospel might say about these structures, it cannot diverge from its own eschatological orientation and hope for the reality of the coming kingdom of God.

Does this mean then that Christianity ought to pursue, or provides the basis for, religious or cultural pluralism or multiculturalism?[33] The problem of a truly pluralist public education, again, is one issue that raises challenges for how best such structures may be engaged.[34] And

---

32. "Public, adj. and n.," *OED Online*, December 2014 (Oxford: Oxford University Press, 2014), http://www.oed.com.libproxy.usc.edu/view/Entry/154052?result=1&rskey=VUMIOq& (accessed January 3, 2015).

33. Miroslav Volf argues for pluralism as a Christian political project in *A Public Faith: How Followers of Christ Should Serve the Common Good* (Grand Rapids: Brazos, 2011), 126–27; for a critical theological approach to multiculturalism (in the UK), and a constructive proposal toward what he calls "multicultural justice," see Jonathan Chaplin, *Multiculturalism: A Christian Retrieval* (London: Theos, 2011).

perhaps it could also be the matter of defining marriage in the contestable public space. Here is where T. F. Torrance's notion of evangelizing the foundations of culture seems entirely wrongheaded. To link such a notion to the need of transformation of mind is one thing, but to assume this can be done for "the mind of human society and culture in which human beings exist" is another thing altogether, which Torrance seems to think is necessary if the church is to put down roots in a particular society and remain genuinely Christian.[35] Much could be said here about the early church existing during its first three centuries on the furthest societal margins, in the darkness as light and operating in a distressed situation (1 Cor 7:26). Torrance may simply be working with the notion of an established church over against a nonestablished setting, in my reading one being more realistic (Augustinian, and affirming the freedom of humans to choose their religion) while the other exudes an unfortunate triumphalism in which even the established church could hope that the Spirit would circumvent to work within. As such, it does not seem at all plausible to say there is, or ever has been, a Christian society; there are only Christians. And they belong to society within public space, to one another, and to the Lord, insofar as they participate in the lives of each.

Accordingly, then, there are no foundations of culture per se. There are only *people* who make culture who are shaped by the culture that others have made, and who either contribute to the advance and health of particular cultures, or else to its decay. Being negotiable at every point, all cultures exist within a constant negotiability of epistemological structures that are present in any given culture.[36] What is not negotiable is ultimate reality and everything good,

---

34. Lesslie Newbigin, *Foolishness to the Greeks: The Gospel and Western Culture* (London: SPCK, 1986), 38–39.
35. Thomas F. Torrance, *Atonement: The Person and Work of Christ*, ed. Robert T. Walker (Downers Grove, IL: IVP Academic, 2009), 444. Although rejecting federal theology, as Paul D. Molnar shows in *Thomas F. Torrance: Theologian of the Trinity* (Farnham, UK: Ashgate, 2008), 181–82, Torrance does not quite dislodge his own theology from what federal theology has bequeathed in the two-kingdoms understanding of the nature of the kingdom today in the world and the role of the church in society. For a critique of this, especially in David M. VanDrunen, see Smith, "Reforming Public Theology," 122–37.
36. George A. Lindbeck, *The Nature of Doctrine: Religion and Theology in a Postliberal Age* (Philadelphia: Westminster, 1984), 32–41.

beautiful, and true, based on and blessed by this ultimate reality of the triune God whose "kingdom" reality is found in the descriptions of the "blessed": the poor in spirit, those who mourn, the meek, those who hunger and thirst for righteousness, the merciful, the pure in heart, the peacemakers, those persecuted for righteousness, the insulted, persecuted, and those falsely accused of all kinds of evil for Jesus's sake and yet who rejoice and are glad.

Torrance himself assumed a situation that Martyn Percy finds also shared between Newbigin and Radical Orthodoxy—in proper nineteenth-century colonialist style—each resembling a stance in Christian mission that insists on "the reality and primacy of Christendom."[37] Torrance, Newbigin, John Milbank, and others may very well insist on this (and whatever Christendom is . . . ), but cannot assert as having any such privilege, much less than secularists or other religious groups can assume privilege.[38] Even with these acknowledgments, the clear demarcations enable various structures to exist in a multicultural or intercultural setting. Such a setting, notwithstanding extreme polarizations, allows for the freedom to change one's mind, as in the well-known case of Peter Berger, himself coming around to agree that the West, with its capitalism and consumerism, is indeed religious. But if it is religious, there is no religious adherence (that is, theology) that is ever expressed in static observance, even though some from different Christian traditions hold their confessions with nothing short of canonical status, as is the case with some Reformed groups and the Westminster Confession of Faith, or in ways that evangelicals hold certain points of a Scripture principle, or the way Catholics hold to the authority of the magisterium. I reckon such a situation is both in keeping with a plausibility structure conducive to Christian conversion as well as revisable Christianity in

---

37. See Martyn Percy, *Engaging with Contemporary Culture: Christianity, Theology, and the Concrete Church* (Farnham, UK: Ashgate, 2005), 68.

38. In some cases, assuming this kind of privilege is a recipe for anarchy, which has riddled otherwise meaningful protests led by activists in the United States in response to the 2014 killings and non-indictments of African Americans Michael Brown in Ferguson, MO, and Eric Garner in New York. 2015 has not been any better with Sandra Bland, Freddie Gray, and Tamir Rice, leading a number of Christian groups into solidarity with the #Blacklivesmatter movement and various features of what it represents amid the realities of white privilege in America.

the Spirit of *semper reformanda*. Much of internal developmental doctrinal discourse takes place both in ongoing dialogue, clarification, and explanatory action among believers and churches as well as while confessing theology in public as part of the church's public missionary task.[39]

## Theology in Public

Whatever public is, it is there that God has called his people to witness to the reality of the gospel. A definition of theology and of the gospel's thick description might be given in this space that others in the public might understand. Sebastian Kim notes that public theology "does not require the privileging of Christianity in public life and its theologians do not necessarily see their work as superseding" other theologies at play in the public arena, namely, liberation and political theology. Kim goes on, "Public theology takes its place in the different contexts of plural and secular societies as a complementary approach alongside many other theologies and philosophies."[40] As such, it also moves in parallel motion with the other religions, and at critical points offers its own propositions, which will give way to a genuine tension and forms of public conflict.

This conflict is not to be asserted or insisted upon by Christian theologians at any point. Rather, the conflict arises from the self-authentication of the biblical message, Spirit-imparted at every level. Contrary to the notion of Christendom, then, public theology is active and on the move, not to control or dominate, but to serve. It transiently exists in various places, prevailing in its followers who are carried along by the Spirit, offering healing, and who are themselves by nature at odds with impulses toward Christendom manifest in the lives of our institutions. They neither seek to avoid the world out of fear nor isolate themselves in hopes of remaining pure. Indeed, as James 1:27 makes

---

39. See Jason S. Sexton, "A Confessing Trinitarian Theology for Today's Mission," in *Advancing Trinitarian Theology: Essays in Constructive Dogmatics*, ed. Oliver Crisp and Fred Sanders (Grand Rapids: Zondervan, 2014), 171–89.
40. Sebastian C. H. Kim, *Theology in the Public Sphere: Public Theology as Catalyst for Open Debate* (London: SCM, 2011), 21.

clear, Christian witness is to be present in the broken places. It works in these "in between" spaces to remove impediments so the church can flourish and so that all humans can have a better chance at a better life here at present and with a view toward the best kind of life to come.[41] Conversely, those who by their own ingenuity try to remain unstained by the world end up stained.

Public Christianity is public then not as it propagates a better hegemony, nor does it aim for this. But it is what it is insofar as it "touches" or carries potentiality to "touch" others in every sphere of society and in any culture with the reality of its hope, shaped then by particular cultural expressions, but also anchored in a revealed reality and translated by the Spirit. Here it makes way for being both a stumbling block and foolishness to others, and yet, being the very power of God unto salvation for all who believe, entailing something only the Holy Spirit enables.

A few more factors are considerable for developing a theology done in public. While various models have been descriptive of the literature, it is clear that many of these are very particularist, and therefore less descriptive for the wider practice of "doing theology." Eneida Jacobsen sketches a number of models for possible appropriation in her own Brazilian context and finds the kind of needful theology she seeks as being "anchored in the lifeworld," "mobilized by the suffering of people," and seeking "to contribute to the expansion of the communicative efforts of a society."[42] If it is the language of the people, it includes media such as poetry, prose, letters, and other forms of regional expressions of life, which Fred Sanders has argued should be made use of for doing theology in the California context.[43] It is a linguistic description of reality known to the common person's experience of the world. But it is still much more than that.

The argument being advanced in this chapter is sympathetic with

---

41. For further reflections on this matter of working in the "in between" spaces to remove impediments and heal, reflecting on the practical matter that directly affects most people at some point in their lives, see Gene L. Green, *The Scalpel and the Cross: A Theology of Surgery*, Ordinary Theology (Grand Rapids: Zondervan, 2015).
42. Eneida Jacobsen, "Models of Public Theology," *International Journal of Public Theology* 6 (2012): 22.
43. Sanders, "California, Localized Theology, and Theological Localism," 19–33.

Pannenberg's disdain for the privatization of religion that emerged again in the post-Reformation era.[44] Rejecting religion's totalizing impulse, religious expression became a matter of private practice, which has especially been amplified in the United States at different points, and not always in the most helpful ways. It became cut off from other cultural issues affecting the church and society, and from other cultural institutions such as the university, only to roar back at different moments in the forms of different reactionary movements that often co-opted faith for different ends. However, the truth at the heart of Christianity still holds the power of transforming lives, of witnessing to the coming kingdom, of proclaiming judgment,[45] and of laboring to love inexplicably.

## Conclusion: Doing Theology That Matters in Public

Much of theology done in public today is not done very well, including evangelical theology. It often retreats into an incubated existence within the life of the church, partitioned off from the world, or else proceeding as suspicious or reactionary when it comes into the public square with any responsible consciousness. So there is one final point worth emphasizing here in conclusion. To reiterate a statement earlier in this essay, there is no "from the church to the world"; but there is the church and its members, functioning in the world as the body of Christ, broken for the world, both shattered and scattered throughout various soils. As such, the church remains the most significant actor in the public square. In the presence of the worshiping members of its community, the church in these particular soils "celebrates the resurrection of Jesus as the ground of assurance that the present and the future are not under the control of blind forces but are open to unlimited possibilities of new life. This is because the living God who was present in the crucified Jesus is now and always the sovereign Lord of history and therefore makes possible a continuing struggle against

---

44. Pannenberg, *Faith and Reality*, 137.
45. Luke Bretherton, *Christianity and Contemporary Politics: The Conditions and Possibilities of Faithful Witness* (Oxford: Wiley-Blackwell, 2010), 148–49.

all that ignores or negates his purpose."[46] This very real struggle denotes the privileged calling believers are blessed to participate in, with frail and fleeting lives as they hold out and hold open with their lives the confession they have been brought into, making manifest the hope of that confession that through Christ, God will one day reconcile all broken things. This will be the greatest day the public has ever known, and every eye will see it.

46. Newbigin, *Foolishness to the Greeks*, 63.

# PART III

# The Practice of
# Shaping Theology for
# Mission

11

---

# The Widening of Christian Mission: C. René Padilla and the Intellectual Origins of Integral Mission

## David C. Kirkpatrick

Ecuadorian theologian C. René Padilla (b. 1932) became a traveling secretary with the International Fellowship of Evangelical Students (IFES) in the late 1950s, a role that required constant contact with a revolutionary Latin American university environment. IFES is the worldwide representative body that arose out of the Inter-Varsity Fellowship (IVF), later known as the Universities and Colleges Christian Fellowship (UCCF) in Britain, and InterVarsity Christian Fellowship-USA (IVCF). In Latin America, the preceding decade saw tectonic shifts in the sociopolitical landscape, spurred on by the Cuban revolution, a rapid spread of repressive military regimes, and vast rural–urban migration—all of which funneled into the Latin American university context.[1] This sociopolitical environment proved particularly salient for the development of social theologies in the second half of the twentieth century, as widely recognized in the rise of liberation theology. During this time, Padilla, along with other Latin American thinkers, began to develop what would later be termed *misión integral,* or integral mission.[2] Padilla is widely considered "the father of integral mission."

The meager historiography on Latin American Protestant evangelical social theology has described it as unidirectional—essentially a Latin American monologue toward the rest of global evangelicalism.[3] Social location alone, however, cannot produce theological methodologies. Theologians do not simply react to contexts; they react to contexts with intellectual resources drawn from a variety of sources. As the first critical study of Ecuadorian theologian C. René Padilla's theology, this chapter will argue that from its very inception integral mission was a global conversation, influenced by voices as diverse as the movement of evangelicalism itself. Influence upon integral mission was multidirectional, mirroring Padilla's educational journey: from Wheaton College to Manchester University and to a missionary-influenced Latin American Protestant landscape. This chapter is essentially a work of intellectual archaeology, attempting to uncover the sources of Padilla's theology, without diminishing its roots in the Latin American context. By challenging the prevailing narrative of integral mission, this chapter invites further reflection on the diversity of evangelical Protestant missiology.

David Bebbington has clearly demonstrated that in the late nineteenth and early twentieth centuries, evangelical social action was largely justified theologically through the removal of "obstacles to the progress of the gospel" or eliminating social sins that contravened

---

1. See David C. Kirkpatrick, "C. René Padilla and the Origins of Integral Mission in Post-War Latin America," *Journal of Ecclesiastical History* 67 (2016): 351–71.
2. This English translation has been adopted by René Padilla himself and will thus be utilized here.
3. See, for example, Sharon E. Heaney, *Contextual Theology for Latin America: Liberation Themes in Evangelical Perspective* (Milton Keynes, UK: Paternoster, 2008). Daniel Salinas, *Latin American Evangelical Theology in the 1970's: The Golden Decade* (Boston: Brill, 2009).

divine commands.[4] In terms of theological methodology, this fit squarely within what David Bosch called a "two mandate approach," which predominated in evangelical theological language prior to the 1970s.[5] This method bifurcated Christian mission into a primary, spiritual mandate and a subordinate (often muted) social mandate. In contrast, integral mission is an understanding of Christian mission which posits that social action and evangelism are both essential and indivisible components of Christian mission—indeed, both central aspects *within* the Christian gospel. (The Spanish word *integral* is used to describe whole-wheat bread or wholeness.) Put more simply, integral mission synthesizes the pursuit of justice with the offer of salvation.

For Padilla, these "wider dimensions" of Christian mission derived from his theology of the kingdom and its eschatological framework, as seen clearly in his most important book, *Mission between the Times: Essays on the Kingdom* (*Misión Integral: Ensayos Sobre el Reino*).[6] Today, the language of integral mission has been increasingly adopted by Christian mission and relief organizations, Christian political activists, official congress declarations, and ecclesiastical movements around the world.

### Padilla at Wheaton College (1953–1960): Arthur F. Holmes and Critical Engagement with Evangelicalism

René Padilla was connected to Wheaton College at a young age: his parents befriended Dr. Victor Raymond Edman (1900–1967), president of Wheaton College during 1940–1965, when Edman was a missionary in Quito, Ecuador (Padilla's hometown), from 1923 to 1928.[7] Padilla

4. David Bebbington, "Evangelicals and Reform: An Analysis of Social and Political Action," *Third Way* (1983): 10–13; Bebbington, *The Nonconformist Conscience: Chapel and Politics, 1870–1914* (London: G. Allen & Unwin, 1982), 37–60.

5. David J. Bosch, *Transforming Mission: Paradigm Shifts in Theology of Mission* (Maryknoll, NY: Orbis, 1991), 403.

6. See especially chap. 10, "The Mission of the Church in Light of the Kingdom of God." C. René Padilla, *Mission between the Times: Essays on the Kingdom*, 2nd ed. (Carlisle, UK: Langham Monographs, 2010), 199–211. =Padilla, *Misión integral: ensayos sobre el Reino y la iglesia* (Grand Rapids: Eerdmans, 1986). This work has also been translated into Portuguese, Swedish, German, and Korean.

addressed both his most effusive praise and his most biting critique to his time at Wheaton in the suburbs of Chicago from 1953 to 1960. In a 2013 interview, one name surfaced repeatedly as crucial in Padilla's theological development: his master's supervisor, Arthur F. Holmes.[8]

Holmes (1924–2011) was born in Dover, England, to a Baptist family (his father was a lay preacher and a school teacher).[9] Holmes later completed his entire education in the Chicago area: he took a BA and MA from Wheaton College in 1950 and 1952, respectively, followed by a PhD in philosophy from Northwestern University in 1957.[10] Holmes taught at Wheaton College for over four decades, chairing the Philosophy Department from its founding in 1969 to 1994. (Prior to 1969, philosophy fell within the Bible and Philosophy Department.)[11] Padilla explicitly chose his philosophy major so that he could take more courses with Holmes.[12] Padilla later cited Holmes's work as providing the raw ingredients for his project of contextualizing the gospel.

In his book, *Mission between the Times*, Padilla turned to what he called "the epistemology of biblical realism" to ground his understanding of the contextualization of the gospel. Padilla expanded his concept of contextualization beyond the historical context to "the metaphysical, the ethical, and the personal."[13] Padilla's three main theses are taken from Holmes's 1971 work *Faith Seeks Understanding*.[14] For example, the idea of knowledge being social, rather than isolated pieces of information for individuals, spoke strongly to a Latin American context

---

7. Wheaton College Archives, V. Raymond Edman papers, SC 08, http://www2.wheaton.edu/learnres/ARCSC/collects/sc08/.

8. Holmes was his first reader. Interview of René Padilla by author, Buenos Aires, Argentina, September 13, 2013.

9. Wheaton College Archives and Special Collections, "Arthur F. Holmes Papers," SC 183, Box 2, Folder "Correspondence," "Chapel Address: 'My Spiritual Pilgrimage, 1982.'" (Researcher's note: WCASC has a separate cataloging system from the Billy Graham Center Archives at Wheaton.)

10. Ibid., "Vita: Arthur F. Holmes."

11. See BGCA, SC 300, Hudson T. Armerding to Arthur Holmes, March 14, 1969, for the announcement of its founding.

12. René Padilla, interview by author, Buenos Aires, Argentina, September 13, 2013 (p. 43 of field notes).

13. Padilla, *Mission between the Times*, 106.

14. Padilla, *Misión integral*, 87; Padilla, *Mission between the Times*, 110–11. Arthur F. Holmes, *Faith Seeks Understanding: A Christian Approach to Knowledge* (Grand Rapids: Eerdmans, 1971), 125, 129.

dominated by premillennial dispensational eschatology and heavy emphasis on "saving souls." In his work, Holmes concluded, "Scripture knows no dichotomy of the physical and spiritual."[15] Ultimately, Holmes's purpose in connecting knowledge to community was effective communication.[16] Holmes provided the philosophical categories that Padilla used to articulate a Latin American contextual evangelical theology inextricably tied to local realities. From Holmes, Padilla gleaned a philosophical grounding in personal knowledge fused to social realities, grounded in a synthesis between the spiritual and the physical, and driven toward effective communication. Here Padilla found some of the raw ingredients that would later constitute his understanding of integral mission.

While Holmes contributed to Padilla's understanding of contextualizing the gospel message, his influence upon Padilla as a mentor was even more significant.

Being British, Holmes occupied a position that made it easier to resonate with international students such as Padilla, and to critique broad Wheaton political loyalty to the Republican Party. Holmes encouraged students to engage critically with evangelical doctrines —even defending the presence of agnostic students against the threat of expulsion via a policy of Wheaton College dean Peter Veltman.[17] Holmes challenged students such as Padilla to wrestle with evangelicalism, even to the point of broadening its tent.[18] It is not surprising, then, that when Holmes lobbied for philosophy to be an independent major at Wheaton, Holmes mentioned Padilla as a positive example of the type of student Wheaton was producing.[19] Holmes could not have foreseen the influence he would later have on Padilla nor the eventual shockwaves sent back to the Wheaton establishment.

In a 2013 interview, Padilla described a conversation that imme-

---

15. Holmes, *Faith Seeks Understanding*, 125, 129.
16. Ibid., 133.
17. WCASC, Arthur Holmes Papers, Box 20, Arthur F. Holmes to Peter Veltman, April 16, 1968.
18. See, for example, Holmes pushing Wheaton president Edman to include Edward Carnell after his involvement in the Fuller Seminary controversy. See Record Group # 2. 5. 0. Provost. Hudson T. Armerding. Box 9, Holmes to Edman, March 27, 1964.
19. Wheaton College Archives, SC 183, Record Group # 2. 5. 0. Provost. Hudson T. Armerding. Box 9, Folder "Arthur Holmes."

diately followed his controversial plenary speech at the Lausanne Congress in 1974, in which he lambasted the exportation of "American culture Christianity" around the world. Padilla recounted that after his speech, he was met on the platform by a "very important leader" from the United States—someone "very, very related with Wheaton College"—whom Padilla did not identify by name. The most probable leader, given his prominence as a Wheaton alumnus and leader on the platform at Lausanne, would be none other than Billy Graham or Wheaton president Hudson T. Armerding (1965–1982). In Padilla's 2013 account, this American leader approached him saying, "How can you say what you said if you graduated from Wheaton?" Padilla said he responded, "Precisely there I learned to do critical thinking." While Padilla's speech signaled the rise of majority world evangelical Protestant leadership, it caused a stir with fellow alumni from Wheaton College—to which he gave credit for forming his critical capacities. What is most clear from Padilla's time at Wheaton is that it grounded him in an intellectually fertile tradition of Evangelicalism, which Padilla would eventually draw upon to critique the very institution that trained him, challenging the foundations of Evangelical mission, for which Wheaton stood as a symbol. Padilla's critique at Lausanne, then, was not simply a Latin American monologue, but the result of a global conversation—from American missionaries in Quito, Ecuador, to Padilla's diverse theological training, both in Wheaton and his PhD research at Manchester under F. F. Bruce.

## Padilla at Manchester University (1963–1965): F. F. Bruce, George Eldon Ladd, and the Theology of the Kingdom

Padilla graduated from Wheaton College with a bachelor of arts (BA) in philosophy in May, 1957, and a master of arts (MA) in theology in January of 1960 in absentia. Padilla was already a traveling secretary with the International Fellowship of Evangelical Students in July of 1959, six months after Fulgencio Batista's regime was toppled in Cuba by forces loyal to Fidel Castro. From Latin America, Padilla then applied to four PhD programs—Harvard University, University of Chicago,

University of Edinburgh, and the University of Manchester. Padilla chose to include Manchester because of the possibility to study under Bruce—Rylands Professor of Biblical Criticism and Exegesis from 1959 to 1978.[20] If the goal was to interact with the best of Euro-American evangelical scholarship, one could hardly do better than Bruce—his star was rising within and outside evangelical circles. Brian Stanley described Bruce as "the most prominent conservative evangelical biblical scholar of the post-war era."[21]

What is perhaps most surprising, however, is the apparent lack of influence Bruce had on Padilla.[22] In a 2013 interview, Padilla recalled only rarely meeting with Bruce regarding his thesis work (though he had various meals at the Bruce home), and eventually stopped scheduling supervision due to lack of constructive comments.[23] Accounts from other students seem to corroborate Padilla's recollection regarding inattentive supervision.[24] Bruce was also a classicist and technical biblical scholar, not a theologian. While Bruce was not a significant *theological* influence on Padilla, he gained from Bruce, more than anything, the academic and evangelical credibility that came along with studying "under" him. For example, John Stott noted in his travel diary in January 1974 that Padilla studied "under F. F. Bruce at Manchester."[25] This entry came just months before the Lausanne Congress, where Stott's relationship with Padilla would prove crucial to the later inclusion of social elements in the Lausanne covenant.[26]

Padilla completed his PhD thesis titled, "Church and World: A Study into the Relation between the Church and the World in the Teaching of Paul the Apostle," in October 1965, graduating in absentia while already back in Latin America, June 1966. He had been named the first

20. Interview of René Padilla by author, Buenos Aires, Argentina, September 13, 2013.
21. Brian Stanley, *The Global Diffusion of Evangelicalism* (Downers Grove, IL: IVP Academic, 2013), 54.
22. See C. René Padilla, "Voces para nuestro tiempo: F. F. Bruce," *Certeza* 13 (1973): 10.
23. René Padilla, interview with author, Buenos Aires, September 15, 2013.
24. Tim Grass, *F.F. Bruce : A Life* (Grand Rapids: Eerdmans, 2012), 107.
25. Lambeth Palace Library, John Stott Papers. John Stott Travel Diary, Mexico, January 9–14, 1974. See also Padilla's early description in *Certeza* magazine identifying him with Bruce. C. René Padilla, "Mensaje bíblico y revolución," *Certeza* 39 (1970): 196–201.
26. Samuel Escobar, interview and translated by author, Valencia, Spain, October 21, 2013.

general secretary for Latin America of IFES in the summer of 1966 prior to his graduation. His PhD research has been often referenced and praised, but never studied. His thesis is a document that reflects its time and location; it is a work of conservative evangelical biblical scholarship, with no reference to the Latin American context or even to what would later be termed integral mission.[27]

Despite the absence of an explicitly missiological dimension to his thesis, Padilla gave credit to his PhD research for providing raw ingredients for his later social theological work—specifically the "the eschatological dimension of the gospel . . . this basic emphasis in the New Testament that we are living between the times, and this is the time when we experience the tension between the already and the not-yet of biblical eschatology."[28] Elsewhere, Padilla expanded that his "Lausanne paper was a synthesis of insights I had gained through my doctoral studies, combined with years of experience in university student work."[29]

Padilla wrote at a time of resurgent emphasis on the kingdom of God as a theological category. Among the various conservative evangelical biblical scholars who wrote on the theology of the kingdom, perhaps foremost in this group was Baptist North American George Eldon Ladd (1911–1982), who, at the time, was a professor of New Testament at Fuller Theological Seminary in Pasadena, California. Ladd taught at Fuller from 1950 to 1980.[30] His 1964 work, *Jesus and the Kingdom: The Eschatology of Biblical Realism* (later republished under the title *The Presence of the Future: The Eschatology of Biblical Realism* in 1974) was the high point of his academic career and the result of over a decade of research (though his work *A Theology of the New Testament* [1974] was also influential).[31] *Jesus and the Kingdom* sought a middle way between the "consistent" or "thoroughgoing eschatology" of Albert Schweitzer

---

27. C. René Padilla, "My Theological Pilgrimage," *Journal of Latin American Theology* 4 (2009): 100.
28. Billy Graham Center Archives, Wheaton College. Interview of René Padilla by Paul Ericksen, March 12, 1987. Collection 361, T1.
29. Padilla, "My Theological Pilgrimage," 105–6.
30. The definitive work on Ladd is John A. D'Elia, *A Place at the Table: George Eldon Ladd and the Rehabilitation of Evangelical Scholarship in America* (Oxford: Oxford University Press, 2008).
31. Ibid., 122.

and the "realized eschatology" of C. H. Dodd, which Ladd described as "synthesis of futuristic and realized eschatology."[32] As fundamentalism and dispensationalism went out of vogue, conservative evangelical biblical scholars searched for alternative understandings of eschatology that would address postwar social realities. Both Ladd and Carl Henry (along with others such as Edward Carnell) held a premillennial eschatology, while sharing discontent with dispensational strands of the eschatological understanding which dominated conservative evangelicalism.[33] In response to this perceived vacuum, many neo-evangelicals turned to the theology of the kingdom.[34]

By the 1960s, there was a growing consensus among neo-evangelicals regarding the present and future characteristics of the kingdom of God.[35] In *Jesus and the Kingdom*, Ladd preferred to use the phrase "eschatological tension" to refer to this middle place of future and present reality—the "already" and "not yet" of the kingdom of God.[36] This eschatological tension Ladd described most clearly by saying, "The church . . . is a people who live 'between the times.' They are caught up in a tension between the Kingdom of God and a sinful world, between the age to come and the present evil age."[37] Ladd ultimately connected his theology of the kingdom to his soteriology: "To be in the Kingdom is to receive the gospel of the Kingdom and experience its salvation."[38]

---

32. In his thesis, Padilla often acknowledged Dodd, but does not follow him in terms of an eschatological system. See, for example, C. René Padilla, "Church and World: A Study of the Relation between the Church and the World in the Teaching of the Apostle Paul" (PhD diss., University of Manchester, 1965), 178. "Schweitzer, Albert," in *Oxford Dictionary of the Christian Church*, ed. F. L. Cross and E. A. Livingstone (Oxford: Oxford University Press, 1997), 1469.

33. See George M. Marsden, *Reforming Fundamentalism: Fuller Seminary and the New Evangelicalism* (Grand Rapids: Eerdmans, 1987), 69, 120. For more on this book's impact, see D'Elia, *A Place at the Table*, xix, and Stanley, *Global Diffusion of Evangelicalism*, 36–38.

34. Marsden, *Reforming Fundamentalism*, 81, 94. See also 135, 204, 211, and Brian Stanley, "Evangelical Social and Political Ethics: An Historical Perspective," *Evangelical Quarterly* 62 (1990): 33.

35. George Eldon Ladd, *Jesus and the Kingdom: The Eschatology of Biblical Realism* (New York: Harper & Row, 1964), xiv.

36. See, for example, George Eldon Ladd, *The Presence of the Future: The Eschatology of Biblical Realism* (Grand Rapids: Eerdmans, 1974), 39, 160, 167–68, 177, 179, 208, 211, 262, 279, 306, 308, 314, 319, 323, 342.

37. Ladd, *Jesus and the Kingdom*, 334.

38. Ladd, *The Presence of the Future*, 203; Padilla, *Mission between the Times*, 95.

Padilla relegated his discussion of the kingdom of God almost entirely to the final two chapters of his thesis—due, in part, to its focus on ecclesiology. In chapter 5, Padilla channeled Ladd's language of *between the times* to speak of the eschatological character of the kingdom of God: "She [the church] looks back to the incarnation and forward to the parousia, and lives 'between the times.'"[39]

The final chapter, which opens under the heading "between the times," is a thematic break from the rest of the thesis, moving from theology to ethics.[40] One might expect to find integral mission themes, given the narrative surrounding the thesis. Yet, rather than containing a fledgling social theology, Padilla's writing fits well within his contemporary conservative evangelical biblical framework. Here, Padilla saw any attempt by the church to reform existing social structures as a dangerous slackening in the eschatological tension of the kingdom of God.[41]

Perhaps the most unique feature of integral mission is its understanding of social ethics as *part* of the gospel, rather than an implication of it (the primary understanding of social ethics within postwar evangelicalism).[42] Yet careful attention to Padilla's social ethics here reveals he had not yet discovered this contribution.[43] Similarly, Padilla spoke of an expanded gospel within his thesis. Yet, what he included in terms of its "wider dimensions" was not social, but rather an ethical separation from worldliness. He wrote, Christians "have their homeland in heaven and this 'otherworldliness' . . . is an integral part of the Gospel."[44]

Padilla had thus discovered the eschatological tension of the "already and the not yet," but had not yet applied it to the fields of social ethics and missions in the way he would from 1974 onward.[45] In contrast, in his PhD thesis, he was still utilizing this eschatological

---

39. Padilla, "Church and World," 190.
40. Ibid., 210.
41. Ibid., 258.
42. See, for example, Gary F. VanderPol, "The Least of These: American Evangelical Parachurch Missions to the Poor, 1947–2005" (ThD diss., Boston University, 2010), 8.
43. Padilla, "Church and World," 245–46.
44. Ibid., 218.
45. See, for example, C. René Padilla, "Luz del mundo, sal de la tierra," *Misión* 8 (1989): editorial.

tension of the kingdom to rebuke those attempting to work toward social transformation.

This literary analysis has revealed that Padilla's thesis cannot be given credit for the genesis of his social theology. It did, however, provide theological ideas *en embryo* which, when fully formed, would serve a critical function within integral mission. In his PhD research, Padilla, through his reading of Ladd, had come to a realization that the kingdom of God was "the heart of [Jesus'] proclamation and the key to his entire ministry."[46] Ladd's phrase "between the times" also later became part of the title of Padilla's *Mission between the Times: Essays on the Kingdom*. The Spanish phrase for "mission between the times" is *misión integral*.

From Ladd, Padilla gained the eschatological framework of the kingdom of God, which would provide the central, organizing principle for his theology of the kingdom. Yet to apply these realities to the Latin American context, Padilla, along with an entire generation of Latin American Protestant evangelicals, found critical congruence with the work of Scottish theologian John A. Mackay.

## Padilla and the Latin American Missionary Context: John A. Mackay's Call for Contextualization

The decades of the 1930s and 1940s represented an intellectual low-water mark for evangelicalism in many parts of the world.[47] Though there were many individual exceptions, Scotland largely stood alone in terms of a robust theological development due to "the combined influence of a dominant Reformed tradition and an unrivalled system of public education."[48] This intellectual tradition, combined with a vigorous missionary-sending culture, produced influence around the world that was disproportional to its size.[49] Most importantly for

46. Padilla, "Church and World," 179. See also Ladd, *The Presence of the Future*, 139; Padilla, *Mission between the Times*, 89.
47. Joel A. Carpenter, *Revive Us Again: The Reawakening of American Fundamentalism* (New York: Oxford University Press, 1997), 244–45.
48. Stanley, *Global Diffusion of Evangelicalism*, 93.
49. For more on the Scottish missionary diaspora, see Andrew F. Walls, *The Cross-Cultural Process in*

purposes here, Scotland provided the foremost Protestant evangelical theologian in Latin America in the first half of the twentieth century: John A. Mackay (1889–1983).

Mackay grew up in the Free Presbyterian Church in Inverness, Scotland, later becoming a missionary of the Free Church of Scotland to Latin America during 1916-1932—though he often visited after his missionary tenure.[50] Mackay studied at the University of Aberdeen, where he earned an honors degree in 1913. He was involved significantly with the Student Volunteer Movement at Princeton Theological Seminary in New Jersey, where he graduated in 1915.[51] After a productive missionary career in Latin America, Mackay was eventually recruited to lead his alma mater Princeton Theological Seminary as president, being formally installed on February 2, 1937.

Mackay's life and work influenced an entire generation of Latin American Protestant evangelical thinkers. They found in Mackay a rare bridge between faithfulness to the Latin American context and to their understanding of evangelical orthodoxy. In a 2013 interview, the researcher asked Samuel Escobar about the progression of understanding social action as not only an *implication* of the gospel message, but *inherent* within it. Escobar was unequivocal: "I believe this is part of the heritage of Mackay." Escobar expanded:

> This had a strong influence, I believe, *possibly in René [Padilla] too*, in my understanding that the idea of loving neighbor and serving as an essential [*constitutiva*] part of the message of the gospel—it wasn't added. So the polemic was always for North American missionaries, and for many pastors, it wasn't part of the gospel. So, in this sense, I believe that we received an inheritance from Mackay.[52]

Elsewhere, Escobar was explicit with regard to Mackay's influence on

---

*Christian History: Studies in the Transmission and Appropriation of Faith* (Maryknoll, NY: Orbis, 2002), 259–72.

50. The definitive biography of Mackay was written by his grandson. John Mackay Metzger, *The Hand and the Road: The Life and Times of John A. Mackay* (Louisville: Westminster John Knox, 2010). See Samuel Escobar, "Legacy of John Alexander Mackay," *International Bulletin of Missionary Research* 16 (1992): 116–17.

51. R. Wilson Stanton, "Studies in the Life and Work of an Ecumenical Churchman" (Princeton Theological Seminary, 1958), 13. Escobar, "Legacy of John Alexander Mackay," 116.

52. Interview of Samuel Escobar by author, Valencia, Spain, October 22, 2013.

his colleagues: "The writings of Latin American ecumenical theologians like Emilio Castro and José Míguez Bonino, or evangelicals like René Padilla and Pedro Arana, show Mackay's pervasive influence."[53] Escobar was not alone in giving Mackay credit for catalyzing social theology. In a 2014 interview, Pedro Arana, successor to Padilla as general secretary for Latin America with IFES, also gave (unprompted) credit to Mackay for providing the category of an expanded gospel message.[54]

In Mackay's most famous work, *The Other Spanish Christ* (1932), he decried a foreign Jesus being imported to Latin America, and declared the pressing need for replacing imported theology with contextual theology and national leadership.[55] Padilla described the book as "an outstanding example of the sort of apologetics that evangelical theologians felt compelled to articulate in the face of Roman Catholic hegemonic power in Latin America."[56] Padilla expanded, "This book became a classic and is still regarded as one of the best explanations of the *raison d'entre'e* [sic] of Protestant Christianity in a Roman Catholic continent."[57] Mackay also saw theological education as a mission field, arguing that theology must be contextualized for Latin Americans to truly grasp Christ.[58] Early in his own career, Padilla noted that Mackay influenced his understanding of the need for Latin American theological education led by Latin Americans themselves—an emphasis that became one of Padilla's enduring legacies.[59] Yet, as Arana and Escobar

---

53. Escobar, "Legacy of John Alexander Mackay," 116. For another mention of Mackay's influence on Padilla, see Allen Yeh, "Se Hace Camino al Andar: Periphery and Center in the Missiology of Orlando E. Costas" (DPhil thesis, University of Oxford, 2008), 78, 81. For Escobar, see especially, Escobar, "The Legacy of John Alexander Mackay." See also Samuel Escobar, "Doing Theology on Christ's Road," in *Global Theology in Evangelical Perspective : Exploring the Contextual Nature of Theology and Mission*, ed. Jeffrey P. Greenman and Gene L. Green (Downers Grove, IL: IVP Academic, 2012), 71.

54. Skype interview of Pedro Arana by author, translated by author, March 11, 2014.

55. John Alexander Mackay, *The Other Spanish Christ: A Study in the Spiritual History of Spain and South America* (London: SCM, 1932), 95.

56. C. René Padilla, "Evangelical theology in Latin American contexts," in *The Cambridge Companion to Evangelical Theology*, ed. Timothy Larsen and Daniel J. Treier (Cambridge: Cambridge University Press, 2007), 261.

57. Ibid.

58. Mackay, *The Other Spanish Christ*, 262.

59. C. René Padilla, "A Steep Climb Ahead for Theology in Latin America," *Evangelical Missions Quarterly* 7 (1971): 41.

wrote above, Mackay's contribution in terms of the social element in the gospel is foremost here. In *The Other Spanish Christ*, Mackay discovered that the kingdom of God had personal as well as social elements. Mackay wrote, "Jesus' concept of the Kingdom of God had a social as well as a personal aspect. It was a state of society as well as a state of the soul."[60] Thus, while Padilla discovered the importance of the kingdom of God through the influence of neo-evangelicals such as Ladd, he applied the kingdom in a personal way through the influence of thinkers such as Mackay. Mackay and Padilla shared the resource of the Latin American context—Mackay wrote *The Other Spanish Christ* from Mexico City, Mexico. Because of this shared resource and Mackay's unique cultural sensitivity, his writing gained broad acceptance.

From 1970 onward, Padilla increasingly addressed contextual realities within his social location. In doing so, his writing shows clear continuity with the emphases of Mackay. In his controversial Lausanne plenary paper, Padilla wrote, "Those of us who live in the Third World cannot and should not be satisfied with the rote repetition of doctrinal formulas or the indiscriminate application of canned methods of evangelization imported from the West."[61] The following year, he first utilized the phrase "the contextualization of the gospel" at an international consultation on evangelical literature in Latin America. The influence of Mackay is again manifest in his words: "It must be admitted that the total panorama of the Church in the Third World continues to be that of a church without theology . . . there is no hope that this situation will change as long as the missions' theological responsibility is conceived of as the exportation of theologies elaborated in the West. Especially in the fields of theological education. And as long as the gospel does not attain a profound contextualization in the local culture, in the eyes of people in that culture it will continue to be a 'foreign religion.'[62]

Continuity with Mackay's emphases also surfaced at the first

---

60. Mackay, *The Other Spanish Christ*, 210.
61. C. René Padilla, *The New Face of Evangelicalism: An International Symposium on the Lausanne Covenant* (Downers Grove, IL: InterVarsity Press, 1976), 140.

gathering of the International Fellowship of Evangelical Mission Theologians (INFEMIT)—a missiological network formed in reaction to the 1980 Lausanne consultation in Pattaya, Thailand, where many Majority World theologians objected to a perceived disregard for the social emphases from the Lausanne Covenant of 1974. At INFEMIT in 1982, Padilla wrote, "The images of Jesus Christ imported from the West into the Two Thirds World are inadequate for the life and mission of the Church in situations of poverty and injustice."[63] Such laments at the isolation of evangelical theology from the daily realities of Latin American life and the importation of a "foreign religion" demonstrate clear continuity with Mackay's emphases. Padilla ultimately channeled this global conversation into contextual Protestant evangelical theological production in Latin America.

### Padilla and the Latin American Theological Fraternity: Defining the Theology of a Movement

In 1972, René Padilla relayed the importance of the kingdom of God to the Latin American Theological Fraternity (LATF)—an influential Latin American Protestant evangelical think tank founded in 1970, launching a theological project that would define the theological movement of contextual evangelical Latin American theology. During December 11–18, 1972, twenty-seven Latin American evangelical leaders gathered at Seminario Bíblico in Lima, Peru, for the second consultation of the FTL under the theme of "The Kingdom of God and Latin America." Padilla's paper at the second consultation of the FTL, titled "The Kingdom of God and the Church," marked the first occasion on which Padilla publicly expounded his understanding of the kingdom of God after engaging academically with the concept in his PhD thesis. Padilla not only shared his discovery with his Latin American colleagues, but

---

62. C. René Padilla, "The Contextualization of the Gospel," *Journal of Theology for Southern Africa* 24 (1978): 22. This was a published version of his speech.
63. Vinay Samuel and Chris Sugden, eds., *Sharing Jesus in the Two Thirds World: Evangelical Christologies from the Contexts of Poverty, Powerlessness, and Religious Pluralism: The Papers of the First Conference of Evangelical Mission Theologians from the Two Thirds World, Bangkok, Thailand, March 22–25, 1982* (Grand Rapids: Eerdmans, 1984), 217.

his writing here formed the basis of a significant portion of "The Mission of the Church in Light of the Kingdom of God"—the final chapter of his masterwork *Mission between the Times.*[64]

In sharing his theology of the kingdom, Padilla drew heavily on his PhD research. Indeed, the influence of Ladd permeates the paper, both through its framing as "already" and "not yet" and through translating Ladd into Spanish.[65] In doing so, Padilla also applied these concepts to unique realities within the Latin American context.[66] He sought a middle way between two opposing sides in Latin America: the dispensational, future-oriented eschatology of the kingdom (represented here by Emilio Nuñez's paper) and the "realized eschatology" of many liberation theologians and participants in the World Council of Churches which was associated with Church and Society in Latin America (*Iglesia y Sociedad en América Latina*, or ISAL).

For the first time, Padilla also expounded his view that the mission of the church finds its nexus in the kingdom of God: "The 'already' of the kingdom of God defines the mission of the Church."[67] This all occurs "between the times of Jesus Christ, between the initial fulfillment and the fullness"—probably the first published mention of Padilla's organizing principle.[68]

Above everything, Padilla later recalled the FTL event as "important" due to "the rediscovery of the centrality of the kingdom of God in the life and ministry of Jesus Christ."[69] Escobar credited Padilla with sharing this concept: "René communicated to us an insistence on his new perspective of the eschatological structure of the New Testament message."[70] This newfound emphasis on eschatological

---

64. C. René Padilla, "*La misión de la iglesia a la luz del Reino de Dios,*" Misión 5 (1986): 122–29.
65. C. René Padilla, "El reino de Dios y la iglesia," in *El reino de Dios y América Latina,* ed. C. René Padilla (El Paso, TX: Casa Bautista Publicaciones, 1975), 8, 44. Padilla, "Church and World," 61, 178. He also interacted with Schnackenburg throughout, but diverged from him on significant passages. For example, Padilla viewed the phrase "fellow-workers for the Kingdom of God" in Col 4:11 as being *present* while Schnackenburg referred to it as *future* (p. 182). Padilla followed him elsewhere (ibid., 184, 199).
66. C. René Padilla, "The Kingdom of God and the Church," *Theological Fraternity Bulletin* 1-2 (1976): 13.
67. Emilio Antonio Nuñez C., "Testigo de un nuevo amanecer," in *Hacia una teología evangélica latinoamericana: ensayos en honor de Pedro Savage,* ed. C. René Padilla (Miami: Editorial Caribe, 1984).
68. Padilla, "El reino de Dios y la iglesia," 53, 57.
69. Ibid., 61.
70. Padilla, *Mission between the Times,* 72, 88–91, 95, 98, 200–201.

tension and the centrality of the Kingdom of God would define both Padilla's theology and the future trajectory of Latin American contextual evangelical theology.[71]

## Conclusion

This chapter has attempted to situate Padilla's theology of the kingdom and understanding of the contextualization of the gospel within its intellectual and theological context. Integral mission was deeply rooted in Latin America and sprang from contextual realities that were unique to this social location. The toolkit, however, from which Padilla drew his contribution was the result of a global conversation that took place within conservative evangelical circles in the second half of the twentieth century. The contours of Padilla's contextualization were initially formed through the mentorship and writings of Wheaton College professor Arthur F. Holmes. Padilla also drew extensively from the work of George Eldon Ladd and his theology of the kingdom, which he discovered in the course of his PhD research at Manchester. Thus Padilla was not unique in his recovery of the kingdom of God as an organizing principle, but was part of a larger intellectual trend that took place around him—particularly in North America. Padilla's writing also found critical continuity with the work of Scottish theologian John Mackay, who decried the importation of foreign theologies and called for the development of contextual ideas and national leadership. In doing so, Mackay influenced an entire generation of Latin American Protestant evangelical thinkers.

This chapter has not attributed his theology to purely Western theological influences or sought to export the credit for the rise of social theology within Latin America to sources within the North. Nor has it provided an exhaustive list of intellectual influences on Padilla. For example, further research is needed on the contribution of American Mennonite theologian John Howard Yoder and Padilla's wife and closest colleague Catharine Feser Padilla. Nevertheless, this

---

71. Padilla, "My Theological Pilgrimage," 104.

chapter has unearthed the extent to which Padilla's formulation of integral mission drew on eclectic theological resources as well as on the Latin American context. The origins of integral mission were, from its earliest stages, grounded in a global dialogue as diverse as evangelicalism itself. These origins reflect Padilla's own journey—global in scope, contextual in impetus and application. This provides a helpful corrective to the current historiography on Latin American Protestant evangelical social theology, which has described this conversation as unidirectional.

Regardless of the efficacy of integral mission as a theological concept, this recognition of multidirectional conversation may provide a way forward in our increasingly diverse world. For the theologian, it is a striking reminder of the need for the inclusion of diverse voices within theological dialogue and development. To editors and publishers, it is a gentle critique of the continued lack of attention to world Christianity within Western theological discourse. To educators, it is an encouragement to foster learning environments that welcome diverse voices and backgrounds.

12

———

# Embodiment as Social Healing between the Church and LGBT Community

## Andrew Marin

I am intensely convinced that all persons of Christian conviction are theologically obligated to at least initiate the pursuit of social healing with their other.[1] I especially believe this to be true within the contemporary disconnect between the church and lesbian, gay, bisexual, and transgender (LGBT) community.[2] Even if the core perceptions of this disconnect are rooted in dual intercommunity rationales that self-justify one specific worldview against the other,

---

1. Practicing social reconciliation through: (1) social humility when being sinned against (Matt 5:38–42; Phil 2:3–4); (2) taking upon oneself another's sins (Gal 6:1–2; Phil 8–21); and (3) social congruency between the belief and practice of love (2 Cor 5:18–19; Col 3:12–17; 1 John 2:9–11).
2. For the argument's readability, I delineate between the church and LGBT community. However, I am acutely aware these are not mutually exclusive categories. There are various extremes and shades of progressive, moderate, and conservative Christians who identify from LGBT to heterosexual.

traumatic experiences[3] continually leave members of each community with unwanted experiences, memories, and stunted relational engagement with their other.[4]

Whether or not these perceptions or experiences are substantiated in the lives of everyone constituting the disconnect, it is ultimately of less consequence than the mandate for Christ followers of any sexual orientation to take the first step toward bringing social healing with their other. Because of this conviction I, a heterosexual Christian, spent over a decade intentionally living in the Boystown neighborhood of Chicago, one of the world's largest contingencies of LGBT persons. My life and mission in Boystown facilitated reconciliation between the LGBT community and social, political, and religious conservatives through a public charity I created called The Marin Foundation (TMF).[5] Rather than reflecting missiologically on that decade of work, I have been asked as a systematician to theologically reflect on TMF's missiological engagement instantiated in a very unique moment in history.

TMF's infancy was in the early 2000s, situated in a cultural and political landscape already relegated archaic by contemporary life. As recent as ten years ago, there was no such thing as legalized same-sex marriage (SSM) in America. In recent years, however, the United States Supreme Court constitutionally struck the Defense of Marriage Act[6] in 2013, and, during the editing of this chapter, in 2015, ruled same-sex couples can legally marry within all fifty states. Dramatic shifts are similarly happening in Britain. In the span of just over one month in early 2014, Scotland, England, and Wales all legalized SSM. With each of these declarative societal movements, the church, its tradition, and

---

3. This chapter's use of "trauma," "perpetrator," "perpetration," "perpetrated," and "victim" do not necessarily reflect acts of violence. They reference any agent involved in anything that results in prolonged dissension between the agent and another person, institution, or system; including arguments, being labeled "the other," or cyber-bullying, among others.

4. Cognitive findings suggest the negative effects associated with physical or emotional trauma act as a formative core to the experience's subsequent memory, making said memory highly durable and immutable to dissolution. Martin Conway, *Flashbulb Memories* (Oxford: Psychology Press, 1995), 113–14.

5. See Andrew Marin, *Love Is an Orientation: Elevating the Conversation with the Gay Community* (Downers Grove, IL: InterVarsity Press, 2009).

6. Defining a legal marriage as solely between one man and one woman.

millennia of teaching have been placed under a multisided crucible of pronouncement to pick only one side, and subsequently forsake the other.[7] Pejorative assertions such as who is already *on the right side of history* are no longer for historians to debate, but normative public declarations.

Whose history, I wonder? And what consensus has been reached to who contemporarily dictates future interpretations? The answers just depend on who is asked.

This chapter, then, will theologically reflect on ecclesial engagement within the ever-changing and often contentious realities of mission in postmodern, pluralistic cultures. Although the following can be generalized to a variety of global ecclesial disconnects, I will specifically focus on the Western church, utilizing TMF's experiences within the LGBT and religious-conservative (for example, church) disconnect as theological grounding for the contemporary praxis of embodiment as social healing.

## Defining Embodiment

The act of forgiveness is widely accepted as *the* main facilitator to a process of social healing between disparate persons, people groups, and worldviews.[8] Though I agree forgiveness is significant, my experience through TMF has shown, time and again, that forgiveness is the second installation to the broader two-part process of social healing. Before forgiveness can take root, an agent must first socially, emotionally, cognitively, and spiritually embody their experienced trauma such that their trauma becomes a remembered, integrated part of their post-trauma identity. Only after can forgiveness sustainably flow through an agent's post-trauma reality to the extent that it initiates their will to engage in a process of social healing with their perpetrator. The fact remains there can be short-term (or even forced)

---

7. For a framework of social change seeking institutional reconciliation around such topics as same-sex marriage, see Andrew Marin, *Our Last Option: How a New Approach to Civility Can Save the Public Square* (ebook) (Colorado Springs: Patheos, 2013).

8. Desmond Tutu, *No Future without Forgiveness* (Kindle version) (New York: Doubleday, 2009), locations 3,589–3,598.

forgiveness without embodiment,[9] but there cannot be a victim's formation of their socially healed post-trauma identity without a sustained work of embodiment playing a central role.

The generational ineffectiveness of a number of global Truth and Reconciliation Commissions (TRC) are justification for such a claim. Within one generation, high-level works of systemic reconciliation have ended up in a reverse recycling of trauma. Forgiveness, which can be easily regulated and quickly implemented, has consistently been politically substituted for the impossible-to-regulate unseen realms, that embodiment addresses.[10] And through a hurried conjoining of politics and religious necessity, the original TRC victims were set up for failure. They were never going to be able to sustain the type of public forgiveness their government demanded of them, because they were not given the tools or time to embody a process of healing created through a post-trauma integration of the trauma itself.[11] Forgiveness was commanded; not felt, remembered, and embodied.

Just the same, the original TRC perpetrators did not willfully recognize their forced public "apology" as a legitimate conciliatory expression of their perpetration.[12] Without the victims or perpetrators embodying the trauma received or caused, the outcome is consistent, no matter the country or scenario—original victims still feel perpetrated against, and eventually act out in anger against their original perpetrators, who still feel no remorse. Thus, forced political forgiveness leads the perpetrated to becoming the new perpetrator.[13] Yet, within any situation of experienced trauma, the act and even the concept of forgiveness must give way to the work of embodiment for any hope of sustained social healing.

Embodiment, then, is traditionally regarded as the physical body's

---

9. Like such ineradicable pop theology phrases as "forgive and forget." Short-term forgiveness without embodying the trauma is also the reason why systemic recycling of trauma remains a constant threat.

10. Including an agent's emotional, cognitive, and spiritual characteristics. Trudy Govier, *Forgiveness and Revenge* (New York: Routledge, 2011), 142–44.

11. Audrey R. Chapman, "Truth Commissions and Intergroup Forgiveness: The Case of the South African Truth and Reconciliation Commission," *Journal of Peace Psychology* 13 (2007): 56.

12. Ibid., 64.

13. Ibid.

conceptualizations of an agent's surroundings influencing their growing awareness of knowledge and self.[14] Though I believe this is a fundamentally accurate definition, I argue, the fullest extent of embodiment touches all realms of not just humanity's knowledge but its entire existence. In its very nature, embodiment is an ontological outworking of an agent's integration of their whole self into their present reality, including the unwanted realities that come with experienced trauma.

Nancy Eiesland suggests embodiment is more than just "overcoming" experienced trauma. It does not seek to deflect truth, attempt to "pass" as okay, or hunt after "rehabilitative normalization."[15] Embodiment is, rather, the process of an agent's physical, emotional, cognitive, and spiritual integration of their experienced trauma such that the experienced trauma is a reflection of the agent's new post-trauma identity, or their new normal.[16]

I am aware of this definition's contradiction. How can an agent's post-trauma identity be rooted in the trauma itself, yet produce a will to forgive? Or further, a desire to engage in social healing with their perpetrator? I will attempt to answer those questions in light of the disconnect between the church and LGBT community, arguing that regardless of which community is in focus,[17] a theology of embodiment can facilitate social healing through three imperative movements: (1) to begin with proximity; (2) to function in reality; and (3) to practice hope.

## Embodiment Begins with Proximity

The largest scientific research study ever conducted on religion and the LGBT community reports that 86 percent of American LGBT persons attend a religious service, group, or event at least one time per

---

14. Elisabeth Moltmann-Wendel, *I Am My Body* (New York: Continuum, 1995), 103; David Nikkel, *Radical Embodiment* (Eugene, OR: Pickwick, 2010), 74.
15. Nancy Eiesland, *The Disabled God: Toward a Liberatory Theology of Disability* (Nashville: Abingdon, 1994), 117.
16. Ibid., 23.
17. Within the contemporary church and LGBT disconnect, both worldviews claim they are being perpetrated against by the other.

week until the age of eighteen.[18] This total is 11 percent higher than the average American. However, after the age of eighteen, 54 percent leave that religion. Although this finding suggests LGBT persons leave their religious communities double the rate than the average American, an astonishing 76 percent who left still remain open to finding an ecclesial community in the future (with only 8 percent reporting they would solely return to a theologically progressive religious community).[19]

From a missiological perspective, this 76 percent openness rate is significant in its offering of hope for future social relations between the church and LGBT community. However, in real time, it also offers one significant problem to a majority of Western faith communities and denominations, which, according to the Pew Forum on Religion and Public Life, are predominantly conservative evangelical Christian churches.[20] Since so many conservative vangelical churches and denominations are in their own contentious process of missiological adjustment to, around, and within culture's rapidly shifting political and orientational normalcies, they are left unequipped to handle what can externally and intercongregationally arise with a potential resurgence of out-LGBT persons in attendance.

Though this adjustment period might take some time—indeed, longer than some would hope for—the study did find one common thread linking LGBT orientation to the 76 percent who left the church yet are opening to making a return: the more an LGBT person accepts their orientation, the stronger their desire to again participate and belong to the religious community they once left.[21] This correlation is not suggesting the propagated fear that once LGBT people accept their orientation, they also begin identifying as partisan activists, want to

---

18. Andrew Marin (The Marin Foundation), Michael Bailey (Northwestern University), and Mark Yarhouse (Regent University). Andrew Marin, *Us versus Us: The Untold Story of Religion and the LGBT Community* (Colorado Springs: NavPress, 2016).
19. Ibid.
20. Pew Research Center, "The Global Religious Landscape," December 18, 2012, http://www.pewforum.org/2012/12/18/global-religious-landscape-exec (accessed December 29, 2015); Dan Cox, "Young, White, Evangelicals," Pew Research Center, September 28, 2007, http://www.pewresearch.org/2007/09/28/young-white-evangelicals-less-republican-still-conservative/ (accessed December 29, 2015).
21. Marin, *Us versus Us*.

be clergy, or desire to overthrow orthodox theology.[22] Many just want to feel that ever-important connection to God through a reflective process of self-honesty, and thus belong to a community that believes in the same process. This type of existential acceptance is a practical outworking of a person's ontological embodiment of their creation as a child of God. An agent's grasping of the nature of their self in the divine provides the boundaries for their continued acceptance of reality—in this case, being sexually attracted to another person of the same sex in conjunction with the knowledge they are still loved by God.

As this narrative becomes ever more normative,[23] how are ecclesial communities to externally engage with the LGBT community's acceptance of their own orientation, identity, faith, and outward longing to return to and engage with the church? The answer is first found in the church's theology of embodiment, and second, in its physical proximity to the LGBT community through *place*.

A theology of embodiment begins with the belief that all human beings are embodied. Among others, a person's gender, orientation, appearance, mind, body, and spirit are all inherent embodied characteristics, irrevocably tying us to who we are. The result from such a metaphysical yet extremely practical intertwining is the greater force an agent chooses to separate themselves from any of their inherent attributes, the more they are damagingly disconnected from their true self, potential long-term stability, and from the reality, knowledge, and embodied understanding of God in humanity.[24] Therefore, any theological response to identity formation *other than* the church's embodiment of an agent's lived reality drives a clear wedge into the Holy Trinity's provision for humanity to partake.[25]

---

22. Wesley Hill, *Washed and Waiting: Reflections on Christian Faithfulness and Homosexuality* (Grand Rapids: Zondervan, 2010); and Shawn Harrison, *Ministering to Gay Teenagers: A Guide for Youth Workers* (Loveland, CO: Simply Youth Ministry, 2014).

23. Two brief caveats: (1) agreement or disagreement with that conclusion is a secondary issue to the reality of the truth that one is sexually attracted to another of the same sex and they have a faith in God; and (2) an LGBT orientation does not automatically define one's understanding and practice of sexual ethics.

24. Karl Barth, *Church Dogmatics*, vol. III, *The Doctrine of Creation*, pt. 2, ed. Geoffrey W. Bromiley and T. F. Torrance (Edinburgh: T&T Clark, 1960), 46.

25. Due to the limitations of the paper's scope and length, there is a lack of treatment and dialogue

Within the trinitarian narrative of embodiment, God created humans in God's own image.[26] Christ's incarnation through his fleshly birth from a virgin teenage Jewish girl was a literal embodiment into humanity.[27] And finally, the Holy Spirit descended upon humanity, continually working in active ways to implement God's plan in partnership with human creation.[28] In this vein, LGBT Christians' existential and theological embodiment include their orientation as people created in God's image.[29] It is only after this realization that the church, in conjunction with LGBT Christians, should turn its concentration onto the study and reflection of sexual ethics.

The church must be accountable, and hold LGBT persons accountable, to work together in this order. Any reversal directly affects the church's mission received by LGBTs, as it implicitly suggests the church's primary concern is with sexual ethics over an agent's knowledge, understanding, and most importantly, belief in Jesus. As Jack Sanders relates, a church that does not give primacy to one's belief in Christ is misappropriating Christ's ethical and eschatological teachings.[30] With this as the church's existential theological foundation, its next move is through its external work of embodiment with the LGBT community. This happens as the church commits to being in proximity with LGBT persons on their terms. Put another way, the church's mission is to focus on the importance of *place* in regard to their other.

Jesus lived in a first-century system where, like today, having power and being labeled an authority were at a premium. Culturally, the Second Temple period highlighted these modes of influence through both the rabbinical and occupying Roman hierarchies. What sociologically separated Jesus from the aforementioned authorities is that as they were constantly in proximity to what they deemed most

---

with the extensive literature on God's image with humanity, God's covenant with humanity, and God's ongoing work with humanity; including the work of Barth, *Church Dogmatics*, III/2:44–45.

26. Gen 1:27.

27. Isa 7:14; Matt 1:20–23; Heb 2:9.

28. John 14:16–17, 26; 20:22–23; Acts 2:4; Rom 5:5, 8:9, 16–17.

29. There are numerous theories why people have same-sex attractions. The reality is that they are all theories and there is no psychological, biological, or theological consensus.

30. Jack Sanders, *Ethics in the New Testament* (London: SCM, 1975), 96.

important, the temple and government buildings, Jesus was constantly in proximity to what he deemed most important—people. His constant proximity, or practice of place within the masses, among those who both revered and hated him, uniquely positioned Jesus as a formidable social, political, and religious figure.[31] For the first time, this suggested that a commitment to external proximity had more temporal leverage than anyone gave it credit.

Contemporary missiology views a commitment to proximity as a tool for evangelistic credibility. Though correct, I feel it is missing the important ramifications of place. No different from the example above, intentional engagement in proximity to one's other has more contemporary social, political, and religious leverage than anyone gives it credit. Since 2009, TMF has regularly been brought in to assist the United Nations, White House, US Congress, Department of State, among others, because by their own admission, TMF is actually able to build bridges through our commitment to place—rather than theorizing from the outside how others should be able to build bridges.

Over a decade of commitment in local proximity within this very real social, political, and religious disconnect has tangibly affected both the individual and systemic relations of Chicago's ecclesial and LGBT communities. TMF's engagement through place took a small, underresourced, unheard-of public charity to directly advising world leaders. It is *because* Chicago's ecclesial and LGBT communities sustainably engage *with* each other in new and unique ways through TMF that local, national, and international credibility was earned. I am not recounting any of this to prop up my charity's work, but rather because I believe such a platform was given to TMF solely because of the importance we put on place. Place means that our life, work, mission, and love cannot be separated from who we are as agents for Christ's work of social healing between disparate communities.

What requisitely makes this so hard is the work of place functions

---

31. Jesus's miracles did initiate much of the original wonderment of the masses. However, his disciples and later apostles carried on the same practice of proximity with the masses, sans miracles, and yet had the same formidable cultural, political, and religious influence (and received-persecution) as Jesus.

in real life, where nothing is ever totally arbitrary.[32] Over two billion people around the world look to find stability and their "whole" through a radically embodied church *in* the world. At the same time, *in* the world is fueled by postmodern assumptions based on a deconstructive lens assessing even the most certain of truths.[33] Therefore, the church cannot effectively practice an existential or external theology of embodiment of place without also being able to highly function in close proximity within a diverse, and sometimes disagreeable, set of realities.

## Embodiment Functions in Reality[34]

I have no interest in philosophically debating the boundaries of reality. I am concerned with how traumatic events influence temporal thoughts, perceptions, and memories, all of which greatly influence people and the church's mission. Epidemiological studies report that over 50 percent of women and 60 percent of men experience at least one traumatic event in their lives.[35] For all the years of training clergy receive in how to research and deliver a sermon, few, if any, are taught how to theologically or practically handle the unstoppable storage of trauma in human memory—the same remembrance that irrevocably ties the victim to the exact trauma they long to forget.[36]

Yet reality proves that experienced trauma can never be unexperienced. Psychologists C. J. Rathbone, C. J. Mouline, and M. A. Conway bluntly state that autobiographical memories are the basis for one's sense of self.[37] For each of the polarities of good and evil that inhabit memory, one cannot be fully human without them. As

---

32. Nikkel, *Radical Embodiment*, 56.
33. Ibid., 64.
34. I first explored a framework of this section in Andrew Marin, "Pastoral Care to Those Suffering from Traumatic Memories," *Bible in Transmission* (2014): 24–26.
35. Daniel Schacter, *The Seven Sins of Memory: How the Mind Forgets and Remembers* (New York: Houghton Mifflin, 2001), 174.
36. Moving forward I am defining *LGBT-church trauma* as the negative emotional, spiritual, and relational events that are cognitively ingrained to the point of being self-identified as abuse (which does not necessarily reference the classic understanding of physical or sexual abuse).
37. C. J. Rathbone, C. J. Moulin, and M. A. Conway, "Autobiographical Memory and Amnesia: Using Conceptual Knowledge to Ground the Self," *Neurocase* 15 (2009): 405.

straightforward as that sounds, most problematic to social healing is Daniel Schacter's cognitive research suggesting the human brain is not able to forget a memory of experienced trauma.[38] In addition, any attempts to avoid or forget traumatic memories (which is, by far, the most frequently attempted coping mechanism) only *further ingrain* the unwanted memories into the forefront of one's consciousness.[39] Therefore, post-trauma consciousness is shaped by two major processes during the brain's formation of memory.

First, during the event itself, as the perpetrated's brain is autonomically forming a short-term memory, one of the most crucial and permanent physiologically and psychologically altering moments occurs: the memory is assigned an emotional context. Once assigned, that emotion and its context of the place(s), person(s), reaction(s), and object(s) involved in the trauma are *indelibly linked to that memory*. When triggered during post-trauma, these indelibly linked emotions show absolutely no reactionary difference in transporting the perpetrated back to their original trauma, even when compared against image-based memories.[40]

Second, the climax of memory retention is reached when the brain *biologically changes* by chemically adapting itself to the experienced trauma solidified into long-term memory.[41] The human brain has no choice in this matter. For better or worse, the retentive process of autonomic memory irrevocably changes and shapes human consciousness.

The irony of such cognitive solidification is that memory is generally bad at its purposed function: "remembering." The percentages of memory's general accuracy range from 65 percent on the high end to 15 percent on the low. These percentages plummet to a dismal 9 percent accuracy when one attempts to correctly recall trauma.[42] This suggests with time, "memory" is only a shell of the original event.

---

38. Schacter, *Seven Sins of Memory*, 183.
39. Ibid., 176.
40. Conway, *Flashbulb Memories*, 95–96.
41. Ibid., 103.
42. Hajime Otani et al., "Emotion, Directed Forgetting, and Source Memory," *British Journal of Psychology* 103 (2012): 343.

Unintentional as it is, if facets of remembered "truth" are corrupted, what is actually being remembered?

Memory, then, must be placed in its proper context. It is an identity-shaping, inaccurate at best, ingrained tool of linked emotions and images that are very real, and yet can be extremely misleading. In this definition, I am not suggesting those who experience trauma do not remember the experience, feelings, and ramifications of their trauma. They most certainly do! What I am suggesting is the formation of memory retention is so unpredictable that the process of post-trauma healing has to begin with an agent's current cognitive understanding of reality in relation to their trauma, whatever that reality looks like.

Thus, the church's agreement or disagreement with certain LGBT perceptions of the church, exegetical interpretations, or systemic ecclesial or cultural involvement are all secondary issues to the church functioning in the LGBT person's reality. As Jesus exemplified through his frequent engagements with those deemed his other, his close involvement in their reality did not threaten for one second the strength of his convictions. What Jesus did was radically embody his other's reality as a faithful act of mission by engaging in the frameworks presented to him, whether he agreed or disagreed. This work foreshadowed core missiological engagement throughout the New Testament[43] and, in my view, the best of contemporary cultural engagement.

### Embodiment Practices Hope

The final movement to practicing a theology of embodiment as social healing centers on the temporal practice of eschatological hope. Miroslav Volf defines eschatology as the triune God's final reconciliation with humanity and humanity's temporal work, culminating in each's purification within the new creation.[44] He theorizes that in the eschaton, God's love will ultimately cause the

---

43. Among other petitions for the same type of engagement: Rom 13:1–3, 5–7, 15:2; 2 Cor 1:5–11; 5:19; Gal 5:13–15; 6:1–5; Eph 4:1–7, 12–13, 29–32; Phil 2:3–4; Col 3:12–14; 4:1, 5; 1 Thess 4:11–12; 1 Tim 1:3–7; 6:1–2; Titus 2:2, 8, 10; 3:1–2; James 2:10, 18; 3:18; 4:11–17; 1 Pet 2:13–17, 23; 3:8–12; 4:8–10; 1 John 2:9–11; 4:20–21.

resurrected to "forget" their traumatic memories as the "last obstacle to an unhindered final reconciliation."[45]

Volf justifies temporal impact from eschatological forgetting by working backward from God's eternal love as the goal for Christians' temporal worldview, believing that eschatology flows from creation's perfect inheritance onto humanity's temporal situations and out-looks.[46] Therefore, he sees a direct correlation between eschatological hope and a reshaped temporal identity, through the temporal know-ledge of eschatological "non-remembrance," providing a hopeful separation from the experienced trauma.[47] This gives those perpetrated against needed reprieve as they attempt to ingrain the hope inherited from the Crucified.[48]

Volf's explanatory process highlights four central questions: (1) Do God's essential attributes include the doctrine of "forgetting"? (2) Does God's love within the eschaton dismiss humanity's temporal toil with trauma by God's forgetting, who then forces forgetfulness upon humanity? (3) Does Scripture theologically promote eschatological forgetting as the final qualification to perfect forgiving? And (4) does the combination of these three ultimately provide humanity with a reshaped temporal identity through eschatological hope? Although exploring each theme is not possible in the constraints of the current chapter, I will briefly respond to Volf's presuppositions in a three-tiered theological progression.

First, God's essential attributes of eternity and omniscience explain who God is in relation to knowledge. Because an eternal and all-knowing God does not make a "choice" to "remember" or "forget," Volf's forgetting exegesis[49] ultimately lacks dimension. I use such a

---

44. Miroslav Volf, Exclusion and Embrace: A Theological Exploration of Identity, Otherness, and Reconciliation (Nashville: Abingdon, 1996), 109–10.

45. Ibid., 140.

46. Ibid., 124, 277.

47. Miroslav Volf, The End of Memory: Remembering Rightly in a Violent World (Grand Rapids: Eerdmans, 2006), 198–99.

48. Ibid., 21.

49. Cf. Isa 43:18–19, 25; 65:17–18; and Jer 31:34. Though Volf's theory has merit in his understanding of God's perfect eschatological community of love, his conclusion of the "final reconciliation" is that God will simply forget humanity's sins and also wash away all of the resurrected's traumatic memories (ibid., 171).

descriptor because Scripture's forgetting texts cannot be substituted for the commonly accepted contemporary Western understanding of what it means "to forget" (for example, I forgot what I did a week ago; I forgot your name; I do not remember doing xyz, and others),[50] which is how Volf defines, uses, and justifies forgetfulness in his theology of hope.[51]

Volf's singularly quoted Old Testament references to "forgetting"[52] cannot be generalized as a temporal *or* eschatological theology of knowledge. Forgetfulness in the Old Testament's prophetic books is more nuanced and contextualized than the contemporary Western definition. Paul Hanson argues that Old Testament references to forgetting fall under the umbrella of God's covenant being fulfilled through God's "memory-then-action commands."[53] In these commands, forgetting is not about non-remembrance. It is about the Israelites remembering the past so as to grasp the overwhelming nature of God's grace with past sins. Thus the Israelites are able to move forward in faith into God's new work.[54]

Second, the Israelites, work of temporally fulfilling God's memory-then-action commands are simultaneously fulfilling their temporal requirement for hope. Their tangible work toward hope in the present through God's directional instructions are leading them into their fulfillment of God's covenant promises.[55] Insofar as the Israelites continue moving in God's new opportunities (for example, forgetting

---

50. Which is quite misleading to the everyday person of Christian conviction reading popular contemporary Bible translations.
51. Including a lengthy argument in *The End of Memory* (152–76) on the merits and applicability of Sigmund Freud's theories justifying forgetting, which psychodynamically have been clinically proven inaccurate decades ago. Ronald Comer, *Abnormal Psychology*, 8th ed. (New York: Worth Publishers, 2013), 53.
52. Isa 43:18–19, 25; 65:17–18; and Jer 31:34.
53. Defined as God stifling the Israelites' over-nostalgic affinity to tradition and the past, which threatens to bind them to the point of unresponsiveness to God's new opportunities. These memory-then-action commands are most directly highlighted in Isa 43:18–19 and 65:17–18. Paul Hanson, *Isaiah 40–66* (Louisville: John Knox, 1995), 71.
54. Ibid.
55. Each reference to God "forgetting" in the Old Testament is not insular. They are God's presuppositions to God's people accepting their new exilic reality (instead of negatively lingering on the past; for example, "forget the past!"), learning how to settle in their new land and promote peace (see Isa 65:16–19; Jer 29:1–14; 31:31–34). Ibid, 73.

the past),[56] all their temporal toil is not done in vain and will not be eschatologically forgotten.[57]

The same hopeful impact of God's eschatological remembrance will protectively frame an agent's temporal cognitive outlook, work, and spiritual hope as they engage in the process of forming their new post-trauma identity. By imbuing their work of traumatic embodiment through God's memory-then-action commands (for example, embodying the toil to free themselves to move into God's new opportunities), an agent has confidence their experienced trauma integrated into their new post-trauma identity will also not be forgotten, but eschatologically remembered in love by God. In this view, an agent's temporal remembrance of the experienced trauma and subsequent embodying process of a post-trauma identity *is* both the temporal and eschatological fulfillment of God's memory of God's covenant in hope and love.[58]

Third, in briefly exploring Christ's life, betrayal, death, resurrection, and ascension, I argue Christ's temporal and eschatological embodiment of remembrance more directly instills temporal hope in an agent's post-trauma identity formation than does Volf's eschatological transition to forgetfulness.

While praying in Gethsemane, Jesus embodied the immanent bloody, torturous, spat-upon, and unimaginably painful reality, regardless of the fact that he did not want to partake in any of the forthcoming evil (Matt 26:38; cf. Heb 5:7–8).

During Jesus's betrayal, he acknowledged what must happen while submitting to embody the torture that lay ahead (Matt 26:50).

While hanging on the cross, Jesus embodied, literally, the trauma forced upon him while offering divine hope to another sharing in this torture (Luke 23:43).

As Christ's resurrection validated death's defeat, the proof of his embodied remembrance of torture was physically scarred into his body by

---

56. Isa 43:18–19.
57. Heb 6:10–11.
58. Deut 6:20–25; 8:1–11.

> the nail holes in his hands and feet, and the puncture of the spear's blade in his side (John 20:26–27).

> Christ did not forget his temporal trauma in his ascension to heaven, but is able to act as humanity's High Priest *through* remembrance of the crucifixion (Heb 4:14–5:3, 7–8).

Thus Christ did not "forget" his temporal experiences in his temporal, resurrected, or ascended states. What Christ did was fully integrate his temporal experiences *into* his resurrected body, embodying his temporal trauma within the larger eschatological narrative. In its simplest form, what is the point of eschatologically forgetting if one is not able to remember the reason for the original sacrifice that brought on the necessity to forget in the first place? Survivors have scars, and that cannot be denied. Yet the instillation process of hope begins when, like Christ, the temporal scars are embodied into the survivor's new narrative, based in God's love in the here and now.

Eschatological hope is a theology of hope indeed. But in post-trauma social healing, eschatology cannot stand on its own, apart from an agent's inclusion of the tangible and temporal practices of hope. Only through temporal involvement in hopeful and redemptive works of building bridges, healing, counseling, and time given to adjust to an agent's new post-trauma normal, among others, are measures that can continue refilling their temporal hope *until* the eschaton, not because of it. Agents of any sexual orientation experiencing trauma with their other will not be able to cognitively or socially find temporal healing through a future expectation of forgetting the trauma ever happened. Such disconnected theologies must be liberated, as each wounded party must work through their own process of embodying the reality of their new, post-trauma reality and identity.[59]

Put another way, the teenage girl who was raped, brutalized, and physically scarred from an attack of unsubstantiated evil feels very little affinity to being told that in heaven that her bodily scar will be removed, virginity restored, and personal and communal knowledge of

---

59. Eiesland, *Disabled God*, 72–74.

love made right. And those with life-altering disabilities (for example, someone wheelchair-bound without use of legs) who are told they will, one day, dance on two legs in heaven with all the saints does not erase their inability to walk down the street. Temporal hope in God's perfect eschatological community of love must be more than a future-realized hope viewed through a temporal lens.

Even if Volf is correct that an agent's reshaped post-trauma identity can be based in the eschatological hope of forgetfulness, the elephants in the room still exist within their temporal traumatic memories and subsequent indelibly linked emotions. The practice of hope, then, must be inseparably combined with an agent's embodied temporal works of hope done for hope's own merit to one day be continued, but *not necessarily dependent upon* its continuation, in the new creation. It is in this space where the temporal-to-eschatological congruency of remembrance fills an agent's pain of experienced trauma with the hope of God's perfect love, as God validates an agent's struggle to embody their trauma just as the agent does not stifle God's new work through an over-affinity with their pretrauma life.

## Conclusion

In a letter from the prophet Jeremiah to those forcefully carried into exile to Babylon, God relays a message of embodiment in the most unlikely of circumstances—that over the next seventy years, God's exiled people must settle in their new land by marrying their sons and daughters to the oppressors. They must seek peace with their new city and diligently work to help their Babylonian perpetrators prosper.[60] A set of extraordinary relational commands, to say the least! Yet they are normative in God's economy. Jeremiah's message stands next to Jesus's words to the Jews struggling with Roman occupation: love your oppressive enemies (Matt 5:44a), pray for those who persecute you (Matt 5:44b), and submit to the unjust cultural system placed upon you.[61] God continually reminds humanity that the best way to handle

---

60. Jer 29:4–10.

perpetration is for those perpetrated against to embody their surroundings in the Crucified's example of service (proximity), remembrance (reality), and love (hope).[62]

Through this path, God continually insists that those perpetrated against must pursue their perpetrator's prosperity even if the perpetrator does not reciprocate.[63] This includes the work of the church seeking (sometimes unsuccessfully) social healing with LGBT people, and LGBT people doing the same (also sometimes unsuccessfully) with the church. Any agent seeking social healing with their other through the work of embodiment brings tangible hope to their existential future, even if nothing external comes from it. God will not forget this work; nor will God's justice forget the perpetrator's role in the trauma (Jer 51:36–58). And through God's divine remembrance, an agent's experienced trauma and corresponding memories will not be forgotten either. Rather, they will be embodied into God's fully realized and perfected narrative of temporal and eschatological love.

Such integrative love gives the one perpetrated against the confidence to work toward an embodied post-trauma identity in hope. Experienced temporal hope, in conjunction with the knowledge of God's eschatological remembrance, gives the one perpetrated against a clear path to engage in a process of social healing with those who caused them harm. And if there is one thing I have learned through TMF over the past decade, the church can live into its mission and bring this sought-after social healing with the LGBT community with as much frequency as they commit to the theological practice of embodiment's imperative movements of living in proximity with their other, functioning in their other's reality, and engaging in the temporal works of hope.

---

61. Andrew Marin, "Winner Take All? A Political and Religious Assessment of the Culture War between the LGBT Community and Conservatives," *Political Theology* 12 (2011): 501–10.
62. Cf. John 13:13–17.
63. As Volf rightly suggests, even if the perpetrator is absent from the process, essential to social healing is the agent's ability to create the space in themselves to embrace their other (Volf, *Exclusion and Embrace*, 68).

# 13

---

# Pioneering Mission for the Church's Theology

## Jonny Baker

### True North

The mission of God, which we seek to discern and join in with, is like the magnetic force of true north. Whatever practice we are engaged in or facilitating, it gets firmly but gently oriented around mission. This might seem like a simplistic image or place to start, but the longer I have thought about this, the more important or profound it has become in my own imagination, in my own life, and certainly in the mission and theological training effort I lead.

As a member of the Church Mission Society (CMS), it may not come as that great a surprise to make this point. CMS is a mission community. Prophetic mission is our charism, our passion, our lifeblood, and our calling. CMS began at the end of the eighteenth century as a voluntary society focused on sending people to share the gospel in other parts of the world—notably in Africa and Asia. It was a big part of the Western missionary enterprise, and through its mission, something like two-thirds of the Anglican Communion was birthed. Since then, CMS has engaged in multiple contexts and pioneered its mission efforts in many forms, always with an awareness and lens of cross-cultural mission. In 1807, CMS developed its own mission and theological training at Aston Sandford in Buckinghamshire.[1] Thomas Scott was a vicar with a large vicarage where potential missionaries would stay and learn biblical knowledge. At the time, there was a college in London for many years, and subsequently one in Birmingham. From the very early days, CMS trained missionaries in a space that was different from the existing theological colleges and seminaries.

I have worked for CMS in various guises for the last twelve years, but the most recent focus of my work has been in mission education, the last five years helping to create and design a training pathway that included a diploma and MA degree. This training is geared toward what in the United Kingdom we call "pioneers" or those who do "pioneer ministry." These are essentially people who start new things in mission to reach beyond the edges of the mission and ministry of the church, beyond business as usual. Many other colleges and seminaries training church leaders have sought to add on pioneer ministry training. Like our predecessors, we have felt the need and the excitement of developing something in another kind of space that is oriented somewhat differently with a different formation, pedagogy, curriculum, and community. At its root, it is this difference in what true north is that has pushed us (or pulled us) in this direction.

This is not solely an effort to make an argument for missiology per se in the academy over and against systematic theology, though I would happily support an argument for the importance of missiology and the dialogue between the two, which is the point of this book. Both have

---

1. See John Scott, *Life Letters and Papers of The Late Thomas Scott* (New Haven: Nathan Whiting, 1827), 191.

their place. There are currently discussions in missiology about its role in how mission encouragingly has become part of the discourse in theology and the church.[2] While this is surely a good thing and a sign of its success, there remains a real danger in assuming one does not need spaces in which mission is particularly studied and reflected upon. The lens that we use for this is, in this sense, missiological, which is a strong thread for us. I have been quite reassured through Stanley Skreslet's review of missiology as a field of study that this is, in some sense, home for us.[3] In some places, the guilt and fear of mission's dark colonial side in its history has meant that a growth of academic departments now are labeled "World Christianity" or "Intercultural Studies." Their different lenses do open up particular insights, but at CMS, our pull and preference remains "mission." We think it is essential and are passionate about it. But it is also a bit more nuanced than that.

Curiously, we have, at times, felt slightly out of place at gatherings of missiological educators. We think this is probably because missiology can get stuck in the academy ironically disconnected from mission itself. So the second crucial aspect of true north for us is practice. The title of the gathering at which the chapters in this book were presented was "Doing Theology For the Church's Mission," but this is problematic. It seems to assume somehow that the thinking part comes first, and then the church's ministry, practice, and mission will change. I am highly suspicious of this way of orienting the conversation. In my experience, all the best theology comes out of practice, out of real questions arising from mission or ministry on the ground, not as something that is worked out in the academy and then banked up for dealing with mission later on. That is why I called my paper at the conference "Doing Mission for the Church's Theology." Our true north is about mission as the orientation of the learning, but also alongside mission practice in a conversation or dialogue between the two. CMS's founders were interested in transformation of the world in sharing the

---

2. See, for example, John Roxborogh, "Missiology after Mission," *International Bulletin of Missionary Research* 38 (2014): 120–24.
3. Stanley Skreslet, *Comprehending Mission: The Questions, Methods, Themes, Problems, and Prospects of Missiology* (Maryknoll, NY: Orbis, 2012).

gospel, in campaigning for the abolition of slavery, and a host of other things. The reason why they learned was to enable this practice, this transformation. Pioneers are similarly about mission on the ground. This is not to devalue the academic. We are passionate about learning and research, but it needs to connect with practice. This now sounds like an argument for practical theology, and I am a big admirer of practical theology, but I also do not want to locate fully there. Practical theology is at its best when it orients around mission. But at times, it feels like practical theology's true north can get pulled in the direction of reflective practice itself, being a reflective practitioner. While this is a good thing—and we hope all of our students will learn this—for us, it is not an end in itself.

The third thread that combines around this image of a compass and true north is pioneering itself, what we think of as the pioneer gift. We are somewhat unusually only training pioneers in mission. I will say a bit more about this, where it comes from and why it is pertinent for the current moment, at least for the church in the West, before reflecting further on the learning we have been doing around mission and theological education itself.

## The Pioneer Gift

The image of a compass is helpful during times when a map is lacking, either because one simply has not brought one or perhaps more so when one is found in unmapped territory. It is hard for us to think of the world being unmapped now, but on old maps, there were sometimes images of dragons on the edge, which were a sign that beyond the edge of the known, mapped world, no one knew what was there—there might be dragons! Other maps sometimes had sections that were off-road, as it were, and labeled *terra periculosa*, or "dangerous land."

The current moment in the Western world feels somewhat like this—it is certainly unknown territory, and in many ways, unmapped. There have been huge changes in the last fifty years that can cause the feeling of being in a new world. It is not the place of this chapter to describe the contours of this terrain—many others have attempted this. It has been described in various ways often with a "post" prefix, signifying it comes after what went before, but not much more. So, we have postmodern, post-Christendom, postcolonial, and so on. It is not news in mission circles that the gospel is always culturally robed, embedded, and embodied in different places and eras in different ways—indeed, in different paradigms that mean that various understandings of theology and mission are quite different. But the church in the West has found this new world somewhat threatening and tricky to navigate. It has found itself more wedded to modernity or to a bygone era than at first it seemed, and it feels like everything is up for discussion. Worship, church, discipleship, spirituality, ministry, leadership, mission, theology, dare I say theological education itself where they once seemed clear and sure are all a bit at sea. I am not suggesting for a moment that what is ancient and wisdom from the tradition is suddenly no longer helpful. But the impact of the changes are huge. David Bosch has the rather lovely phrase in his book *Transforming Mission* that the church needs to prolong the logic of the ministry of Jesus in each era. How do we do that in all of these areas in the United Kingdom or the United States or whatever country we find ourselves in, or our local neighborhoods? And for the question raised by the current book, do we have the courage to really take a good hard look at the ways theological education has been inculturated in particular ways to a modern Western culture that no longer constitutes the world we are living in?

One encouraging thing in this changed context is how mission has come to the fore in discussions around the way forward. This is on a scale that was unimaginable fifteen or twenty years ago. There has been a growing realization that the West is a mission context itself and that the skills, imagination, and lens of cross-cultural mission that is nurtured when a missionary travels to another country or culture is precisely the kind of thing we need for our own contexts now. It is why I feel so at home in CMS because we have a lot of experience and wisdom in this area.

In this new unmapped, uncharted world, we clearly need people who are prepared to go into the land of dragons and to travel beyond the edges of the known world into *terra periculosa*. It certainly will not be everybody's call, but thank God for those who are energized by the adventure. We call these people "pioneers" or "mission entrepreneurs" in the United Kingdom. These two terms have largely come to the fore because they were the terms used in the recommendations of the report "Mission Shaped Church."[4] This report recognized that in this new emerging culture, there was a need for a different kind of designation for ministry, a different set of skills, a different disposition for those who could sail beyond the edges of the reach of existing churches and grow fresh expressions of church and mission community in the soils of the new culture(s). It has been a surprise to many that an old denomination seemingly in decline could break open the possibility for this newness, but it has been a hugely encouraging story with a lot of new churches and mission leading both to genuine growth and transformation. The report also recommended that these pioneers and entrepreneurs should be trained through the lens of cross-cultural mission, which is how we at CMS came to be involved in the training of both lay and ordained pioneers.

People who are pioneers bring an amazing gift.[5] This gift is about seeing and building. Pioneers imagine and see new possibilities in the way things are, reflecting afresh on business as usual, and they are then able to build a pathway to make real what they see and imagine. The word *entrepreneur* comes from two French words that mean "to take between"—that is, to innovate in a gap or a space. The simplest description I have come across is from Beth Keith, who puts it this way: "A pioneer is someone who sees future possibilities and works to bring them to reality."[6] This is actually important in every culture, business, organization, and church, but perhaps especially so when things have

---

4. This was a report published by the Church of England and Methodist Church in 2004 to reflect on the emerging church planting and fresh expressions of church in the changing context in Britain.
5. See Jonny Baker and Cathy Ross, eds., *The Pioneer Gift: Explorations in Mission* (Norwich: Canterbury Press, 2014), which reflects more on the nature of pioneer ministry.
6. David Goodhew, Andrew Roberts, and Michael Volland, *Fresh! An Introduction to Fresh Expressions of Church and Pioneer Ministry* (London: SCM, 2012), 137.

become somewhat stuck. And of course, it is not actually new. It is an interesting exercise to go through a calendar of saints remembered by the church and biblical characters and think about which of them were pioneers and which were more pastoral. A huge number were pioneers, including many of the heroes of faith, such as Abraham, who set off in faith without knowing where he was going, leaving the security of his known world. Jesus is described in Heb 12:2 as the pioneer of our faith. He certainly saw and built something very new.

Having worked with those who, under various guises, have been on the journey to the new—in youth ministry, alternative worship, emerging church, mission communities, new monasticism, fresh expressions of church, and particularly through the pioneers who have come and trained with us at CMS in the last few years—we have found this gift delightful, multifaceted, intriguing, hard to nail down. The journey to the new is by definition unknown and unpredictable, but the church has had great wisdom in recognizing the need for it even if she is struggling to know quite what do with it ever since. I think it would be a lot easier for the church, and indeed, maybe for everybody if pioneering were simply a case of taking what worked in the old world and transplanting it into the new—simply jumping from one to the other. But in practice, that seems to be successful in limited scenarios. For example, a church plant may reach a similar demographic as its members had in the sending church. However, this lacks the depth of change required if real newness is to emerge that is truly inculturated in new cultures that are substantially different. We have found through the pioneers that the journey to the new involves grief, a letting-go, an undoing. In many ways, this is the language and experience of the prophets—Walter Brueggemann has suggested that only grief leads to newness.[7] It is difficult. It invariably has to go through a liminal space, the wilderness, before hope and newness can begin to emerge. And often, the new because it requires, by definition, a new imagination, theology, set of practices, is misunderstood and perceived as a threat

---

7. Walter Brueggemann, *Hopeful Imagination: Prophetic Voices in Exile* (Minneapolis: Fortress Press, 1986), 9.

by those wedded to the old ways. So, alongside the difficulty of pioneering something new is the political negotiations with those in power, especially if money is involved. And usually those in power have a vested interest in business as usual. In some sense, they are the guardians of the status quo. It takes a secure leader to encourage and create space for pioneers. This courage is itself a form of dissent, what Gerald Arbuckle[8] calls authority dissenting, fitting well with pioneers who are also dissenting as pathfinding dissenters. It is actually the combination and interplay of these two kinds of dissent that opens up the possibility of real change taking root. Cultures of churches, and indeed, theological seminaries, are often much more powerful than people assume. At a recent research day with our pioneers in Oxford, Arbuckle put it this way: "Culture eats strategies for lunch." In the light of these anthropological insights, perhaps it is not surprising that the church has found that this gift is difficult as much as it is essential.

All this is by way of saying that we have found ourselves at CMS creating an environment and learning community with these kinds of wonderful people who are creative, interesting, imaginative, entrepreneurial engaged in the practice of this pioneering ministry of seeing and building something new. We sometimes use a shorthand for this gift as the gift of not fitting in because invariably there is some sense of not fitting in with the way things are. It is this gift and this community that is then our third thread around our true north—pioneering. While we are still discovering what it is, what it might mean, how best to nurture it, and so on, alongside mission education and mission practice is a mission that is pioneering and prophetic.

### What Are We Learning?

We have been discussing at CMS what we are learning about theological or missiological education and what is underneath our pedagogy, and I would like to tentatively offer some thoughts in this

---

8. Gerald A. Arbuckle, *Refounding the Church: Dissent for Leadership* (London: Geoffrey Chapman, 1993).

area. I have been helped by a few others who have thought about these things and taken the time to publish them, for which I am grateful,[9] although it remains difficult to find much consensus. At one level, the curriculum looks like a lot of others; so we cover the Bible, ministry, pastoral care, leadership, spirituality, mission, mission history, theology, skills, theological reflection, and probably a few things that others do not, such as crossing cultures, theology in global perspective, and missional entrepreneurship, which we could say a lot more about. But that easily misses how the approach we are taking is different to some others. I am taking as prior what I have already described above as true north that orients our approach.

## Formation Formission

Formation is a word that gets knocked about in theological education a lot. I have grown to quite like it as a word—it is quite rich and broad in its possibilities. It stems from a recognition that theological education is not just about something academic, but about forming people for life, for Christian discipleship, to follow in the way of Christ, to develop character, maturity, and integrity, and so on. But I have also grown suspicious of the word partly because it gets talked about in somewhat mystical tones or hushed whispers, often assuming that everyone knows or shares an understanding of what we mean. And to put it bluntly, some of this assumed shared understanding of formation does not seem to help form people for pioneering mission. My hunch around this in the culture of theological colleges in the United Kingdom is that their understanding of formation is quite influenced by Benedictine spirituality, which, of course, is great. But this was for a context in which people were cloistered, in residential community, and ends up requiring stability and predictability or it simply is not going to work. However, the kind of formation developed by the likes of St. Francis or St. Ignatius for the communities of friars who are spread out and live in the world required something very different—flexibility,

9. For example, Robert Banks, Parker Palmer, Perry Shaw, Darren Cronshaw.

adaptability, response to different cultures. The purpose of formation in these communities is inculturation and prophetic ministry to the world. Usually, it would include placements or substantial periods of living with and among the poor—that is, being formed in the context of mission.[10] This is an overstatement, but it seems as though the emphasis for one is a kind of con-formation—to the tradition, habits, and practices of the church—designed to knock off any edges. But the other emphasizes trans-formation in and of the world. It is formation that is formission. We do share, I am sure, common ground in relation to the soul work that students (and indeed, staff) find themselves engaged in as issues surface in their lives and they seek to grow as mission disciples; so these are not completely separate entities. But I have begun to reflect that we are involved with pioneers in the formation for pioneering and prophetic ministry that is more like this second kind. CMS has become a religious community of the Church of England in the last few years—technically, an acknowledged community. This is, therefore, a spread-out mission community that is ecclesial, gathered around a second-order commitment to pioneering mission, so it is extraordinary how wonderful a home and good fit this has become for the formation and community of pioneers.

## Practice

All pioneers participate in mission in local contexts. Those contexts might be geographical, a particular housing estate, and/or it might be with a particular people—spiritual seekers or those who are homeless and struggling with addiction. So the learning community is a space in which we reflect on real questions that haunt people through their practice. As suggested above, formation is for mission in the world. To give an example of this, one student working with women who have issues dealing with shame has explored in theology and missiology what can be learned about shame. She is developing an ecclesiology of shame-resilient communities in contrast with many of women's

---

10. I have been very helped by Gerald Arbuckle's thinking in *From Chaos to Mission: Refounding Religious Life Formation* (Collegeville, MN: Liturgical, 1997), where he looks at refounding formation.

experiences where liturgies and church practices compound their shame. Another student has explored salvation as the healing and redemption of all things, and this has freed him up to connect his work with mission so that he is now renewing town-center high streets. In other words, the theological questions arise in the context of crossing borders into new landscapes where the systematic theology supposedly being done for the church's mission does not seem to have the answers, or at least, its answers are to slightly (or sometimes very) different questions, and even assuming a different system(atic). It is not that there is no gift in systematic theology for pioneers—of course there is. But minimally, there is a lot more theologizing to be done in the context, a lot more local theology. Much of our Western theological tradition is indebted to philosophy—the questions it generates are, in some respects, philosophical and abstract, which has made them somewhat distant from current concrete realities. It is highly conceptual, separating thought and action. We are seeking a way of doing theology that refuses this separation. It would be unhelpful to then create a new binary opposition of local versus systematic theology.[11] This is not a new tension—liberation theology grappled with this and what the role of the professional theologian might be in relation to the grassroots. A grasp, for example, of how systematic theology has understood the incarnation will play an important role in the development of local theologies. The theologizing done in context is likely to be richer the more it improvises in and out of the resources of the tradition. We also ask students to undertake placements in other contexts and have a host of practitioners share their stories and reflections across the curriculum. There is a growing swell of opinion on this in global theology—theology that is divorced from action ends up being irrelevant. Kevin Vanhoozer suggests that laypersons would be within their rights to sue systematic theologians for criminal pastoral and missiological negligence![12] In educational theories,

---

11. Robert Schreiter resolves this by describing tradition as a series of local theologies which then positions systematic theology as one or more such local theologies. Robert Schreiter, *Constructing Local Theologies* (Maryknoll, NY: Orbis, 1985).
12. Kevin J. Vanhoozer, "One Rule to Rule Them All: Theological Method in an Era of World

learning is nearly always understood as taking place when it is holistic. For example, a popular and influential way of speaking about this is Benjamin Bloom's cognitive, affective, and behavioral domains[13]—that is, thinking, feeling/emotions, and skills or psychomotor. Too often, education, at best, gives a nod in the direction of the affective and behavioral while putting all its energy, including the way assessments are designed, into the cognitive. It seems depressingly hard to shift this culture in the West. But the location in context ensures something more rounded, more integrated. I cannot emphasize enough the significance of the students' mission contexts and practice, along with the energy these bring into the learning community when we gather. This is not to give the impression that a different educational methodology on its own will change things. Educational methodology is also important, but not on its own. Yet the case I am making is methodological!

There is a second aspect of practice that relates to those who are teaching. It is extremely demanding being involved in teaching, especially if one leads a program, department, or college.[14] So, it seems almost an unreasonable value, but those who teach at CMS have to connect with practice in some meaningful way. True north is not just something we are trying to teach students—it must be displayed in our lives too. Parker Palmer suggests that to know truth, we must follow it with our lives and describes how words dried up for him as a teacher when he was disconnected from practice.[15]

## Context

Related to this is this little word *context*, which may eventually undo the edifice on which many of our systems are built, which is why many

Christianity," in *Globalizing Theology: Belief and Practice In An Era Of World Christianity*, ed. Craig Ott and Harold A. Netland (Downers Grove, IL: InterVarsity Press, 1997), 93.

13. Benjamin S. Bloom et al., eds., *Taxonomy of Educational Objectives: The Classification of Educational Goals; Handbook I: Cognitive Domain* (London: Longmans, 1956).

14. See Dan Strange's comment on this in his chapter about implications of Kirsteen Kim's work as it relates to "a mission stream in [the] curriculum" of the academic institution he helps lead.

15. Parker J. Palmer, *To Know As We Are Known: Education as a Spiritual Journey* (San Francisco: Harper & Row, 1983).

people are probably rightly afraid of it. The tide is only going one way on this, and we'd better get with it if we do not want to end up washed up on the beach. The turn to context is massive. Context has become primary for the theological task. It ought to be a big relief to realize that what in the West has been purported to be (and has been presented as) "doctrine" or "theology" is really local Western theology, and large parts of the world are now doing theology "after the West." There is an irony here in the pioneer training. We are now focused in mission education and theology on the specifics of Western contexts, yet find that enterprise informed by our relationship (which is the essence of CMS) with the global church. We need the global to be truly and authentically local. This is a great gift of postmodernity—to see our embeddedness and situatedness, which calls for humility and the need to sit and share and learn from others in multiple contexts about the unseen insights we might learn from the gifts of the global church. For pioneers, it is also a context that is peculiarly local—the resources of local theology, contextual theology, and indeed ordinary theology are wonderful gifts that enable actually doing theology in the new context.[16] This is, of course, then set within the wider canon and catholicity such that its improvisation is not disconnected, simply made up, or thinly constructed, but it remains faithful in the mission theodrama that is unfolding.

## Theological Homelessness

Something we have observed in the pioneer journey is a theological homelessness. Cathy Ross has reflected on this in *The Pioneer Gift*. This is how she describes it:

> For many, the theology that they grew up with, or have been introduced to, does not seem to engage with reality as they experience it. I suspect this is because we are all trying to take our contexts seriously and some of our theology may not. So a kind of theological "leaving home" begins to take place. This means that home and the theology with which we were nurtured is never quite the same. Theological homelessness can be

16. There are now books and conversations in all three categories named here.

painful. It may leave us stranded between two or more worlds. It forces us to look at our theological upbringing with new eyes. This discomfort may be a good thing.[17]

To engage in mission well requires a spirituality of letting go for the sake of discovering God afresh in new contexts. It requires the ability to hold a space where people can make this journey, ask difficult questions, be unsettled in liminality, as it were, and crucially press into those questions with faith seeking understanding. Again, this requires a very different posture and approach in education to one in which the important thing is seen as learning all the right doctrines and so on, and indeed, there is a fear of this kind of questioning and letting go. I have observed in some circles a journey of theological homelessness that people go on in relation to postmodern culture that seems to end up with them cut adrift from church and even from theism. I am not advocating this, and we are not really seeing that with pioneers. I think this is because for pioneers at CMS, this exploration is held within a community that is oriented around the true north of mission.

### Trust Not Fear

There is such energy in discerning God's presence in mission, joining in, and unfolding new language and theology. God is a migrant. We are a migrant people, and things change when you cross borders. But so much of the church seems afraid and threatened. Fear and defensiveness can somehow become default positions, with the church seeing itself almost exclusively as defenders of truth, of right doctrine, of right behavior, the right way to worship, even of church cultures. How did we become so defensive? I sometimes wonder what it is that we are afraid of. I have come to discover more and more that there is great freedom in Christ. Globally, there is a growing sense of freedom in mission. I love the energy in the pope's recent encyclical on evangelism, which is titled *The Joy of the Gospel*[18] as well as the energy in the WCC statement *Together towards Life*.[19] We have found that the

---

17. Cathy Ross, "Pioneering Missiologies: Seeing Afresh," in Baker and Ross, *The Pioneer Gift*, 31–34.
18. Pope Francis, *Evangelii Gaudium* (London: Catholic Truth Society, 2013). See also, http://w2.

opposite to fear—trust and love—creates the environment in which pioneers flourish. Trust God, trust the Spirit, trust the process, trust the community, trust the leaders.

This is not to banish fear. It is very important that an environment in which fears can be talked about is created. And it is actually important that the teacher is able to share their own fears and lead the way in vulnerability. There is plenty of research around about what makes a good teacher. One of the key things is the quality of relationship with students, which Shaw calls a hospitable relationship.[20] In other words, the teacher is able to create an environment of openness, trust, welcome, and value students' contributions. Sometimes, there is an unspoken assumption in education that teachers need to keep emotional distance from students and even from one another to be professional. But this kind of a picture of what a teacher is leads to disconnection. At CMS, we hope to create an environment of trust and hospitality, and as a teaching staff, we see ourselves as friends as well as colleagues. And I think we have a sense of being in it together with students with whom, in appropriate ways, we are also a community of friends. We recently had a student who visited for a semester from New Zealand who commented that one of things he really appreciated was that one minute, someone might be teaching, and the next in the class as a learner.

## Everyone Has a Piece of the Wisdom

One of the phrases we have come to use in our training is this: "Everyone has a piece of the wisdom." Our observation is that many colleges and books on theological education have great ideas about pedagogy and reimagining it, but the experience on the ground is curiously dominated by lectures from experts, with students taking

vatican.va/content/francesco/en/apost_exhortations/documents/papa-francesco_esortazione-ap_20131124_evangelii-gaudium.html.

19. *Together towards Life: Mission and Evangelism in Changing Landscapes*, ed. Joseph Keum (Geneva: WCC, 2013) is an affirmation statement of mission and evangelism from the World Council of Churches in 2012.

20. Perry Shaw, *Transforming Theological Education: A Practical Handbook for Integrative Learning* (London: Langham Global Library, 2014), 262.

notes. In some forms of training for ministry, what people have previously done or all the life experience they bring is sometimes ignored or discounted or not perceived to be relevant. There is a gap between the rhetoric and the reality. We probably flip the balance too much the other way, but we value the gifts of people in the room and the experience, wisdom, and insight they bring, and seek to draw these out in conversation. Of course, a good teacher will manage to combine this with bringing teaching and insights into that mix. Our class layouts tend to be informal, and we have a lot of conversation. We were recently visited by a diocesan member of staff who was visiting one of the pioneer ordinands he is responsible for who was training with us. This member of the diocese has visited several colleges and remarked with surprise how much learning and content seemed to be happening across the room in conversation, and not just from the front. In pioneer training, we genuinely do not think we have all the answers, although, hopefully, have some wisdom to bring to bear, but there is a lot more when everyone's voice is heard.

## Heat and Hunger

One way we have come to think of one aspect of our learning we denote with the idea, "heat in the room." Sometimes, indeed quite often, somebody interjects something—a question, or something from their own experience—and it can be intense. The temptation as a teacher (depending somewhat on your personality) is to want to stick with what you have prepared. But we have learned to go with the heat in the room. Often this is where connections are made with what is being taught, the live questions, and the real struggles. This relates to the previous points—pioneer training requires an environment that is hospitable and teaching staff who are comfortable in holding a generous space open for conversation. It has to be a space in which there is trust and safety and where genuine doubt and struggle can be part of the conversation. If we think learning is about the right answers, this approach simply will not do.

Finally, as we have reflected on what we are up to, we love the hunger in the staff team, both core and guest teachers. We are all on an adventure, a quest around theology and mission and love learning from one another, from the practice of students. We are as likely to be seeking out a book from their portfolio references as they are to pick one up that we recommend. If this curiosity and ongoing faith seeking understanding to join in with God's mission eludes us or runs dry, it is time to leave and do something else.

## To Make a Way Where There Is No Way

At our first graduation, we wanted to give students a memento, a sign, a symbol of the journey. We worked with British sculptor Iain Cotton, who produced a unique object for each student—a piece of stone, a landscape, in which a new path has been carved, literally chiseled out. It is a sign of making a way where there is no way. He described it by saying this:

> This carving is one of a series investigating the idea of a carved path. Each path is set out with a chisel edged brush and carved with a hammer and chisel in a slate tile, metaphorically making a way across a new landscape. The brush gives the forms a calligraphic quality, traversing the stone from left to right like a written text but the language is a mystery. A new language or a speaking in tongues? Each path is unique. A new expression of the journey.

We loved the path and the connection with calligraphy—the paths look like a language, a speaking in tongues in the new landscape. The journey to the new requires the gift of the Spirit and the discovery of new language on the way to a new world, both in the practice of the mission and ministry of the church, but also in the practice of theological education.

# 14

---

# Adopting a New Theological Paradigm for Doing Theology for the Church's Mission

### Krish Kandiah

### Of Narcissism and Narrative

The request to give a theological account of my own work elicited the same awkward feeling I get when I have to watch a video of myself preaching. I am nervous of narcissism and nonplussed about navel-gazing. But I also recognize that there is always a lot to learn and ways I can improve my ministry, so I gladly take this opportunity to ask for a constructive critique. What follows is a theological reflection on my work, which attempts to bridge the gap between the academy and the church, and so this chapter will reflect some of that interaction. I consider myself in some form a "reflective practitioner," and so this chapter will seek to reflect on practice and practice the reflection. This chapter also reflects on my work as executive director for churches in mission at the Evangelical Alliance,[1] a position I held for seven years.

My theology has always been a "theology on the run," seeking wisdom to know how to join in with God's mission in the world. Because of the often reactive and dynamic nature of the alliance's work, theology on the run is definitely a helpful virtue to develop. We are constantly responding to media invitations, questions from both individual members as well as organizational members, and there seems to always be some impending theological or relational crisis to tackle. But the alliance is seeking not just to be a reactive institution functioning as an evangelical organizational version of a marriage counselling service or a modern-day version of the Athenian Areopagus where the latest ideas are discussed. The alliance also seeks to be a catalytic movement, and both internally and externally, we draw inspiration from the collective activism of Wilberforce and Shaftesbury and the Clapham sect. There are thus some ongoing initiatives where the alliance staff team seeks to gather and galvanize evangelicals, to learn from one another, but also, inject into the evangelical imagination intellectual capital and innovation. This is where my work with the alliance[2] fits in. I carried a portfolio of projects. Rather than offer a cursory tour of the different facets of my work, I will attempt to offer a deeper, perhaps "thicker" theological analysis of one aspect of my work—namely, Home for Good, an initiative to see more Christians consider fostering and adoption as part of their Christian service.

## Of Home for Good

There are unprecedented numbers of children coming into the UK care system to the extent that one child every twenty minutes is being removed from their family and brought into care. There are not enough foster carers to cope with this demand, with a shortfall of around nine thousand carers.[3] At the same time, there are four

---

1. The Evangelical Alliance is the largest body serving the 2 million evangelical Christians in the UK.
2. See the Evangelical Alliance website, www.eauk.org.

thousand[4] children who have been made available for adoption by the legal system, and yet, because they have additional needs, are older children, have siblings, or are from black and minority ethnic families, they are not wanted by the many adopters who are currently in the adoption system awaiting an adoptive placement.

This crisis situation prompted immediate personal and theological reflection from a number of evangelical Christians and led to the development of the Home for Good initiative, which is calling the church to step up to meet the need for both adopters for "hard to place children," and also to recruit Christians to meet the national shortfall in foster carers. Theologically, there are two aspects of adoption that warrant further reflection, for the sake of clarity. While I am not entirely happy with the nomenclature, I will refer to God's adoption of sinners into his family as "spiritual adoption" or "vertical adoption" and families' adoption of vulnerable children as "human adoption" or "horizontal adoption."[5] Because of limited space, I will focus my reflection on adoption for the bulk of this chapter and return to fostering again toward the end.

### Of Orthopraxis, Orthodoxy, and Orthopathos

My theological instincts mean that before my team at the alliance would seek to embark on an ambitious project like this, it would be wise to explore the theological landscape around fostering and adoption. This is where I hit a few roadblocks.

I remember being severely challenged by a paper published in the evangelical theological journal *Themelios* in 1995, written by Regent College's R. Paul Stevens,[6] which articulated a nagging suspicion that

---

3. http://www.fostering.net/news/2014/follow-road-fostering#.U4bqLF4Xfhg.
4. The UK is not alone in this challenge. In the USA, in 2012, there were 102,000 children in foster care who were eligible for adoption. See Jedd Medefind, *Becoming Home: Adoption, Foster Care, and Mentoring—Living Out God's Heart for Orphans* (Grand Rapids: Zondervan, 2014), 26. A staggering 30,000 in Canada, which has a much smaller population; see Bruce Clemenger and Tracy Clemenger, "Canada's 30,000 Adoptable Children," *Faith Today* (2010): 18.
5. This language is borrowed from Dan Cruver, ed., *Reclaiming Adoption: Missional Living through the recovery of Abba Father* (Hudson, OH: Cruciform Press, 2010), 7.
6. R. Paul Stevens, "Living Theologically: Toward a Theology of Christian Practice," *Themelios* 20 (1995): 4–8.

I had recognized with my own Christian worldview. He explained the relationship between orthodoxy (right confession), orthopraxy (right action), and orthopathy (right feelings and affections). I recognized in my own evangelical subtribe that a huge emphasis was placed on theology leading to orthodoxy, but very little attempt at translation into orthopraxis or orthopathy. This recognition led to some changes in my personal discipleship, but it also made a deep impression on my study of theology. My area of research was the theology of evangelism, and within it I found an extraordinary, difficult-to-comprehend bifurcation in theological taxonomy such that evangelism was designated or possibly "relegated" to the catchall miscellaneous pile that is "practical theology." I have been frustrated with the implied division of theology into practical and nonpractical, or even worse, "impractical" theology! The existence of a discipline known as practical theology calls into question the nature and purpose of theology in general, a subject too vast to be explored here,[7] but suffice to say that an operating assumption in my approach to theology is that the purpose of Christian theology is to serve God's purposes, which are intrinsically tied to the *missio Dei.*

In light of this bifurcation in theology between the practical and theoretical, I find it interesting to reflect on where human adoption or fostering and the care of vulnerable children fits into current theological taxonomy. If the practice of human adoption appears anywhere, it is most likely to be under "pastoral" or "practical" theology. But I would argue that human adoption is best located in the context of discussion of the *missio Dei.*

The three main places where the apostle Paul outlines his theology of spiritual adoption are these: Rom 8:14–17; Gal 4:4–7; and Eph 1:3–10. In all three of these passages, we see the purpose of the sending/mission of the Son includes the adoption of sinners into the family of God. In all three passages, we see the three persons of the Trinity

---

7. Although, see the chapters in this volume written by self-proclaimed systematic theologians (Stratis, Green, Strange, Sexton), or theologians of another kind (for example, Kim and Elliott). For a fuller exploration of this, see J. Andrew Kirk, *The Mission of Theology and Theology as Mission* (London: Continuum, 1997).

specifically named. In all three passages, there is a connection with our personal eschatological hope and of the consummation and restoration of all creation. That spiritual adoption plays such a pivotal role in the purpose of God for his cosmos means that it should perhaps receive not only more theological reflection than it has but also that it should inform our preaching, disciple making, and liturgies more than it does.

## Of Systematic Theology

My role at the Evangelical Alliance meant that I have to travel extensively both geographically around the United Kingdom, and also theologically, moving across denominational and tribal boundaries both within and outside of evangelical circles. From this wide exposure to the UK church scene, I can report that in evangelical circles, adoption is a missing feature of our soteriology. There are, of course, passing mentions of adoption in the Bible commentaries that engage with the relevant passages, but adoption is not a common theme in either the hymnody or the homiletics of our churches. There are also a couple of notable outliers: 1987's "Father God I wonder," and Mark Stibbe's initiative "The Father's House,"[8] which has sought to rehabilitate the concept of adoption as part of a Christian's self-identity. Sadly, the ministry lost a lot of momentum after its founder resigned due to moral failure. Despite these two examples, adoption has not caught the imagination of the wider church. In neither our evangelistic literature nor our discipleship material is adoption a prevalent theme. Adoption was not one of the dominant metaphors in the evangelistic preaching that I assessed in my tenure as director for the Oxford Centre for Christian Apologetics, nor as a tutor at Wycliffe Hall, nor as an external examiner at Oak Hill College, nor in the numerous UCCF evangelistic missions I witnessed and participated in. The dominant metaphors for salvation were forgiveness, justification, penal substitution, and redemption. This also rings true in evangelistic courses, such as Alpha and Christianity Explored. Adoption is not often

---

8. See Mark Stibbe, *I am Your Father: What Every Heart Needs to Know* (Oxford: Monarch Books, 2010).

part of the figurative lexicon of most evangelists. Similarly, adoption is not a common theme in the ongoing discipleship of the church. Despite the lofty place that evangelical theologian James Packer offers the doctrine of adoption—justification is the basic blessing, on which adoption is founded—adoption is the crowning blessing, to which justification clears the way.[9]

Evangelicals who hold a high view of Scripture should need little more argument than the scriptural emphasis on spiritual adoption to feel the force of this critique. But on top of this, there are pastoral implications of being inadequately established in our identity in Christ. Emphasizing the forensic (justification) or the financial (redemption) images of our salvation are all well and good—they, of course, have clear biblical precedent and frequency—but to never mention adoption seems woefully remiss. Justification and redemption emphasize changes in status—once we were guilty, now we are declared righteous, or once we were enslaved and now through Christ our ransom, we are free. Dan Cruver argues that "through adoption God graciously brings us to participate in the reciprocal love that ever flows between the Father and his Son. Not only is this the very heart of adoption; it is also the very heart of the gospel."[10] Adoption does offer a change in status; this theme is present in the Galatians and Romans passages, which emphasize the status of an adopted son in contradistinction to slavery and underline our status as heirs awaiting our inheritance. But the biblical theology of spiritual adoption emphasizes both a change in identity and a radical relational intimacy with God.

Recently, Kevin Vanhoozer offered a way through a shibboleth in evangelical theology—namely, the competing theologies of justification. This division is a symptom of the division and suspicion between evangelical tribes personified in the writings of N. T. Wright and John Piper.[11] Vanhoozer argues that the impasse between John Piper's approach to "imputed righteousness" and N. T. Wright's

9. J. I. Packer, *Concise Theology: A Guide to Historic Christian Beliefs* (Wheaton: Tyndale House, 1993), 167.
10. Cruver, *Reclaiming Adoption*, 26.
11. See John Piper, *The Future of Justification: A Response to N. T. Wright* (Wheaton: Crossway, 2007); and N. T. Wright, *Justification: God's Plan and Paul's Vision* (Downers Grove, IL: IVP Academic, 2009).

approach to "incorporated righteousness"[12] could be solved through a reemphasis of a theology of adoption.

> I submit that adoption, first cousin as it were to union with Christ, is the perfect mediating category inasmuch as it pertains both to the question of covenant membership (that is, who is in God's family) *and* of legal standing before God (that is, right so inheritance). Hear again the word of Calvin: "as soon as you become engrafted into Christ through faith, you are made a son of God, an heir of heaven, a partaker in righteousness.[13]

Not only has a lack of emphasis on God's vertical adoption of sinners into his family left us theologically bereft and experientially challenged, but perhaps this lack of emphasis on a theology of adoption has left the church hard-hearted and ambivalent toward the plight of vulnerable children in our communities.

Why is there the lack of emphasis on vertical adoption in the shared life and liturgies of our churches? Perhaps it is due to the passive nature of adoption not fitting in with the context of post-Enlightenment individualism. In the words of William Ernest Henley's well-known "Invictus," we like to consider ourselves the captains of our souls. Adoption is a passive metaphor for conversation as the decision to adopt is not in our hands, but God's. And yet the praxis of our church life may also exasperate this cultural trend. Evangelical churches have a strong emphasis on conversionism, which is one of the corners of David Bebbington's evangelical quadrilateral, "the belief that lives need to be transformed";[14] and this is often understood as performed through the crisis of conversion. So, if preaching for conversion is a normal practice of the church, then adoption appears to be a difficult metaphor to do that from. Even in the New Testament in the evangelistic speeches in Acts, there is not a clear emphasis on adoption, so if we as evangelicals have a predominantly evangelistic

---

12. See Kevin J. Vanhoozer, "Wrighting the Wrongs of the Reformation? The State of the Union with Christ in St. Paul and Protestant Soteriology," in *Jesus, Paul and the People of God: A Theological Dialogue with N. T. Wright*, ed. Nicholas Perrin and Richard B. Hays (Downers Grove, IL: IVP Academic, 2011), 235–61.

13. Ibid., 254, citing Calvin's *Institutes* 3.15.6.

14. David W. Bebbington, *Evangelicalism in Modern Britain: A History from 1730s to the 1980s* (New York: Routledge, 1989), 3.

thrust to our preaching and teaching, perhaps it is understandable that adoption is not a commonly spoken about theme. This points to a flaw in homiletic practices of the church. As an evangelist, I delight in the church's commitment to evangelistic preaching, but this cannot be at the expense of the discipleship and biblical literacy of the church. If vertical adoption is a forgotten theme in our evangelization, it pretty quickly becomes a forgotten theme in the church's life. If this happens, an important narrative bridge is broken between the orthodoxy of the church and its orthopraxis.

The book of Deuteronomy builds an important link between the historical narrative of God's engagement with his people and the expectation of the praxis of the community.

> Do not deprive the foreigner or the fatherless of justice, or take the cloak of the widow as a pledge. Remember that you were slaves in Egypt and the Lord your God redeemed you from there. That is why I command you to do this. When you are harvesting in your field and you overlook a sheaf, do not go back to get it. Leave it for the foreigner, the fatherless and the widow, so that the Lord your God may bless you in all the work of your hands. When you beat the olives from your trees, do not go over the branches a second time. Leave what remains for the foreigner, the fatherless and the widow (Deut 24:17–20).

For Israel, remembering their history, their former circumstances, and God's redemptive work in the nation's life was supposed to soften the hearts of God's people toward the needs of the poor and marginalized among them. The transformation of Israel from slaves to the redeemed people of God was to set the tone for Israel's relationship with marginalized peoples. In fact, a dominant trope in the book of Deuteronomy is the need to remember that history: "it has become clear . . . that the Bible contains a theology of recital. The book of Deuteronomy holds a key place in the Bible's theology of recital."[15] Similarly, Duane Christensen comments: "We are in constant danger of forgetting God, and we need to find new ways to remember his mighty acts in times past."[16] Remembrance holds a vital link in covenantal

15. Edward P. Blaire, "An Appeal to Remembrance: The Memory Motif in Deuteronomy," *Interpretation* 15 (1961): 42.

faithfulness. Israel is warned in Deuteronomy that in times of plenty, they are likely to forget their history and give up on the covenant. John Arthur Thompson argues, "For Israel there could have been no prosperity had not Yahweh brought them out from the slavery of Egypt and cared for them during the wanderings. . . . There is always a danger that men's hearts might become lifted up with pride . . . and, forgetful of the facts of the case."[17] Following this logic, if our vertical adoption narrative is forgotten, then it is not surprising that horizontal adoption will be ignored too. Perhaps a recovery of the doctrine of the believers' privilege and experience of spiritual adoption will help the church to remember our past identity as vulnerable children in need of God's adopting love and make us more receptive to the needs of those in our communities who are need of families? Perhaps even to see that adoption can be a living parable of the gospel?

### Of Missiology

Horizontal adoption is not often considered part of the mission of the church. I have found no reference to it in any of the major missiological journals. Perhaps this results from a failure in missiology to demonstrate truly integrative approaches to mission. We often separate mission into word and deed, proclamation and presence. But these still seem restricted to the corporate activities of the church or to the personal activities of individual believers—but are rarely connected with the family unit.

Perhaps the problem is that we have understood mission to be an epistemological entity rather than an ontology[18]—a way of *being* in the world. So, in common parlance, church leaders often talk about "doing mission" or going "on a mission," rather than the mission of God setting the tone for a way of being in our world. There is hope that

---

16. Duane L. Christensen, *Deuteronomy 1-21:9*, 2nd ed., Word Biblical Commentary 6A (Dallas: Word, 2001), 175.
17. John Arthur Thompson, *Deuteronomy: An Introduction and Commentary*, Tyndale Old Testament Commentary 5 (Nottingham, UK: Inter-Varsity Press, 1974), 153.
18. This insight was prompted by the comment on Oliver O'Donovan's ecclesiology in Luke Bretherton, *Hospitality as Holiness: Christian Witness amid Moral Diversity* (Farnham, UK: Ashgate, 2006), 4.

this might change, thanks to rediscovery of the concept of the *missio Dei* across the evangelical movement. Missiologists such as David Bosch and Lesslie Newbigin and theologians such as Jürgen Moltmann are increasingly cited in this regard. Moltmann: "It is not the church that has a mission . . . it is the mission of the Son and the Spirit through the Father that includes the church."[19] Similarly, Bosch writes, "Mission is not primarily an activity of the church, but an attribute of God. God is a missionary God."[20]

The recovery of the *missio Dei* is why many evangelical churches no longer talk about missions as if there was a plurality, but simply mission because the church is caught up in the singular mission of the triune God. Thus the ontological nature of mission has an entrée into the communal life of the church. Yet, there is still a disconnect between mission and the home life of the average Christian. Mike Breen, the director of 3DM and an evangelical thought leader has written:

> Here's the problem. For far too long, many of us felt we were pushed into having to make this false dichotomy: Is it family OR mission?
>
> Rightly recognizing we shouldn't sacrifice our families, we started to put some healthy boundaries in place, but also some unhealthy ones. So we started to compartmentalize. But I believe it's part of the progression. So for many of us, this is now the question of our time: Is it family AND mission?
>
> But when we learn to integrate our life and live well as a people participating in the mission of God each and every day and as we listen to the mission God is calling our family to, this is the next progression: Is it family ON mission?[21]

This is a very welcome next step toward a more integrated understanding of mission. The battle for evangelicals about the integrated nature of mission consisting of words and actions, proclamation, and presence was effectively won back at the 1974 at the inaugural

---

19. Jürgen Moltmann, *Church in the Power of the Holy Spirit* (London: SCM, 1976), 64.
20. David J. Bosch, *Transforming Mission: Paradigm Shifts in Theology of Mission* (Maryknoll, NY: Orbis, 1991), 389–90.
21. Mike Breen, "Sacrificing Mission on the Altar of Family?," personal blog, February 21, 2012, http://mikebreen.wordpress.com/2012/02/21/sacrificing-mission-on-the-altar-of-family/ (accessed January 2, 2016).

Lausanne Congress on Global Evangelization. This affirmed, alongside a clear commitment to evangelism, that "God is both the Creator and the Judge of all people. We therefore should share his concern for justice and reconciliation throughout human society and for the liberation of men and women from every kind of oppression."[22]

This approach to integral mission has been widely accepted and adopted in the vast bulk of evangelical missiological literature, with a few notable exceptions.[23] But as Breen notes, there is another level of integration that is needed—particularly in Western contexts, where we suffer from the bifurcations of the public and the private,[24] between home and church, between nuclear and extended family. Perhaps this explains why fostering and adoption rarely appear in missiological literature as family life remains relatively uncharted missiological territory. The missiological ontological penny has not yet dropped such that family is something we are, whereas mission is still perceived as something we do. Even in Mike Breen's new nomenclature of church life as "family on a mission," the idea of an inclusive, welcoming family that includes the marginalized and excluded into its very heart is missing.

### Of Tribal Interventions

In some contexts, this lack of missiological reflection has had a positive effect. Home for Good was a church facing a campaign focusing on fostering and adoption and has acted as a workaround for some evangelical traditions, which are often ambivalent to a missiology that includes social transformation and social engagement. Perhaps this results from the emphasis being on families playing their part in caring for the vulnerable, rather than the church (though as we shall see this is not a wholly accurate understanding of the campaign). Thus,

22. Lausanne Committee for World Evangelization, *The Lausanne Covenant*, http://www.lausanne.org/en/documents/lausanne-covenant.html.
23. Kevin DeYoung and Greg Gilbert, *What Is the Mission of the Church? Making Sense of Social Justice, Shalom, and the Great Commission* (Wheaton: Crossway, 2011).
24. See Lesslie Newbigin, *Truth to Tell: The Gospel as Public Truth* (Grand Rapids: Eerdmans, 1991), and also chap. 10 of the present volume.

perhaps by avoiding the scrutiny of the missiological radar, the Home for Good campaign may have a wider appeal to some churches who would critique or ignore some of the dominant voices in the wider missiological discourse.

It is the hope that Home for Good will have a subversive missional impact on the whole evangelical movement. As James K. A. Smith has insightfully argued, noting the effects that repeated practices have on affective transformation, "Our hearts are oriented primarily by desire, by what we love, and because those desires are shaped and molded by the habit-forming practices in which participate."[25]

So the daily practice of church families caring for vulnerable children, identifying their emotional, physical, spiritual, and political needs and seeking to meet them will develop godly virtues that will shape the desires and affections of those Christian caregivers. It is in sincere hope that this will have a knock-on effect in their churches such that engagement with the poor will not be a periphery element of a church's life, a transitory sortie into foreign territory, or limited to a client and provider relationship.

Similarly, if the goals of Home for Good are even partially achieved, then church members who do not become foster carers or adoptive carers will have a greater degree of contact with vulnerable children.[26] These children will often hail from different class, educational, cultural, and ethnic backgrounds from the typical church communities that make up the evangelical constituency. It is hoped that this contact through church services and depending on the ecclesiology of the churches involved through the ongoing "life together" of the community of believers will have a knock-on effect on the worldview, affections, and communal life of the whole church. Perhaps this will be another pedagogy for mission. This missiological pedagogy recognizes that we are more than "brains on a stick"; just as we see in the Trinity,

25. James K. A. Smith, *Desiring the Kingdom: Worship, Worldview, and Cultural Formation* (Grand Rapids: Baker Academic, 2009), 25.
26. Of course, robust child protection procedures are assumed to be in place—this has been helped by the role that the Churches Child Protection Advisory Service has played as an early partner in the initiative.

we are "beings in communion,"[27] and thus the community we inhabit forms us as persons. So then, the continual practice of caring for the vulnerable within the contexts of our biological and ecclesiological families forms us into the image of a God who reveals himself as a "Father to the fatherless" (Psalm 68).

I grew up in a wing of the evangelical tradition that tended to describe godliness in terms of abstinence.[28] Godliness involves fleeing youthful desires, abstaining from certain forbidden "worldly" vices: smoking, gambling; in my tradition, imbibing alcohol was part of this worldliness. We were not alone. In the 1980s, David Bosch provided a very helpful schema to compare two major missiological conferences that took place in the Southern Hemisphere. Bosch was involved with both consultations to a significant degree. The first took place in Melbourne, Australia, and was organized by the "ecumenical" stream of the church under the auspices of the Commission for World Mission and Evangelism. The second took place in Pattaya, Thailand, and was organized by the "evangelical" stream under the auspices of the Consultation on World Evangelization. Bosch analyzed the differences between these conferences in a number of papers,[29] and the most pertinent contrasts are collated and outlined in the table below.

27. John D. Zizioulas, *Being as Communion: Studies in Personhood and the Church* (Crestwood, NY: St. Vladimir's Seminary Press, 2000).
28. For an American version of this, see Sara Moslener, *Virgin Nation: Sexual Purity and American Adolescence* (New York: Oxford University Press, 2015).
29. David J. Bosch, "Evangelism and Mission: The Contemporary Debate," *Church Scene*, March 8, 1985, 10–11.

| Melbourne "Ecumenical" Commission for World Mission and Evangelism | Pattaya "Evangelical" Consultation on World Evangelization |
| --- | --- |
| Favored Jesus language of the Gospels | Favored language of Paul's epistles |
| Man's disorder | God's design |
| Emphasized deed (orthopraxy) | Emphasized word (orthodoxy) |
| Social involvement part and parcel (or all?) of Christian mission | Social involvement as separate from mission, or as a result of conversion. |
| Societal macro-ethics important | Personal micro-ethics important |
| Liberation | Justification |
| World main arena of God's activity | Church main arena of God's activity |
| Proclivity to socialism | Proclivity to capitalism |
| Church's credibility | Church's opportunity |

Bosch notes, "There can be little doubt that the ecumenical theology of mission is indeed at decisive points a corrective to its evangelical counterpart."[30] I transitioned into a tribe that recognized the confession of orthodoxy as the key marker of godliness. For example, when I was one the leaders of a large student campus group, I was meticulous to make sure that any speakers coming to talk at the campus group that I led were able to sign our doctrinal statement —even to the point that if someone arrived to speak and had not signed it, we would ask them to do so before standing up to address the gathered students. There was no equivalent orthopraxy statement—someone was deemed able to speak to us as long as they believed the right things. There was never any scrutiny that these truths were converted into right living. According to Scripture orthodoxy, literally right worship must include provision for the poor (Isa 1; 1 John 3). Similarly, the closest we get to this challenge to the worshiping life of the church in the New Testament is in the book of James, where we are told that godliness is not merely abstinence of sinful behavior, not merely the correct observation of ritual, or

---

30. David J. Bosch, *Witness to the World: The Christian Mission in Theological Perspective* (Atlanta: John Knox, 1980), 212.

even the right confession of doctrine. Godliness must include the demonstrating of God's character toward those in need (James 1:27).

## Of Political Theology

As Home for Good has sought to call the whole evangelical community to step up to meet the needs of the vulnerable children in our communities, we have sought to work across the subtribes and denominations that make up the evangelical constituency. As we have worked across tribal lines, we have come across a range of implicit political theologies operating within the churches. Some churches maintain a Christendom posture toward the culture. As Lamin Sanneh puts it, Christendom "refers to the medieval imperial phase of Christianity when the church became a domain of the state, and Christian profession a matter of political enforcement."[31]

Christians operating under a Christendom mind-set seek to put Christians into positions of power because they believe intrinsically that Christians should be running things because we should chase power and influence because we can wield it better than anyone else. They would cite Daniel or Esther as a model of taking on such power and influence. The Christendom model led to both a fight and flight instinct. Because Christians would be better at running things, they should fight their corner so that they get the opportunity to do so. If they do not get to control the power and influence in their institutions, they should steer clear of them and take flight from them. One of the dangers of this political theology is that it can appear that we are only interested in serving our communities on our terms—like a child who is losing a game of football deciding to take his football home and end the game if his team is not winning.

When it comes to fostering and adoption, these same Christians had a predominantly nervous posture toward secular social services and would often seek to fight for Christian rights within the system. For these Christians, the right for families to discipline through the

---

31. Lamin Sanneh, *Whose Religion is Christianity? The Gospel beyond the West* (Grand Rapids: Eerdmans, 2003), 23.

use of corporal punishment, the opposition to same-sex marriage, and the placement of children within same-sex couples were reason to steer clear of adoption and fostering. A very small minority even said they would be willing to lie in order to meet the requirements of the assessing social worker on issues such a corporal punishment perhaps because they did not recognize the authority of the social workers to evaluate their parenting abilities.

At the opposite end of the political spectrum were the churches operating with an implicitly post-Christendom posture. These Christians did not expect to be given any special privileges in their engagement with political life. They believed that Christians did have a role to play in civic and public life, but did not feel that they had an intrinsic right to lead or that thanks to common grace Christians were any more gifted to lead than anyone else. These Christians seemed to have negotiated a new way of living in a multicultural democracy. They were nervous about exerting any kind of power that if an atheist or a Muslim were to use in the same way, for their agenda would make them feel uncomfortable. This approach to politics runs the risk of seeking very little systemic change because it has so little confidence that the gospel is able to bring societal transformation. We end up having a parasitic relationship with the political system—largely ignoring it in the same way that parasites often ignore the life journey and overall direction of the host on which they travel.

When it comes to fostering and adoption, they are very willing to play their part in doing good to those in need. They are often relaxed about same-sex unions (including marriage) outside of the church (though some would be relaxed about this from confessing Christians too).

These polarized positions are surprisingly often exhibited with mediating positions in between infrequently being adhered to. In *Hospitality as Holiness*, Luke Bretherton offers a different paradigm for Christian moral and political engagement in a world of conflicting moral claims.

This approach has some endorsement from Rodney Stark's popular book *The Rise of Christendom*,[32] in which Stark argues that Christians ended up having a hugely significant impact on the social and moral fabric of their society through hospitality. The precursor to the Constantinian settlement that we came to know as Christendom was not a deliberate attempt to seize power, but rather a grassroots transformative influence that demonstrated the compassion and grace of God in the middle of a crisis. In Stark's historical case study, it was the church's response to the great plagues of the second century that formed the tipping point for explosive growth of Christianity from "a tiny and obscure messianic movement from the edge of the Roman Empire" to "the dominant faith of Western civilization." By Stark's estimation, this must have been of the order of 40 percent growth rate per decade for three centuries.

Stark argues that a key factor was the selfless acts of mercy and charity of Christians toward their neighbors that made such a huge impression on the population of plague-ridden Europe in the second century.[33] It was not that "the Romans knew nothing of charity, but it was not based on service to the gods. Pagan gods did not punish ethical violations because they imposed no ethical demands."[34] This puts him at odds with part of the thesis behind James Davison Hunter's book *To Change the World*.[35] His argument is that we should target the social elites and network them together to leverage greater impact. Hunter does not engage with the practice of Jesus to spend most of his ministry not focusing on the seat of power nor the opinion formers or influencers, but instead, on the marginalized and the poor. Perhaps it is not an either/or strategy. We need both a ground level, working out of the gospel, and one that targets the cultural elites and decision makers in a particular society.

---

32. Rodney Stark, *The Rise of Christianity: How the Obscure, Marginal Jesus Movement Became the Dominant Religious Force in the Western World in a Few Centuries* (San Francisco: HarperSanFrancisco, 1997), 3.
33. Ibid., 87–88.
34. Ibid., 88.
35. James Davison Hunter, *To Change the World: The Irony, Tragedy, and Possibility of Christianity in the Late Modern World* (Oxford: Oxford University Press, 2010).

## Of Integrative Theology

One of the challenges of having a wider portfolio and only limited time is the temptation to seek to integrate the various parts of one's job together. Of course, this can be abused, but it also can help integrate otherwise disparate theological projects.

When it comes to spiritual formation, I have been greatly appreciative of James K. A. Smith's two volumes from the Cultural Liturgies series with Baker Academic, which both offer a helpful critique of the reductionist pedagogy at play in much Christian education and approaches to spiritual formation. Smith argues that the liturgy and practice of the churches' corporate worship gatherings can have a large habit-forming effect and help redirect our affections toward God. This is good and true, but focusing on the gathered corporate worship of the church is itself a reductionist approach that encourages a public/private dichotomy, and an unfortunate sacred/secular bifur-cation. It is not just the corporate. No place in Smith's work so far is given to the formative influence of the family. As my own children become young adults, I have been very interested to observe the formative practices that we, as a family, introduce to help them develop into adult believers. One of those practices is to be part of a family that offers hospitality to the vulnerable. I have spoken to many families who can report that after years of foster care, they can see how being a foster carer helped to develop virtues of hospitality, compassion, kindness, patience, and generosity in their own birth children. This conscious development of strong but porous boundaries between family and community have modeled something of the hospitality of God involving children in the *missio Dei*, in an ongoing rather than episodic manner—mission becomes a way of being as a family. Of course, foster caring is not the panacea for the discipleship deficit and will not singlehandedly help young people to fully transition from childhood faith to adult faith. It simply offers another perspective in which to understand faith development.

A factor appearing to limit a willingness for Christians to share their faith is the perception of Christians in the media. If, when a Christian self-identifies as a believer in public, they have to overcome the negative perceptions that this involves: "I am a Christian, but not that kind of Christian." This may be especially true of evangelical Christians. Don Carson testifies to this when he states:

> If I was living in New York with my dear friend Tim Keller, I would never call myself an evangelical unless I was in a very friendly group . . . because by and large in Manhattan evangelical means the Christianized version of the Taliban. It roughly means right wing, stupid, ignorant, hate filled, bomb throwing people and I don't think of myself in that way. . . . It is why when we were putting together the organization the Gospel Coalition, it was not called the Evangelical Coalition.[36]

In the United States, this experience was born out in their UnChristian report, which surveyed sixteen- to twenty-nine-year-olds who are classified as outsiders to the church and asked them about their perceptions of Christianity. They were presented with the prompt: "Here are some words or phrases that people could use to describe a religious faith. Please indicate which of these phrases describes present day Christianity."[37]

|  | A lot | A lot or some |
| --- | --- | --- |
| Anti-homosexual | 66% | 91% |
| Judgmental | 57% | 87% |
| Hypocritical | 54% | 85% |
| Too involved in politics | 46% | 75% |
| Out of touch with reality | 37% | 72% |

These are pretty damning figures, and sadly, there is no comparison figure in the UK, but it is not too strange to extrapolate that in a country with a lot less church attendance than in the United States, there is not much reason to expect the figures to be any better.

36. D. A. Carson, "What is an Evangelical?," mp3 recording from January 28, 2008, Grace Fellowship Church, Toronto, Canada.
37. Dave Kinnaman and Gabe Lyons, *Unchristian: What a New Generation Really Thinks About Christianity . . . and Why it Matters* (Grand Rapids: Baker, 2007), 28.

In this kind of environment, the church has an opportunity to enact in front of a watching world a living parable of the gospel in stepping forward to adopt the "unwanted children" left behind in the system. The church has the opportunity to see a sea change in perceptions of what the church is and what the gospel is that we believe carries power that forms who we are. Just as God used, among other things, the prophetic lifestyle of the church in the second century, could the increased engagement with the poor and vulnerable help turn the tide as outsiders see the churches' "good deeds and praised their father in heaven" (Matt 5:16)? This is not a shift to a social gospel, but rather a recognition that the common life of the church lived out in public is one of the most persuasive arguments for the best apologetic of the gospel we believe. As Newbigin explains, "The best apologetic of the gospel is a congregation that lives by its message." If the church lives its life in the public eye and offers help, hope, and hospitality to the most vulnerable in our communities, this creates the plausibility structure in which the gospel makes sense when it is preached.[38]

## Conclusion

Home for Good seeks to integrate a number of different elements of the church's life. It seeks to integrate worship, doctrine, practice, and experience. Recognizing the need for a truly orthodox approach to Christian mission will involve attending to the parts of the Bible that we often neglect, and thus, by highlighting the biblical doctrine of spiritual adoption, we seek to help the church remember its history. All of us were vulnerable children in great need, and due to his great compassion, God the Holy Trinity intervened in human history to make possible our adoption as sons and daughters of the living God. This right confession will lead to the right praise of God in the practicing of the characteristics of God's compassion, mercy, kindness, and love toward a world in need. This continual praxis reshapes the emotional and affectionate life of the people of God. As we do this, we are both

---

38. Lesslie Newbigin, *The Gospel in a Pluralist Society* (Grand Rapids: Eerdmans, 1989), 223–24.

proclaiming a powerful metaphor that lies at the heart of the gospel and visibly demonstrating the privilege at the heart of the coming kingdom of God. This provides a plausibility structure in which the gospel of the kingdom will make sense and offers to a skeptical world a context for the gospel to be seen and heard. This approach to mission will help mission stop being a part-time activity of the church and instead become a normative way of being in the world for the people of God that transcends the barriers between home and church, nuclear and extended family.

# Afterword


## Christopher J. H. Wright


Anyone who has persevered through all the substantial chapters of this book will perhaps join me in a single afterword—Phew! The range and depth of the conversation that these chapters represent is remarkable, and we can only hope that the conversation will continue through many more consultations such as the one that gave birth to these studies.

My second thought in reading them has been, "What a change fifty years has brought!" As I said in my introduction to *The Mission of God*, I studied theology at Cambridge University in the 1960s as the son of missionary parents with a strong personal interest in all things "missionary." But that spiritual commitment had very little, if any, bearing on the content of my theological studies, or vice versa. Many other evangelical students were also interested in missionary issues, but hardly any were studying theology. And most of my fellow theology students had no particular interest in "the mission field." And certainly, there was no connection at that time between theology and mission in the Divinity Faculty (and missiology was not even a word I ever remember hearing back then, although from the historical surveys in this book, it certainly did exist, apparently confined to

Scotland . . .). So, for all that Brian Stanley laments that theological issues still tend to be bracketed out from the academic discipline of "world christianities" (which cannot avoid the empirical facts of Christian mission), at least mission studies (by various names) hold a legitimate and more respected place in the academy. I am encouraged by that, even if there is a long way to go before theology as a whole discipline is shaped by its "end," in serving the life and mission of the church.

During the years I taught at All Nations Christian College (1982–1983 and 1988–2001), we had a slogan that we were not teaching theology *and* mission, but theology *for* mission. We took it seriously. All courses were approached from the angle, "How does this or that subject relate to the mission of God, the mission of the church, and the mission that these students will very soon be engaging in (or in most cases had already some experience of)?" That applied to courses in biblical exegesis, Christian doctrine, ethics, pastoral studies, as well as the more obviously "missional" subjects such as cultural anthropology, other faiths, or the history of Christian mission. Of course, this ambition was greatly helped by the fact that almost all the faculty had personal experience of serving in mission in other cultures, and that the students were heading in that direction too. About half the students actually came from outside the United Kingdom, so cultural diversity was a lived experience. The whole ethos of the institution was shaped by its commitment to training for hands-on mission and preparing for the challenges of understanding other cultures and thinking hard about how the Bible, the gospel, and the whole Christian tradition of doctrine and ethics could be lived out and communicated in other cultures.

I'm sure that the way we thought (and taught) about "cultures" was strongly conditioned by those currents of missionary thinking in the mid-twentieth century, and would be susceptible to the thoroughly researched critique of Kirsteen Kim (herself a graduate of All Nations!). However, second-year students were required to read not only evangelical documents, such as those emerging from the Lausanne movement, but also some of the Roman Catholic and ecumenical ones Kirsteen mentions. So there was a strong desire to help students think through how their personal faith commitments related not only to the wider world of religious and cultural diversity but also to the breadth of "world Christianities"—other than the evangelical tradition. It was a constantly stimulating place to live and teach, and inevitably, it contributed substantially to the thinking and research that eventually solidified into *The Mission of God.*

That book, of course, has been my own attempt to combine theology and mission within a biblical perspective on both. I have often said that it is not so much a biblical theology of mission, as a missional theology of the Bible. It may sound disingenuous to describe a book of such size (though there is another Wright who has far surpassed it for sheer bulk) as tentative—at least in the process of working on it. I remain as convinced as ever of the conclusions it reaches, but what I say in the epilogue is the straightforward truth: "This book has indeed been a journey of discovery for its author." I began the writing, after years of teaching on Bible and mission at All Nations, with the strong (but untested) intuition that a missional perspective could be defended as at least one valid angle of approaching the task of biblical hermeneutics. But once I made the paradigm shift from thinking of the word *mission* as solely a collective term for a whole range of *human* activities (missions, and missionaries, and mission fields), and recognized that it needs to be applied *primarily* to the mission of God—in the sense of God's ultimate plan and purpose for his whole creation—then it became clear that a missional hermeneutic in *that* carefully defined sense (which critics often ignore) could apply throughout the whole canon of Scripture. And as I worked through the great trajectories of the biblical narrative—creation, election, redemption, covenant, and others—that conviction grew through constant exegetical reinforcement and hermeneutical fruitfulness.

Since then, it has been a further encouragement to find that doing theology *for* mission, even if it has not yet permeated (or subverted) the secular academies where theology as a discipline still manages in various ways to survive, has been taken up among a growing number of seminaries and institutions of theological education around the world. An illustration of this was the triennial conference of the International Council for Evangelical Theological Education (ICETE) in Nairobi in 2012, where the theme was "Rooted in the Word; Engaged in the World"—exploring how theological education can be both faithful to the nonnegotiables of the biblical Christian faith and contextually shaped, engaged, and applied in all our global diversities. A number of seminaries are now submitting their whole curriculum to a "missional audit"—to ensure that their theology and training is, in the proper sense of the phrase, "fit for purpose"—God's purpose for the church and all who serve God's purposes in the world. May their tribe increase.

# Bibliography

Andersen, Wilhelm. *Towards a Theology of Mission: A Study of the Encounter between the Missionary Enterprise and the Church and Its Theology.* London: SCM, 1955.

Anderson, Gerald H., and Thomas F. Stransky, eds. *Mission Trends 3: Third World Theologies.* New York: Paulist, 1976.

Andrews, Jake. "Farewell to Theology?" *Anglican Theological Review* 96 (2014): 715–25.

Arbuckle, Gerald A. *From Chaos to Mission: Refounding Religious Life Formation.* Collegeville, MN: Liturgical, 1997.

_____. *Refounding the Church: Dissent for Leadership.* London: Geoffrey Chapman, 1993.

Arendt, Hannah. *The Human Condition.* 2nd ed. Chicago: University of Chicago Press, 1998.

Baker, Jonny, and Cathy Ross, eds. *The Pioneer Gift: Explorations in Mission.* Norwich, UK: Canterbury Press, 2014.

Barber, John. *The Road from Eden: Studies in Christianity and Culture.* Dublin: Academia Press, 2008.

Barker, Chris. *Cultural Studies: Theory and Practice.* London: Sage, 2000.

Barth, Karl. *Church Dogmatics.* Edited by G. W. Bromiley and T. F. Torrance. London: T&T Clark, 2003.

_____. *Dogmatics in Outline.* London: SCM, 1949.

_____. "Die Theologie und die Mission in der Gegenwart." *Zwischen den Zeiten* 10 (1932): 189–215.

Bartholomew, Craig G., and David J. H. Beldman, eds. *Hearing the Old Testament: Listening for God's Address*. Grand Rapids: Eerdmans, 2012.

Bauckham, Richard. "Mission as Hermeneutic for Scriptural Interpretation." Currents in World Christianity Position Paper, 106 (1999).

____. "Mission as Hermeneutic for Scriptural Interpretation." In *Reading the Bible Missionally*, ed. Michael W. Goheen. Grand Rapids: Eerdmans, 2016.

Bavinck, J. H. *An Introduction to the Science of Missions*. Philadelphia: P&R, 1960.

Bebbington, David W. *Evangelicalism in Modern Britain: A History from 1730s to the 1980s*. New York: Routledge, 1989.

____. "Evangelicals and Reform: An Analysis of Social and Political Action." *Third Way* (1983): 10–13.

____. *The Nonconformist Conscience: Chapel and Politics, 1870–1914*. London: G. Allen & Unwin, 1982.

Bergen, Doris L. *Twisted Cross: The German Christian Movement in the Third Reich*. London: University of Carolina Press, 1996.

Berger, Peter. *The Sacred Canopy*. New York: Doubleday, 1967.

Berkouwer, G. C. *The Return of Christ*. Grand Rapids: Eerdmans, 1972.

____. *The Second Vatican Council and the New Catholicism*. Translated by Lewis B. Smedes. Grand Rapids: Eerdmans, 1965.

Bevans, Stephen B. *Models of Contextual Theology*. 2nd ed. Maryknoll, NY: Orbis, 2002.

Bevans, Stephen B., and Roger P. Schroeder. *Constants in Context: A Theology of Mission for Today*. Maryknoll, NY: Orbis, 2004.

____. *Prophetic Dialogue: Reflections on Christian Mission Today*. Maryknoll, NY: Orbis, 2011.

Blaire, Edward P. "An Appeal to Remembrance: The Memory Motif in Deuteronomy." *Interpretation* 15 (1961): 41–47.

Blauw, Johannes. "The Mission of the People of God." In *The Missionary Church in East and West*. Edited by Charles C. West and David M. Paton. London: SCM, 1959.

Bosch, David J. *Believing in the Future: Toward a Missiology of Western Culture*. Valley Forge, PA: Trinity Press International, 1995.

____. "Evangelism and Mission: The Contemporary Debate." *Church Scene*, March 8, 1985.

____. "Theological Education in Missional Perspective." *Missiology: An International Review* 10 (1982): 13–34.

____. *Transforming Mission: Paradigm Shifts in Theology of Mission.* Maryknoll, NY: Orbis, 1991.

____. *Witness to the World: The Christian Mission in Theological Perspective.* Atlanta: John Knox, 1980.

Bretherton, Luke. *Christianity and Contemporary Politics: The Conditions and Possibilities of Faithful Witness.* Oxford: Wiley-Blackwell, 2010.

____. *Hospitality as Holiness: Christian Witness Amid Moral Diversity.* Aldershot: Ashgate, 2006.

____. "A Postsecular Politics? Inter-faith Relations as a Civic Practice." *Journal of the American Academy of Religion* 79 (2011): 346–77.

Brown, Robert McAfee. *Theology in a New Key: Responding to Liberation Themes.* Louisville: Westminster John Knox.

Bruce, Steve. *Secularization: In Defence of an Unfashionable Theory.* Oxford: Oxford University Press, 2011.

Brueggemann, Walter. *The Bible Makes Sense.* 2nd ed. Louisville: Westminster John Knox, 2001.

____. *Hopeful Imagination: Prophetic Voices in Exile.* Minneapolis: Fortress Press, 1986.

Busch, Eberhard. *Karl Barth: His Life from Letters and Autobiographical Texts.* Translated by John Bowden. London: SCM, 1976.

Cady, Linell E. "Public Theology and the Postsecular Turn." *International Journal of Public Theology* 8 (2014): 292–312.

Calvin, John. *Commentaries on the Epistles to Timothy, Titus, and Philemon.* Translated by William Pringle. Edinburgh: Calvin Translation Society, 1856.

Cameron, Helen, et al. *Talking about God in Practice: Theological Action Research and Practical Theology.* London: SCM, 2010.

Cameron, Nigel M. de S., ed. *Dictionary of Scottish Church History and Theology.* Edinburgh: T&T Clark, 1993.

Carney, J. J. *Rwanda before the Genocide: Catholic Politics and Ethnic Discourse in the Late Colonial Era.* New York: Oxford University Press, 2014.

Carpenter, Joel A. *Revive Us Again: The Reawakening of American Fundamentalism.* New York: Oxford University Press, 1997.

Carson, D. A. *The Gagging of God: Christianity Confronts Pluralism*. Grand Rapids: Zondervan, 1996.

____. "Maintaining Scientific and Christian Truth Claims in a Postmodern World." *Science and Christian Belief* 14 (2002): 107–222.

Chaplin, Jonathan. *Multiculturalism: A Christian Retrieval*. London: Theos, 2011.

Chapman, Audrey R. "Truth Commissions and Intergroup Forgiveness: The Case of the South African Truth and Reconciliation Commission." *Journal of Peace Psychology* 13 (2007): 51–69.

Christensen, Duane L. *Deuteronomy 1–21:9* 2nd ed. WBC 6A. Dallas: Word, 2001.

Clarke, Peter D., and Tony Claydon, eds. *The Church, the Afterlife and the Fate of the Soul: Papers Read at the 2007 Summer Meeting and the 2008 Winter Meeting of the Ecclesiastical History Society*. Studies in Church History 45. Woodbridge, UK: The Boydell Press for the Ecclesiastical History Society, 2009.

Conn, Harvie, ed. *Eternal Word and Changing Worlds: Theology, Anthropology, and Mission in Trialogue*. Grand Rapids: Zondervan, 1984.

____. *Inerrancy and Hermeneutic: A Tradition, a Challenge, a Debate*. Grand Rapids: Baker, 1988.

____. "The Missionary Task of Theology: A Love/Hate Relationship?" *Westminster Theological Journal* 45 (1983): 1–21.

Conway, Martin. *Flashbulb Memories*. Oxford: Psychology Press, 1995.

Corrie, John, and Cathy Ross, eds. *Mission in Context: Explorations Inspired by J. Andrew Kirk*. Farnham, UK: Ashgate, 2012.

Cruver, Dan, ed. *Reclaiming Adoption: Missional Living through the Recovery of Abba Father*. Hudson, OH: Cruciform Press, 2010.

Davaney, Sheila Greeve. "Theology and the Turn to Cultural Analysis." In *Converging on Culture: Theologians in Dialogue with Cultural Analysis and Criticism*, edited by Delwin Brown, Sheila Greeve Davaney, and Kathryn Tanner. Oxford: Oxford University Press, 2001.

D'Costa, Gavin, and Ross Thompson, eds. *Buddhist-Christian Dual Belonging: Affirmations, Objections, Explorations*. Farnham, UK: Ashgate, 2016.

D'Costa, Gavin, Paul Knitter, and Daniel Strange. *Only One Way? Three Christian Responses to the Uniqueness of Christ in a Religiously Pluralist World*. London: SCM, 2011.

D'Elia, John A. *A Place at the Table: George Eldon Ladd and the Rehabilitation of Evangelical Scholarship in America*. Oxford: Oxford University Press, 2008.

Dempsey, Michael T., ed. *Trinity and Election in Contemporary Theology*. Grand Rapids: Eerdmans, 2011.

DeYoung, Kevin, and Greg Gilbert. *What Is the Mission of the Church? Making Sense of Social Justice, Shalom, and the Great Commission*. Wheaton: Crossway, 2011.

Dickson, J. P. *Mission-Commitment in Ancient Judaism and in the Pauline Communities: The Shape, Extent and Background of Early Christian Mission*. WUNT II 159. Tübingen: Mohr Siebeck, 2003.

Duraisingh, Christopher, ed. *Called to One Hope: The Gospel in Diverse Cultures: Report of the Conference of the CWME, Salvador, Brazil, 1996*. Geneva: WCC, 1998.

Dyrness, William A. "Evangelical Theology and Culture." In *The Cambridge Companion to Evangelical Theology*, edited by Timothy Larsen and Daniel J. Treier. Cambridge: Cambridge University Press, 2007.

Edwards, Jonathan. "Concerning the End for Which God Created the World." In *Works of Jonathan Edwards*. Vol. 8, *Ethical Writings*, edited by Paul Ramsey. New Haven, CT: Yale University Press, 1987.

Eiesland, Nancy. *The Disabled God: Toward a Liberatory Theology of Disability*. Nashville: Abingdon, 1994.

Elphick, Richard. *The Equality of Believers: Protestant Missionaries and the Racial Politics of South Africa*. Charlottesville, VA: University of Virginia Press, 2012.

Escobar, Samuel. "Doing Theology on Christ's Road." In *Global Theology in Evangelical Perspective : Exploring the Contextual Nature of Theology and Mission*, edited by Jeffrey P. Greenman and Gene L. Green. Downers Grove, IL: IVP Academic, 2012.

———. "The Legacy of John Alexander Mackay." *International Bulletin of Missionary Research* 16 (1992): 116–22.

Fiddes, Paul S. *Seeing the World and Knowing God: Hebrew Wisdom and Christian Doctrine in a Late-Modern Context*. Oxford: Oxford University Press, 2013.

———. *Tracks and Traces: Baptist Identity in Church and Theology*. Carlisle, UK: Paternoster, 2003.

Flett, John G. *The Witness of God: The Trinity*, Missio Dei, *Karl Barth, and the Nature of Christian Community*. Grand Rapids: Eerdmans, 2010.

Forrester, Duncan B. *Theology and Politics*. Oxford: Basil Blackwell, 1988.

Frame, John M. *The Doctrine of the Christian Life*. Phillipsburg, NJ: P&R, 2008.

Furani, Khaled. "Is There a Postsecular?" *Journal of the American Academy of Religion* 83 (2015): 1–26.

Giddens, Anthony. *Runaway World: How Globalization Is Reshaping Our Lives*. 2nd ed. London: Profile, 2002.

Goheen, Michael W. *As the Father Has Sent Me*. Zoetermeer: Boekencentrum, 2000.

____. *A Light to the Nations: The Missional Church in the Biblical Story*. Grand Rapids: Baker, 2011.

____. "A Missional Reading of Scripture, Theological Education, and Curriculum." In *Reading the Bible Missionally*, ed. Michael W. Goheen. Grand Rapids: Eerdmans, 2016.

Goodhew, David, Andrew Roberts, and Michael Volland. *Fresh! An Introduction to Fresh Expressions of Church and Pioneer Ministry*. London: SCM, 2012.

Gorringe, T. J. *Furthering Humanity: A Theology of Culture*. Aldershot, UK: Ashgate, 2004.

Govier, Trudy. *Forgiveness and Revenge*. New York: Routledge, 2011.

Grass, Tim. *F. F. Bruce : A Life*. Grand Rapids: Eerdmans, 2012.

Green, Gene L. *The Scalpel and the Cross: A Theology of Surgery*. Ordinary Theology. Grand Rapids: Zondervan, 2015.

Gregory, Brad S. *The Unintended Reformation: How a Religious Revolution Secularized Society*. Cambridge, MA: Harvard University Press, 2012.

Griffith, H., and J. R. Muether, eds. *Creator, Redeemer, Consummator: A Festschrift for Meredith G. Kline*. Greenville, SC: Reformed Academic Press, 2000.

Guder, Darrell. "From Mission and Theology to Missional Theology." *Princeton Seminary Bulletin* 24 (2003): 36–54.

____. "*Missio Dei*: Integrating Theological Formation for Apostolic Vocation." *Missiology: An International Review* 37 (2009): 63–74.

____. *Missional Church: A Vision for the Sending of the Church in North America*. Gospel & Our Culture. Grand Rapids: Eerdmans, 1998.

Guest, Mathew. *Evangelical Identity and Contemporary Culture: A Congregational Study in Innovation*. Aldershot, UK: Ashgate, 2007.

Hanson, Paul. *Isaiah 40–66*. Louisville: John Knox, 1995.

Hardy, Edward R., ed. *Christology of the Later Fathers.* Louisville: Westminster John Knox, 1954.

Härle, Wilfred. *Sein und Gnade: Die Ontologie in Karl Barths Kirchliche Dogmatik.* Berlin: Walter de Gruyter, 1975.

Harrison, Shawn. *Ministering to Gay Teenagers: A Guide for Youth Workers.* Loveland, CO: Simply Youth Ministry, 2014.

Hastings, Adrian. *The Shaping of Prophecy: Passion, Perception and Practicality.* London: Geoffrey Chapman, 1995.

Hauerwas, Stanley. *The Peaceable Kingdom: A Primer in Christian Ethics.* Notre Dame: University of Notre Dame Press, 1991.

Healy, Nicholas. *Church, World and the Christian Life: Practical-Prophetic Ecclesiology.* Cambridge: Cambridge University Press, 2000.

Heaney, Sharon E. *Contextual Theology for Latin America: Liberation Themes in Evangelical Perspective.* Milton Keynes, UK: Paternoster, 2008.

Hegstad, Harald. *The Real Church: An Ecclesiology of the Visible.* Eugene, OR: Wipf & Stock, 2013.

Herder, Johann Gottfried. *Philosophical Writings.* Translated and edited by Michael N. Forster. Cambridge: Cambridge University Press, 2004.

Heschel, Susannah. *The Aryan Jesus: Christian Theologians and the Bible in Nazi Germany.* Princeton: Princeton University Press, 2008.

Hiebert, Paul G. *Anthropological Insights for Missionaries.* Grand Rapids: Baker, 1985.

Hill, Wesley. *Washed and Waiting: Reflections on Christian Faithfulness and Homosexuality.* Grand Rapids: Zondervan, 2010.

Holmes, Arthur F. *Faith Seeks Understanding: A Christian Approach to Knowledge.* Grand Rapids: Eerdmans, 1971.

Holmes, Stephen R. "Trinitarian Missiology: Towards a Theology of God as Missionary." *International Journal of Systematic Theology* 8 (2006): 72–90.

Hunsberger, George R. "The Newbigin Gauntlet: Developing a Domestic Missiology for North America." *Missiology: An International Review* 19 (1991): 391–408.

Hunter, James Davison. *To Change the World: The Irony, Tragedy, and Possibility of Christianity in the Late Modern World.* Oxford: Oxford University Press, 2010.

Huntington, Samuel P. *The Clash of Civilizations and the Remaking of the World Order*. London: Free Press, 2002.

Jacobsen, Eneida. "Models of Public Theology." *International Journal of Public Theology* 6 (2012): 7–22.

Keller, Timothy. *Ministries of Mercy*. Grand Rapids: Zondervan, 1989.

Kelsey, David H. *Eccentric Existence: A Theological Anthropology*. Vol. 1. Louisville: Westminster John Knox, 2009.

Keum, Joseph, ed. *Together towards Life: Mission and Evangelism in Changing Landscapes*. Geneva: WCC, 2013.

Keysser, Christian. *A People Reborn*. Translated by Alfred Allin and John Kuder. Pasadena: William Carey Library, 1980.

Kim, Kirsteen. "Edinburgh 1910 to 2010: From Kingdom to Spirit." *Journal of the European Pentecostal Theological Association* 30 (2010): 3–20.

____. *The Holy Spirit in the World: A Global Conversation*. Maryknoll, NY: Orbis, 2007.

____. *Joining in with the Spirit: Connecting World Church and Local Mission*. London: SCM, 2012.

Kim, Sebastian C. H. *Theology in the Public Sphere: Public Theology as Catalyst for Open Debate*. London: SCM, 2011.

Kinnaman, Daven and Gabe Lyons. *Unchristian: What a New Generation Really Thinks about Christianity . . . and Why It Matters*. Grand Rapids: Baker Academic, 2007.

Kirk, J. Andrew. *The Mission of Theology and Theology as Mission*. London: Continuum, 1997.

Kirkpatrick, David C. "C. René Padilla and the Origins of Integral Mission in Post-War Latin America." *Journal of Ecclesiastical History* 67 (2016): 1–21.

Knitter, Paul F. *One Earth Many Religions: Multifaith Dialogue and Global Responsibility*. Maryknoll, NY: Orbis, 1995.

Köstenberger, Andreas J., and P. T. O'Brien. *Salvation to the Ends of the Earth: A Biblical Theology of Mission*. New Studies in Biblical Theology 11. Downers Grove, IL: InterVarsity Press, 2001.

Kraemer, Hendrik. "Continuity or Discontinuity." In *The Authority of Faith: International Missionary Council Meeting at Tambaram, Madras*. London: Oxford University Press, 1939.

Kraft, Charles H. *Anthropology for Christian Witness*. Maryknoll, NY: Orbis, 1996.

____. *Christianity in Culture*. Maryknoll, NY: Orbis, 1979.

Kreitzer, Mark. *The Concept of Ethnicity in the Bible: A Theological Analysis*. London: Edwin Mellen, 2008.

Ladd, George Eldon. *Jesus and the Kingdom: The Eschatology of Biblical Realism*. New York: Harper & Row, 1964.

____. *The Presence of the Future: The Eschatology of Biblical Realism*. Grand Rapids: Eerdmans, 1974.

Letham, Robert. *The Holy Trinity: In Scripture, History, Theology, and Worship*. Phillipsburg, NJ: P&R, 2004.

Lightfoot, J. B. *Saint Paul's Epistle to the Philippians*. London: Macmillan, 1885.

Lindbeck, George A. *The Nature of Doctrine: Religion and Theology in a Postliberal Age*. Philadelphia: Westminster John Knox, 1984.

Lints, Richard, Michael Horton, and Mark R. Talbot. *Personal Identity in Theological Perspective*. Grand Rapids: Eerdmans, 2006.

Luhrmann, T. M. *When God Talks Back: Understanding the American Evangelical Relationship with God*. New York: Vintage, 2012.

Mackay, John Alexander. *The Other Spanish Christ: A Study in the Spiritual History of Spain and South America*. London: SCM, 1932.

Marin, Andrew. *Love Is an Orientation: Elevating the Conversation with the Gay Community*. Downers Grove, IL: InterVarsity Press, 2009.

____. *Our Last Option: How a New Approach to Civility Can Save the Public Square*. Colorado Springs: Patheos, 2013.

____. "Pastoral Care to Those Suffering from Traumatic Memories." *Bible in Transmission* (2014): 24–26.

____. *Us versus Us: The Untold Story of Religion and the LGBT Community*. Colorado Springs: NavPress, 2016.

____. "Winner Take All? A Political and Religious Assessment of the Culture War between the LGBT Community and Conservatives." *Political Theology* 12 (2011): 501–10.

Marsden, George M. *Fundamentalism and American Culture*. 2nd ed. New York: Oxford University Press, 2006.

____. *Reforming Fundamentalism: Fuller Seminary and the New Evangelicalism*. Grand Rapids: Eerdmans, 1987.

Marshall, I. Howard. *New Testament Theology: Many Witnesses, One Gospel.* Downers Grove, IL: InterVarsity Press, 2004.

Martin, James, ed. *Antonio Gramsci: Critical Assessments of Leading Political Philosophers.* Vol. 4, *Contemporary Applications.* London: Routledge, 2002.

Matthey, Jacques, ed. *"You Are the Light of the World": Statements on Mission by the World Council of Churches 1980-2005.* Geneva: WCC, 2005.

Mbiti, John S. *New Testament Eschatology in an African Background: A Study of the Encounter between New Testament Theology and African Traditional Concepts.* London: Oxford University Press, 1971.

McGavran, Donald A. *The Bridges of God: A Study in the Strategy of Missions.* New York: Friendship Press, 1955.

McGrath, Alister E. *The Genesis of Doctrine: A Study in the Foundation of Doctrinal Criticism.* Grand Rapids: Eerdmans, 1990.

McLuhan, Marshall. *Understanding Media: The Extensions of Man.* New York: McGraw Hill, 1964.

Medefind, Jedd. *Becoming Home: Adoption, Foster Care, and Mentoring—Living Out God's Heart for Orphans.* Grand Rapids: Zondervan, 2014.

Metzger, John Mackay. *The Hand and the Road: The Life and Times of John A. Mackay.* Louisville: Westminster John Knox, 2010.

Miyamoto, Ken Christoph. "A Response to 'Mission Studies as Intercultural Studies and Its Relationship to Religious Studies.'" *Mission Studies* 25 (2008): 109–10.

Molnar, Paul D. *Thomas F. Torrance: Theologian of the Trinity.* Farnham, UK: Ashgate, 2008.

Moltmann, Jürgen. *Church in the Power of the Holy Spirit.* London: SCM, 1976.

Moltmann-Wendel, Elisabeth. *I Am My Body.* New York: Continuum, 1995.

Moslener, Sara. *Virgin Nation: Sexual Purity and American Adolescence.* New York: Oxford University Press, 2015.

Muggeridge, Malcolm. *A Third Testament: A Modern Pilgrim Explores the Spiritual Wanderings of Augustine, Blake, Pascal, Tolstoy, Bonhoeffer, Kierkegaard, and Dostoevsky.* New York: Little, Brown, 1976.

Muller, Richard A. *Post-Reformation Reformed Dogmatics: The Rise and Development of Reformed Orthodoxy, ca. 1520 to ca. 1725.* 4 vols. 2nd ed. Grand Rapids: Baker Academic, 2003.

Naugle, David K. *Worldview: The History of a Concept.* Grand Rapids: Eerdmans, 2002.

Newbigin, Lesslie. *Foolishness to the Greeks: The Gospel and Western Culture.* London: SPCK, 1986.

_____. *The Gospel in a Pluralist Society.* Grand Rapids: Eerdmans, 1989.

_____. *Honest Religion for Secular Man.* Philadelphia: Westminster, 1966.

_____. *One Body, One Gospel, One World.* London: International Missionary Council, 1958.

_____. *Trinitarian Doctrine for Today's Mission.* Eugene, OR: Wipf & Stock, 2006.

_____. *Truth to Tell: The Gospel as Public Truth.* Grand Rapids: Eerdmans, 1991.

Nikkel, David H. *Radical Embodiment.* Eugene, OR: Pickwick, 2015.

Nikolajsen, Jeppe Bach. *The Distinctive Identity of the Church: A Constructive Study of the Post-Christendom Theologies of Lesslie Newbigin and John Howard Yoder.* Eugene, OR: Pickwick, 2015.

Nuñez C., Emilio Antonio. "Testigo de un nuevo amanecer." In *Hacia una teología evangélica latinoamericana: ensayos en honor de Pedro Savage,* edited by C. René Padilla. Miami: Editorial Caribe, 1984.

O'Donovan, Oliver, and Joan Lockwood O'Donovan. *Bonds of Imperfection: Christian Politics, Past and Present.* Grand Rapids: Eerdmans, 2004.

Oberman, Heiko Augustinus. *The Harvest of Medieval Theology: Gabriel Biel and Late Medieval Nominalism.* Cambridge, MA: Harvard University Press, 1963.

Oborji, Francis Anekwe. "Missiology in Its Relation to Intercultural Theology and Religious Studies." *Mission Studies* 25 (2008): 113–14.

Oden, Thomas C. *After Modernity . . . What? Agenda for Theology.* Grand Rapids: Zondervan, 1992.

Omer, Atalia. "Modernists Despite Themselves: The Phenomenology of the Secular and the Limits of Critique as an Instrument of Change." *Journal of the American Academy of Religion* 83 (2015): 27–71.

Ormerod, Neil J., and Shane Clifton. *Globalization and the Mission of the Church.* London: T&T Clark, 2009.

Otani, Hajime, et al. "Emotion, Directed Forgetting, and Source Memory." *British Journal of Psychology* 103 (2012): 343–58.

Packer, J. I. *Concise Theology: A Guide to Historic Christian Beliefs.* Wheaton: Tyndale House, 1993.

____. *Knowing God.* London: Hodder and Stoughton, 2004.

Padilla, C. René. "Church and World: A Study of the Relation between the Church and the World in the Teaching of the Apostle Paul." PhD Thesis, University of Manchester, 1965.

____. "The Contextualization of the Gospel." *Journal of Theology for Southern Africa* 24 (1978): 12–30.

____. "El reino de Dios y la iglesia." In *El reino de Dios y América Latina*, edited by C. René Padilla. El Paso, TX: Casa Bautista Publicaciones, 1975.

____. "Evangelical Theology in Latin American Contexts." In *The Cambridge Companion to Evangelical Theology*, edited by Timothy Larsen and Daniel J. Treier. Cambridge: Cambridge University Press, 2007.

____. "The Kingdom of God and the Church." *Theological Fraternity Bulletin* 12 (1976): 1–23.

____. "Luz del mundo, sal de la tierra." *Misión* 8 (1989): 4–5.

____. *Misión integral: ensayos sobre el Reino y la iglesia.* Grand Rapids: Eerdmans, 1986.

____. *Mission between the Times: Essays on the Kingdom.* 2nd ed. Carlisle, UK: Langham Monographs, 2010.

____. "My Theological Pilgrimage." *Journal of Latin American Theology* 4 (2009): 91–111.

____. *The New Face of Evangelicalism: An International Symposium on the Lausanne Covenant.* Downers Grove, IL: InterVarsity Press, 1976.

____. "A Steep Climb Ahead for Theology in Latin America." *Evangelical Missions Quarterly* 7 (1971): 99–106.

Palmer, Parker J. *To Know As We Are Known: Education as a Spiritual Journey.* San Francisco: Harper and Row, 1983.

Pannenberg, Wolfhart. *Systematic Theology.* Translated by Geoffrey W. Bromiley. 3 vols. Grand Rapids: Eerdmans, 1991–1998.

Pecklers, Keith, ed. *Liturgy in a Postmodern World.* London: Continuum, 2003.

Percy, Martyn. *Engaging with Contemporary Culture: Christianity, Theology, and the Concrete Church.* Farnham, UK: Ashgate, 2005.

Perkins, John. *A Quiet Revolution: The Christian Response to Human Need . . . A Strategy for Today.* Waco, TX: Word, 1976.

Picketty, Thomas. *Capital in the Twenty-First Century.* Cambridge, MA: Belknap Press of Harvard University Press, 2013.

Piper, John. *The Future of Justification: A Response to N. T. Wright.* Wheaton: Crossway, 2007.

Rathbone, C. J., C. J. Moulin, and M. A. Conway. "Autobiographical Memory and Amnesia: Using Conceptual Knowledge to Ground the Self." *Neurocase* 15 (2009): 405–18.

Ridderbos, Herman N. *Redemptive History and the New Testament Scriptures.* Translated by H. De Jongste. Revised by Richard B. Gaffin, Jr. Phillipsburg, NJ: P&R, 1963.

Robbins, Joel. *Becoming Sinners: Christianity and Moral Torment in a Papua New Guinea Society.* Berkeley: University of California Press, 2004.

Robertson, Roland. *Globalization: Social Theory and Global Culture.* London: Sage, 1992.

Roxborogh, John. "Missiology after Mission." *International Bulletin of Missionary Research* 38 (2014): 120–24.

Saayman, Willem, and Klippies Kritzinger, eds. *Mission in Bold Humility: David Bosch's Work Considered.* Maryknoll, NY: Orbis, 1996.

Salinas, Daniel. *Latin American Evangelical Theology in the 1970's: The Golden Decade.* Boston: Brill, 2009.

Samartha, Stanley J. *Courage for Dialogue: Ecumenical Issues in Inter-Religious Relationships.* Geneva: WCC, 1981.

____. *Guidelines on Dialogue.* Geneva: WCC, 1979.

Samuel, Vinay, and Chris Sugden, eds. *Mission as Transformation: A Theology of the Whole Gospel.* Oxford: Regnum, 1999.

____, ed. *Sharing Jesus in the Two Thirds World: Evangelical Christologies from the Contexts of Poverty, Powerlessness, and Religious Pluralism: The Papers of the First Conference of Evangelical Mission Theologians from the Two Thirds World, Bangkok, Thailand, March 22–25, 1982.* Grand Rapids: Eerdmans, 1984.

Sanders, Fred, and Jason S. Sexton, eds. *Theology and California: Theological Refractions on California's Culture.* Farnham, UK: Ashgate, 2014.

Sanders, Jack. *Ethics in the New Testament.* London: SCM, 1975.

Sanneh, Lamin. *Translating the Message: The Missionary Impact on Culture.* Maryknoll, NY: Orbis, 1989.

____. *Whose Religion Is Christianity? The Gospel beyond the West*. Grand Rapids: Eerdmans, 2003.

Schacter, Daniel. *The Seven Sins of Memory: How the Mind Forgets and Remembers*. New York: Houghton Mifflin, 2001.

Scherer, James A., and Stephen B. Bevans. *New Directions in Mission and Evangelization 3: Faith and Culture*. Maryknoll, NY: Orbis, 1999.

Schilder, Klaas. *Christ and Culture*. Winnipeg: Premier Printing, 1977.

Schleiermacher, Friedrich. *On Religion: Speeches to Its Cultured Despisers*. Translated by John Oman. London: Kegan Paul, Trench, Trubner, 1893 (1879).

Schreiter, Robert. *Constructing Local Theologies*. Maryknoll, NY: Orbis, 1985.

Scott, John. *Life Letters and Papers of The Late Thomas Scott*. New Haven: Nathan Whiting, 1827.

Sexton, Jason S. "A Confessing Trinitarian Theology for Today's Mission." In *Advancing Trinitarian Theology: Essays in Constructive Dogmatics*, edited by Oliver Crisp and Fred Sanders. Grand Rapids: Zondervan, 2014.

____. *The Trinitarian Theology of Stanley Grenz*. London: T&T Clark, 2013.

Shaw, Perry. *Transforming Theological Education: A Practical Handbook for Integrative Learning*. London: Langham Global Library, 2014.

Shenk, Wilbert R. *History of the American Society of Missiology, 1973–2013*. Elkhart, IN: Institute of Mennonite Studies, 2014.

Silva, Moisés. *God, Language, and Scipture: Reading the Bible in the Light of General Linguistics*. Vol. 4, *Foundations of Contemporary Interpretation*. Grand Rapids: Zondervan, 1991.

Singh, David Emmanuel, and Bernard Farr, eds. *Christianity and Cultures: Shaping Christian Thinking in Context*. Oxford: Regnum, 2008.

Skreslet, Stanley. *Comprehending Mission: The Questions, Methods, Themes, Problems, and prospects of Missiology*. Maryknoll, NY: Orbis, 2012.

Smith, Christian. *The Secular Revolution: Power, Interests, and Conflict in the Secularization of American Public Life*. Berkeley: University of California Press, 2003.

Smith, James K. A. *Desiring the Kingdom: Worship, Worldview, and Cultural Formation*. Grand Rapids: Baker Academic, 2009.

____. "Reforming Public Theology: Two Kingdoms, or Two Cities?" *Calvin Theological Journal* 47 (2012): 122–37.

Stanley, Brian. *The Bible and the Flag: Protestant Missions and British Imperialism in the Nineteenth and Twentieth Centuries.* Leicester, UK: Apollos, 1990.

____. "Conversion to Christianity: The Colonization of the Mind?" *International Review of Mission* 92 (2003): 315–31.

____. "Evangelical Social and Political Ethics: An Historical Perspective." *Evangelical Quarterly* 62 (1990): 19–36.

____. "Founding the Centre for the Study of Christianity in the Non-Western World," in *Understanding World Christianity: The Vision and Work of Andrew F. Walls,* ed. William R. Burrows, Mark R. Gornik, and Janice A. McLean. Maryknoll, NY: Orbis, 2011.

____. "From 'the Poor Heathen' to 'the Glory and Honour of All Nations': Vocabularies of Race and Custom in Protestant Missions, 1844–1928." *International Bulletin of Missionary Research* 34 (2010): 3–10.

____. *The Global Diffusion of Evangelicalism.* Downers Grove, IL: InterVarsity Press, 2013.

____. *The World Missionary Conference, Edinburgh 1910.* Grand Rapids: Eerdmans, 2009.

Stark, Rodney. *The Rise of Christianity: How the Obscure, Marginal Jesus Movement Became the Dominant Religious Force in the Western World in a Few Centuries.* San Francisco: HarperSanFrancisco, 1997.

Stevens, R. Paul. "Living Theologically: Toward a Theology of Christian Practice." *Themelios* 20 (1995): 4–7.

Stibbe, Mark. *I Am Your Father: What Every Heart Needs to Know.* Oxford: Monarch Books, 2010.

Strange, Daniel. "Rooted and Grounded? The Legitimacy of Abraham Kuyper's Distinction between Church as Institute and Church as Organism, and Its Usefulness in Constructing an Evangelical Public Theology." *Themelios* 40 (2015): 429–44.

____. *Their Rock Is Not Like Our Rock: A Theology of Religions.* Grand Rapids: Zondervan, 2015.

Swinton, John, and Harriet Mowat. *Practical Theology and Qualitative Research.* London: SCM, 2006.

Tanner, Kathryn. *Theories of Culture: A New Agenda for Theology*. Minneapolis: Fortress Press, 1997.

Taylor, John V. *The Go-between God: The Holy Spirit and the Christian Mission*. London: SCM, 1972.

Thompson, John Arthur. *Deuteronomy: An Introduction and Commentary*. TOTC 5. Nottingham, UK: Inter-Varsity Press, 1974.

Tidball, Derek J., Brian S. Harris, and Jason S. Sexton, eds. *Revisioning, Renewing, and Rediscovering the Triune Center: Essays in Honor of Stanley J. Grenz*. Eugene, OR: Cascade, 2014.

Tillich, Paul. *Theology of Culture*. Oxford: Oxford University Press, 1959.

Tippett, Alan R. *Introduction to Missiology*. Pasadena, CA: William Carey Library, 1987.

Toon, Peter. *The Development of Doctrine in the Church*. Grand Rapids, 1979.

Torrance, T. F. *Atonement: The Person and Work of Christ*. Edited by Robert T. Walker. Downers Grove, IL: IVP Academic, 2009.

_____. *Reality and Evangelical Theology: The Realism of Christian Revelation*. Downers Grove, IL: InterVarsity Press, 1999.

Trites, Alison A. *The New Testament Concept of Witness*. Cambridge: Cambridge University Press, 2004.

Trueman, Carl R. *The Creedal Imperative*. Wheaton: Crossway, 2012.

Tutu, Desmond. *No Future without Forgiveness*. New York: Doubleday, 2009.

Tylor, E. B. *Primitive Culture: Researches into the Development of Mythology, Philosophy, Religion, Language, Art, and Custom*. London: John Murray, 1920 (1871).

Ustorf, Werner. "The Cultural Origins of 'Intercultural Theology.'" *Mission Studies* 25 (2008): 229–51.

_____. *Sailing on the Next Tide: Missions, Missiology, and the Third Reich*. Oxford: Peter Lang, 2000.

Van Til, Henry. *The Calvinistic Concept of Culture*. Grand Rapids: Baker, 2001.

VanderPol, Gary F. "The Least of These: American Evangelical Parachurch Missions to the Poor, 1947–2005." ThD Diss., Boston University, 2010.

Vanhoozer, Kevin J. "One Rule to Rule Them All: Theological Method in an Era of World Christianity." In *Globalizing Theology: Belief and Practice In An Era*

*Of World Christianity*, edited by Craig Ott and Harold A. Netland. Downers Grove, IL: InterVarsity Press, 1997.

——. "Wrighting the Wrongs of the Reformation? The State of the Union with Christ in St. Paul and Protestant Soteriology." In *Jesus, Paul and the People of God: A Theological Dialogue with N. T. Wright*, edited by Nicholas Perrin and Richard B. Hays. Downers Grove, IL: IVP Academic, 2011.

Vanhoozer, Kevin J., Charles A. Anderson, and Michael J. Sleasman. *Everyday Theology: How to Read Cultural Texts and Interpret Trends*. Grand Rapids: Baker Academic, 2007.

Vanier, Jean. *Encountering "the Other."* Mahwah, NJ: Paulist Press, 2005.

Volf, Miroslav *After Our Likeness: The Church as the Image of the Trinity*. Grand Rapids: Eerdmans, 1998.

——. *Exclusion and Embrace: A Theological Exploration of Identity, Otherness, and Reconciliation*. Nashville: Abingdon, 1996.

——. *A Public Faith: How Followers of Christ Should Serve the Common Good*. Grand Rapids: Brazos, 2011.

Walls, Andrew F. *The Cross-Cultural Process in Christian History: Studies in the Transmission and Appropriation of Faith*. Maryknoll, NY: Orbis, 2002.

Ward, Pete, ed. *Liquid Church*. Peabody, MA: Hendrickson, 2002.

——. *Perspectives on Ecclesiology and Ethnography*. Grand Rapids: Eerdmans, 2012.

Warneck, Gustav. *Modern Missions and Culture: Their Mutual Relations*. Translated by Thomas Smith. Edinburgh: James Gemmell, 1883 (1879).

Wells, David F. *The Courage to Be Protestant: Truth-lovers, Marketers, and Emergents in the Postmodern World*. Grand Rapids: Eerdmans, 2008.

Woodbridge, John D., and Thomas Edward McComiskey, eds. *Doing Theology in Today's World: Essays in Honor of Kenneth S. Kantzer*. Grand Rapids: Zondervan, 1993.

World Missionary Conference. *The History and Records of the Conference (IX)*. Edinburgh: Oliphant, Anderson, and Ferrier, 1910.

——. *Report of Commission I: Carrying the Gospel to All the Non-Christian World*. Edinburgh: Oliphant, Anderson, and Ferrier, 1910.

——. *Report of Commission VI: The Home Base of Missions*. Edinburgh: Oliphant, Anderson, and Ferrier, 1910.

_____. *Report of Commission IV: The Missionary Message in Relation to Non-Christian Religions*. Edinburgh: Oliphant, Anderson, and Ferrier, 1910.

_____. *Report of Commission V: The Preparation of Missionaries*. Edinburgh: Oliphant, Anderson, and Ferrier, 1910.

Wright, Christopher J. H. "Mission and Old Testament Interpretation." In *Hearing the Old Testament: Listening for God's Address*, edited by Craig G. Bartholomew and David J. H. Beldman. Grand Rapids: Eerdmans, 2012.

_____. "Mission as a Matrix for Hermeneutics and Biblical Theology." In *Out of Egypt: Biblical Theology and Biblical Interpretation*, edited by Craig Bartholomew, Mary Healy, Karl Möller, and Robin Parry. Grand Rapids: Zondervan, 2004.

_____. *The Mission of God: Unlocking the Bible's Grand Narrative*. Downers Grove, IL: IVP Academic, 2006.

Wright, N. T. *Bringing the Church to the World: Renewing the Church to Confront the Paganism Entrenched in Western Culture*. Minneapolis: Bethany House, 1992.

_____. *Justification: God's Plan and Paul's Vision*. Downers Grove, IL: IVP Academic, 2009.

_____. *Scripture and the Authority of God*. San Francisco: HarperOne, 2011.

_____. *What Saint Paul Really Said: Was Paul of Tarsus the Real Founder of Christianity?* Grand Rapids: Eerdmans, 1997.

Yates, Timothy. *Christian Mission in the Twentieth Century*. Cambridge: Cambridge University Press, 1994.

Zizioulas, John D. *Being as Communion: Studies in Personhood and the Church*. Crestwood, NY: St. Vladimir's Seminary Press, 2000.

# Index